A MOTHER'S STORY

"I have never in my life seen so many get-well cards for one boy. I think you should go in the *Guinness Book of Records*."

I knew the doctor was just joking, but . . .

If some old gypsy had told me that over the next four years Craig would receive more than one hundred million get-well cards from caring people all over the world . . . that the cards were going to take over my life . . . that every week for nearly four years I'd have to rope in dozens of friends to help open Craig's mail, would I have believed it? And more important, would I still have gone ahead?

I like to think I would. Because one thing is certain, if I hadn't, my son Craig Shergold would not be alive today.

The "Get-Well" Kid

A MOTHER'S STORY OF A MIRACLE

MARION SHERGOLD
with Pamela Cockerill

AVON BOOKS ◆ NEW YORK

Published in Great Britain as *Craig Shergold: A Mother's Story*

"I Just Called to Say I Love You" by Stevie Wonder © 1984. Reproduced by permission of Jobete Music Co., Inc./Black Bull Music.

AVON BOOKS
A division of
The Hearst Corporation
1350 Avenue of the Americas
New York, New York 10019

Original Copyright Material © 1993 by Marion Shergold
Text Copyright © 1993 by Pamela Cockerill
Front cover photo by Peter Pugh-Cook Photography
Published by arrangement with Transworld Publishers, Inc.
Library of Congress Catalog Card Number: 94-96271
ISBN: 0-380-77827-0

First Avon Books Printing: March 1995

AVON TRADEMARK REG. U.S. PAT. OFF. AND IN OTHER COUNTRIES, MARCA REGISTRADA, HECHO EN U.S.A.

Printed in the U.S.A.

RA 10 9 8 7 6 5 4 3 2 1

This book is dedicated to the brave men in my life,
Ernie, Steven and Craig—all my love, always—
and to my wonderful mum, Kate,
who is forever by my side.
Thanks, Mum, for teaching me the power of love.

I also dedicate this book to all the families
who have suffered the heartbreak of losing a child.
My thoughts and prayers are with you.

Acknowledgments

I feel that I am the luckiest woman alive and I owe my thanks to so many people that it is difficult to know where to start—or end! But my love and special thanks go to:

Mr. John Kluge—our guardian angel who gave me back my world. I am forever in your debt; Professor Neal Kassell—our supercalifragilistic hero who performed a miracle while the world watched and waited; all the doctors, nurses and medical staff here and in America who, through their skill and devotion, helped to save my son; every man, woman and child who took the time and trouble to send a card or a token of love. Each and every one of you played a part in this miracle that united the world and proved to me the power of love; all the volunteers who opened the cards. Your hard work has been a true labor of love for which I am eternally grateful; Bill Wyman, a great mate and a true friend who has always been there for us; Ronnie Wood, who painted me a miracle that I will never forget; Linda and Arthur Stein of The Children's Wish Foundation, Craig's Fairy Godparents, who prove over and over again that wishes really do come true; Kate and Sharon, who helped to make the dark clouds slip away; Pamela Cockerill, a treasured friend and patient saint with whom I shared tears and laughter during the writing of this book.

And finally I would like to thank God who sustained me through my darkest hours and answered my prayers, and the prayers of millions of people across the world. I feel truly blessed.

Foreword

I first met Craig Shergold in December 1990 at a fund-raising event at my London restaurant "Sticky Fingers" and upon being introduced, we immediately took to each other.

Craig was, at that time, a very sick boy. I was made aware however that, despite his own "fight for life," he was devoting every minute of his free time working hard to raise money for the Royal Marsden Hospital.

His great courage, his immense sense of humor and his sheer determination not to give up his fight for life, was inspiring enough. However, what totally won me over was his desire to go out of his way to help others through his numerous fund-raising projects—becoming the youngest person ever to raise so much for charity.

Since our first meeting Craig and I have collaborated on many fund-raising events for the Royal Marsden Hospital and have become, to quote Craig, "great mates."

Much love and congratulations, Craig.

Your "Great Mate"
BILL WYMAN

Introduction

It all began as a bit of a joke really. Not that you're in the mood for jokes when you've just been told your child might be dying, but Richard Hayward was good at getting people to smile. He always had a twinkle in his eye and the whole ward used to brighten up when he came in to see his patients. That morning Dr. Hayward was doing his rounds with a team of student doctors and he stopped, as he always did, at the foot of Craig's bed.

"How are you feeling today, Craig? How's the earache?"

"Well . . ." Craig screwed up his face. "I reckon it's not quite as bad as it was yesterday," he said slowly. His voice sounded strange. Something had happened to it in the few days since he'd been rushed to Great Ormond Street Hospital. He was drawling his words and leaving long gaps between them. Sometimes he almost sounded drunk. I couldn't get used to it. It was as if some other child was in Craig's body. I think Dr. Hayward knew how I felt because he looked over at me and smiled—he always met your eyes, not like some of the doctors. "All right, Mother?"

I nodded. I couldn't trust myself to speak. Part of me was still hoping I'd wake up soon and find the whole thing had been a bad dream.

Dr. Hayward checked the side of Craig's head where his brain shunt had been put in three days before. They'd shaved half his hair off and the dark-red scar stood out like a half-moon against his white scalp.

"That looks fine to me, Craig. All being well we should be able to do the next operation on Monday as we planned." Dr. Hayward gave me a quick look. I think he was expecting me to ask him something, but I didn't have any questions that day. I knew much more than I wanted to already.

Then, as he turned to go, Dr. Hayward stopped in his tracks and I knew he'd noticed the walls around Craig's bed for the first time.

"My goodness, someone's been busy."

I felt a bit embarrassed. It had taken hours to put up all Craig's get-well cards and even though it had been Dr. Hayward's idea I still wasn't sure it had been the right thing to do. I was worried it might look as if we were showing off.

Up until yesterday there'd only been about thirty get-well cards on Craig's wall—they were the ones that had come in the first day or two after we got there. Since then, as more and more of our friends and family had heard the news, lots more cards had arrived. But I hadn't put them up. Instead, each morning, after Craig had opened them I'd piled them on his bedside locker. I was afraid we might make the other kids in the ward jealous if we made a big show of them. Not all of them had dozens of uncles and aunties like Craig, and some of the children from abroad only had a few cards behind their beds.

But the day before, when he'd been doing his ward rounds, Dr. Hayward had spotted this great wobbly pile of cards on Craig's bedside locker and he'd given me a real ticking off. "What are they doing there? Get them up where he can see them." He'd spread his arms out wide. "I want this child to have as much spiritual upliftment as possible."

After he'd gone the nurses had kept on at me. "Come on, Marion. You heard what he said. Let's get them up." And they'd helped me string all the cards round the walls. There were hundreds of them by now. Big ones, little ones, funny ones, and what Craig called "soppy" ones. There were cards from the family and neighbors, home-made cards from every child in Craig's school, cards from all my friends at work and from Ernie's mates at the London Electricity Board. By the time we'd finished putting them all up there was hardly an inch of wall-space showing around Craig's bed from floor to ceiling. But I had to admit that Dr. Hayward had been right. It had cheered Craig up. He'd taken more of an interest in these cards than in anything since he'd been in hospital.

Now, as Dr. Hayward saw the result of his instructions, he put on a great act for Craig's benefit, turning slowly round and round, as he stared at the walls. Then he dropped his jaw and made his eyes go wide as if he was seeing things. "I just don't believe it," he said at last. "I have never in my life seen so many get-well cards for one little boy." Craig chuckled and a little bit of the old sparkle came back into his eyes. "It's good, innit?" he said.

"It certainly is. You must have more friends than anyone I know." Dr. Hayward turned to the students standing behind him. "I think he should go in the *Guinness Book of Records*, don't you?"

They laughed politely. "Yeh! Go for it, Craig!" one of the nurses called across the ward as Dr. Hayward moved on to the next bed.

He hadn't meant it seriously. I knew that. It was my friend Alison who took him at his word. She'd been sitting next to me while Dr. Hayward was doing his rounds and for the rest of the morning she seemed lost in thought. I didn't pay her too much attention to be honest. I was too worried about Craig. He looked awful. His face had swollen up and his skin was turning a terrible yellow color. He'd been asleep since Dr. Hayward left him but he was getting very restless. Every so often he'd moan and his body would give a great jerk as if he'd had an electric shock. Anyone could see the pain was getting worse. I couldn't understand why Craig hadn't told Dr. Hayward the truth. I sat on my chair beside the bed, rocking backward and forward in despair.

"Marion—why don't we try for it?" Alison said suddenly.

I stared at her. "What are you talking about?"

"The *Guinness Book of Records.*"

"What?" I thought she'd gone off her trolley. "Alison, Dr. Hayward was only kidding. He didn't mean it for real."

"I know that. I still think we should do it."

I couldn't believe she was serious. I had no idea what

the world record for get-well cards was, but it was a pretty safe bet it would take more than our wall-full to beat it. And in any case what did it matter? What was a world record? Craig was dying. I didn't care a fig about the *Guinness Book of Records*.

But Alison was bubbling over with the idea. "Come on, Marion!" she begged. "Say yes."

I shook my head. "What's the point, Alison?"

"It would give Craig something else to think about instead of just being ill," she said. "That's the point. And you too. It would help take your mind off all this." She waved her hand at the drip bottles behind Craig's bed.

I hesitated. I knew there was some sense in what she was saying. "What would we have to do?"

"We'd launch an appeal asking people to send him get-well cards," Alison said. "I could ring all our customers at work for a start. Write to a few local companies. Maybe the *Sutton Guardian* would run a story about it. What do you think? There's no harm in trying, is there? Go on. Say yes!"

"I'm not sure." But she was beginning to talk me into it. "How many cards do you think we'd have to get?"

"Oh, I don't know . . ." Alison waved her hand in the air as though it wasn't important. "A thousand? Two thousand?"

I thought. A couple of thousand cards didn't seem an impossible target. Craig must have received over two hundred already.

"If we don't do it the cards will stop coming soon," Alison urged. "You can't have many friends who haven't sent one yet. And you know how Craig loves getting his cards."

It was true. That moment, at eleven or twelve o'clock, when the porter brought in the ward post and shouted, "More for Craig" was the highlight of his day. He wouldn't let me touch them. He wanted to open every one himself. It was the only time he really seemed to wake up.

"Oh all right then, Alison," I said. "I suppose it can't do any harm. Let's go for it . . ."

* * *

Introduction

If some old gypsy had read my tea-leaves that day in Great Ormond Street Hospital and told me that over the next four years Craig would receive more than one hundred million get-well cards from caring people all over the world, I wonder if I'd have believed her.

And if that same gypsy had told me that "the cards" were going to take over my life. That our small council house would overflow with sackfuls of get-well cards. That our car would have to sit out on the road because our garage was packed to the roof with cards. That every week for nearly four years I would have to rope in dozens of friends and neighbors to help me open Craig's mountain of mail, would I have believed that? And, what's more important, if I had believed it, would I still have gone ahead?

I like to think I would. I pray I would. Because one thing is certain. If I hadn't said yes to Alison's idea that afternoon, my son Craig Shergold would not be alive today.

Chapter 1

THERE'D BEEN no reason to think on the night that Craig was born that he wasn't going to grow up to be a healthy little boy.

He came into the world at 10:30 P.M. on June 24, 1979—Midsummer night—in St. Helier Hospital, South London, just down the road from Carshalton where Ernie and I lived. It was a perfectly straightforward, normal birth except for one thing—both the parents were in floods of tears.

"No need to cry, Mrs. Shergold." The midwife was shaking her head and laughing at the pair of us as she lifted the baby off the scales. "You've got a lovely baby boy. Seven pound fifteen ounces," and she put him into my arms.

I was so excited I couldn't speak. It was only when I twisted over in the delivery bed to show him to Ernie that I saw the tears rolling down his cheeks too. "A little boy!" he kept saying, "It's a little boy!" and for the next five minutes we just hugged each other and cried.

I know every baby is a miracle to its own mum and dad but Craig was extra special for us because we'd had to wait twelve whole years for him. Steven, our first baby, had been born in 1967, when I was nineteen, and we'd always planned to give him a little brother or sister. But for some reason it just hadn't happened (though I used to tell anyone who was nosy enough to ask that we were having lots of fun trying!). Then in November 1978, when we'd just about given up hope, I'd found I was pregnant again. We'd thrown such a party to celebrate—I'd bought a new dress and made poor Ernie wear his best suit and tie. We were absolutely over the moon. The singing and dancing had gone on all night and most of the next day.

And now, at last, our new baby was safely here and our family was complete. After Ernie had given us both a last kiss, he left for home and the nurse tucked me up in bed in a side ward with Craig snug in a cot beside me. "Now sleep, Mrs. Shergold," she ordered, and she switched out the light. Sleep? She'd be lucky! The minute the door closed I flicked the light back on and dived into the cot. I unwrapped the blankets and carefully checked every inch of him, wanting to see for myself that he was perfect. He was.

He had a mop of the most wonderful dark hair. As I ran my fingers through it and saw the big fat neck underneath I started to giggle. That was Ernie's neck—there was no mistaking it. Still, at least he hadn't got my nose, poor child. In fact he was such a pretty baby, with his long dark eyelashes and rosebud mouth, that he almost looked like a girl. When I was pregnant I'd hoped for a girl but looking at my adorable son now I had no regrets. I wrapped him carefully back up and cradled him in my arms. In my whole life I'd never felt such happiness. The feeling was so strong it frightened me and I remember I said a little prayer. "Dear God. Please, please, don't let anything happen to him. I love him so much already."

Behind the bed there was a headset for the hospital radio, and I slipped on the earphones and heard the wonderful deep voice of Ray Charles singing "I Can't Stop Loving You"—my favorite song. I may not have the best voice in the world but I've never let that stop me. I rocked Craig in my arms and sang happily along with Ray.

I was so lost in the music that I didn't notice the door burst open. But I did notice when the headphones were suddenly wrenched off my head and a cross voice shouted in my ear, "Mrs. Shergold. You're a very naughty girl. You're waking up the whole ward!" The nurse snatched Craig from me and plonked him back in his cot. I tried to look apologetic. "Sorry," I said as she snapped off the light. But it was a fib really. I wouldn't have cared if I'd woken up the whole of London that night. Next day I did have the grace to apologize to the other mums for putting them through such torture. "It's all right, love. It didn't worry us," one of them laughed. "We thought Shirley Bassey must be in labor . . ."

We decided to call our new baby Craig, which was a name I'd found in a book of Christian names someone had given me. "It means strong and enduring, like a rock," I told Ernie. "I like that." For his second name we settled on Thomas, after my dad.

Steven was used to being the only child and I'd been afraid he might feel left out with all the fuss over the new baby but I needn't have worried. He was as thrilled with his little brother as we were—he even wrote a poem about him and brought it into the hospital to give me. That was a big effort for Steven because at the time he hated school and English lessons were real torture for him. I found the poem the other day, tucked between the pages of Craig's baby photo album.

> *Our Baby.*
> *Oh what a sweet little baby,*
> *So pretty and small,*
> *Oh how I love to cuddle his body so small.*
> *His name is Craig.*
> *To me he is the best baby of all!*

Well, maybe it wouldn't win any prizes, but for me it put the icing on the cake that wonderful week.

The day before I was due to take Craig home from hospital my best friend Carol came in to see him. Carol and I go back a long way—she was in my gang at school—and she probably knows me better than anyone. She was cuddling Craig and admiring him, when out of the blue I said to her, "Do you know, Carol, if anything happened to him I just couldn't bear it. I think I'd die."

She gave me a funny look. "Nothing's going to happen to him, Marion. What on earth made you say that?"

I didn't know myself. "It's hard to explain," I said. "It's just that I'm so happy now and sometimes when I look at him I get this awful feeling that something is going to come along to spoil it. I don't know why. I wasn't like this with Steven." I could feel my eyes filling up.

Carol put her arm around me. "Don't be so daft, Marion," she said. "Craig's going to be fine. You've got the baby blues, that's all."

I told myself she was right and after that, whenever the terrible flashes of doubt rose up I did my best to push them away. Of course nothing was going to happen to Craig, I told myself. It was just my hormones making me over-anxious, like Carol said. Gradually as the weeks passed, the feeling came less and less often. But it never quite went away.

Even before I had kids of my own I'd always believed that family life was the most important thing in the world. I grew up in a big tenement building in the Boro'—the local name for the Borough of Southwark just south of the Thames. We only had two rooms, one for eating and one for sleeping, and the mod. cons. in Peabody Buildings left a lot to be desired. Twelve families had to share the toilet on our landing, and every Friday night Dad would carry in our tin bath (marked with a bright-red M5 so he could tell it from the eleven others hanging in the laundry), put the water on to boil, and we would all bathe in front of the fire—first our maiden-aunt Anne, who lived on the next landing, then me, then my brother Kevin, then Mum (I never worked out when Dad took his own bath!).

But even though we were short of home comforts I did have a really happy childhood. My mum came from a very big family and our living room was always full of people. Uncles and aunties used to pop in and out, and there'd always be a kiss and a hug for Kevin and me. We grew up surrounded by singing and laughter and love, and I wanted that for my own kids too. I've always been a great believer in the power of love. I've never had time for those people who think you can spoil kids by showing them too much affection.

So, though Ernie and I were often short of money and there weren't many toys while Craig was growing up I made sure, like I had with Steven, that there were always plenty of cuddles. I don't know if that was why, but Craig

grew into a very contented baby. He was always smiling
and laughing, and boy, did he love an audience! Even before he was walking he was making people laugh. He was
a real performer.

He was musical too. In 1979 that song "Didn't We Have
a Loverley Day, the Day We Went to Bangor" was in the
top ten—and it was his absolute favorite. I'd put it on the
record player and he'd get on his hands and knees and be
rocking to this song and laughing at us because he knew
we were watching him. That Christmas when he was six
months old I took Craig up to Allders, the big department
store in Sutton, to have his photo taken. Dad came with
us. Craig was looking very serious—he just would not
smile until Dad went, "Didn't we have a loverley day . . ."
and it was just like pressing a button. Craig started rocking
away and chuckling and we got the most beautiful picture.

Soon Craig was doing the singing himself. Almost from
the day he could talk he could sing. My mum had a lovely
voice and she and Dad taught him the same old cockney
songs that they'd taught me and Kevin—I think some of
those songs must have gone back to the Boer War. Craig had
a very good memory and by the time he was three or four
years old he knew them all off by heart. As well as being a
good singer my mum was a brilliant mimic and I think it
was watching her that set Craig off doing impressions. To
start with he used to imitate our friends, but before long he
was taking off characters and adverts on telly too (I wasn't
always happy about that—when the "Shake and Vac" adverts
came out my carpets used to be full of Vim . . .). He got
very good at his impressions. Every Christmas we used to
have a family concert where everyone had to do a turn—sing
a song, recite a monologue or tell a joke—and Craig's
"Hylda Baker" always stole the show.

When he was five Craig announced that he wanted to be
an actor when he grew up. I took him seriously. To me it
seemed a perfectly sensible thing to want to do. Per-
forming is in the blood on my side of the family. My
mum's father was a musician and played the trumpet in
some famous band before I was born. He passed his love
of music and the stage on to my mum. Dad was a pretty
good piano player too in his day. When we were growing

up in the Boro' he boosted his wages from the brewery by playing the piano and singing down the pub every Saturday night. Sometimes my mum would sing as well and if Kevin and I behaved ourselves we were allowed to sit in a corner of the Rose and Crown with a glass of lemonade and a packet of potato chips and listen. My sister Kate was born after we moved from the Boro' and she never saw those pub concerts but whatever it was in Mum and Dad's blood, they must have passed on to her because she grew up to be a professional singer.

Sadly the family voice missed me out, but I did inherit the Blydes' love of an audience. Ernie always tells people that the restaurant is my stage and in a funny way I think he's right. You have to be a bit of an actress when you work as a waitress. You put on different faces for different occasions—I used to anyway. Jolly and jokey for a football club dance. Polite and respectful for a black-tie dinner. Deadpan when a married boss was wining and dining his secretary. I could put on different voices too. I'd drop the cockney and talk as if I'd been to finishing school if I was serving at a Buckingham Palace garden party. But in the clubhouse serving breakfast to the Chelsea team after training you'd never know I'd left the Boro'. Being a waitress didn't feel like work to me. It was one long performance, and I loved it!

When Craig was very small I only worked at lunchtimes and at night after he was safely tucked up in bed. I hadn't intended to work at all. While I was pregnant I'd decided I was going to stay at home and be a full-time mum. After waiting so long for him I wanted to enjoy every minute with my new baby. But it didn't work out that way. When Craig was only two months old Ernie lost his job and I was forced to ask my boss Derek for my old job back as head waitress at the Grange Restaurant. Luckily he hadn't replaced me and I was soon back into the swing of things. Although I hated leaving Craig, I told myself that with my mum, Ernie *and* Steven watching over him he'd have all the loving care he could possibly need. And looking back, I think it was all for the best. Being a full-time housewife, cleaning and cooking with no one to talk to all day would probably have driven me mad. I need people around me. People and parties have always been like food and drink to me.

In that way I'm quite different from Ernie who's quiet and shy by nature and a bit of a loner. We're different in other ways too. For instance Ernie is very easy-going and doesn't get worked up about things as easily as me. We do have plenty of things in common as well but actually I think it's our differences which have helped Ernie and me through the rough times. Our temperaments seem to balance each other out.

In those first few years of his life I often thought I'd chosen the wrong name for Craig. "Strong as a rock" sometimes seemed like a bad joke. Steven had never suffered from a single childhood illness, but Craig caught just about everything. If there was a bug going round, he was guaranteed to get it. One June, just before he was four years old, he was really poorly with chickenpox. Only a month afterward he went down with measles. And he'd only just got over those two when he caught whooping cough (he hadn't been vaccinated because one of Ernie's nephews had epilepsy). That whooping cough really scared me. I'd never seen a child so ill. He whooped and whooped until he foamed at the mouth. It went on for weeks and by the end of every day he had a blinding headache from coughing so much. At least I used to think then it was from the coughing. Sometimes now I wonder.

It was in March 1984 that Craig gave us the biggest fright. One morning when I went in to the bedroom to wake him up he wouldn't get out of bed, so I tickled his feet under the covers. "Come on, lazy-bones. You'll be late for nursery."

He looked up at me and his face was white. "Mum," he said, "I can't walk."

All the fears which had haunted me when Craig was a small baby came back in one blinding flash. I was terrified he was going to die. My legs turned to jelly and I had to sit down on the edge of his bunk.

"What do you mean you can't walk?"

"I can't move my legs. I feel funny," he said.

Ernie and I carried him downstairs and put him on the settee and I called the doctor. I was beside myself with worry, but the doctor didn't seem very concerned. "It's just a virus," he said when he'd examined Craig. "It's made him feel weak, that's all. It'll pass."

But it didn't pass. It got worse. The next day Craig was admitted to hospital and he stayed there for five days. During those five days Ernie and I hardly left his bedside, but Craig wouldn't have known if we were there or not. He just slept and slept. Then slowly he started to be more alert and once he was able to stand up and hobble around they let him come home again. They did all sorts of tests on him but they never found anything wrong. "Don't worry about it, Mrs. Shergold. There's no reason anything like it should happen again," the consultant assured me. But I did worry. Afterward, sometimes when Craig hugged me good night or came for his morning cuddle before he went to school, a feeling of dread would come over me. I loved my little boy so much it scared me.

Craig took to school like a duck to water. There wasn't a keener kid in Carshalton and from the start his reports were good. I'm not pretending he was perfect. Like most kids he could be a holy terror and he got into scrapes like any small boy, but he could usually talk his way out of trouble. Even the day I caught him hanging off the back of the milk-float getting a tow on his skate-board I couldn't stay cross with him for long. Steven didn't often lose his temper with him either, though Craig used to push him to the limit. He always wanted to play with Steven and his friends, but being twelve years older, they didn't always want him hanging around. "Upstairs! Hop it!" Steven would say when his mates came in. But Craig would pull a pathetic face and go, "Ohhhh Ugly!" (Ugly was his pet-name for Steven) and Steve would end up letting him stay. Craig was very good in an argument. He had all the answers. And if all else failed he knew he could always make Steven laugh and get what he wanted that way. Sometimes Steve would shake his head and say, "He's going to be a train-robber, Mum. He'll finish up in prison—he's too clever for his own good."

Craig got hooked on football at the same time as I started working at the Chelsea Football Club at Stamford

Bridge. I was doing freelance waitressing at that time and I worked all over the place—I didn't mind where I went as long as the hours suited. The job at Chelsea involved serving breakfast to the players after training and dinners to the directors on match days. The team breakfasts were very informal and I soon got to know the players. It was quite a coincidence really that it was Chelsea, rather than one of the other London teams, that I found a job with because Ernie and his whole family had always been mad keen Chelsea fans. With me working there as well, there was only one team that Craig could possibly support. Though "support" doesn't describe it properly. He was a fanatic about Chelsea. Chelsea F.C. was the business! His bedroom was a shrine to the team. He had all the gear—scarves, rosettes, duvet cover, photos of players all over the wall ... Even his pop idol, Kylie Minogue, had to take second place to Chelsea and her pictures were squashed together to make room.

Steven wasn't too pleased about it. He shared Craig's bedroom and he was keener on rugby and kung fu than on football. But he put up with it. Steven had other things on his mind now. He'd left school, got himself a job and started courting ...

When he was eight Craig started to play Little League football and Ernie used to take him to the school gym on a Monday night for coaching. The Tigers played their matches on Saturday mornings at the playing field up the road. I don't think Craig would ever have been a star but he loved it and like every other kid in the team he dreamed of playing for Chelsea when he grew up. After the Tigers match, if there was a home game, Ernie would take Craig to see Chelsea play at Stamford Bridge. Ernie had always spent a lot of time with Craig when he was small and now they were growing into really good mates.

But that year was a bad time for me. My mum found a lump on her breast and a few days later the doctors told her it was cancer. I gave up work and when they'd finished giving her chemotherapy treatment at the Royal Marsden Hospital I nursed her at home until she died in July 1988. Her death hit the whole family hard. Everyone had loved my old mum. She was a big personality—a real old-type cockney who called a spade a spade. She could swear a bit too, but not in a way that anyone would take offense at because she was so funny with it. She'd had Parkinson's disease for most of her life so she hadn't ever been able to go out to work, and it had always been a struggle for her to make ends meet. She'd never been abroad or even slept in a hotel bed until the year before she died when we took her to Spain. But I never once heard her complain. Her family was always much more important to her than money. She would have killed for her kids. And for her grandchildren too. Craig was the apple of her eye.

After she died I felt really tired and low and I started to have bad dreams. One terrible night in September I dreamed that Craig was dead and lying in a white coffin across my feet on the bed. It was so real I felt I could reach out and touch him. His head was on my left and his face was looking up at me with his eyes closed while all around his face were layers of pleated white lace and silk. And although in my dream I was still in my own bed, the wall of my bedroom had turned into the wall of Alf Smith's funeral parlor where my mum had been laid out. I screamed. When I woke up the sweat was rolling off me and Ernie was shaking me. "What's the matter, Mal? What is it?"

"I've got to see Craig," I was trembling like a leaf. "I've got to see if he's all right . . ."

"Of course he's all right," Ernie tried to calm me down. "It was just a nightmare, that's all."

But I couldn't rest until I'd been into Craig's bedroom and put my face close to his mouth and checked that he was still breathing.

Of course he was. But when I came back to bed I cried and cried while Ern held me tight in his arms. "Ern, if anything happens to him I'll die," I sobbed. "I can't live without him."

For days afterward the image of Craig in his coffin haunted me. I saw it everywhere I looked. I knew I had to pull myself together. I was run down. What I needed was a holiday.

I've always been a great one for holidays. Ever since we'd been married if I ever had a bit of spare money I'd go down to the travel agents and book a cheap package deal. Material things have never really bothered me. If people say, "Oh come and see my new oven . . ." I yawn. Forget it. Holidays are what count. Holidays and flowers are the two things I never grudge spending money on.

We booked a week in Benidorm in November. We hadn't been there before. By the time November came around a whole crowd of friends and family had cottoned on to the idea and there were thirty-six of us! It was going to be a real old-fashioned knees-up. Steven and Ernie took a week off work—Ernie was a delivery driver for the London Electricity Board now—and we got permission to take Craig off school. We even persuaded my old dad to come along, and on November 19 we all set off from Heathrow.

We had a terrific time. None of us was impressed with Benidorm, which was colder than Russia that week, but the night-life was great. I took my party-music tapes and we played them every night in the bar and stayed up till the early hours dancing and singing. The barman did such good trade that week that he offered to buy my tapes off me!

Craig joined in everything we did. There were only a couple of other kids in our party and no way was he going to be left out of the grown-up fun. I wouldn't have left him on his own in the hotel room anyway, so I used to make him take a long nap in the afternoon, so he could keep going at night. Not that he ever had much trouble keeping going. Craig was a party person like me. It was always Ernie and Steve who'd be yawning before him.

One night toward the end of the week there was a lottery in one of the bars and Craig won it. It was about a hundred pounds but they gave it to him in pesetas, nearly 21,000 of them! He had notes spilling everywhere. "What a lucky boy, Craig," the barman said. "God smiles on you, eh?" Craig had always wanted a radio-control car and I promised him he could buy one with the money when we got home.

On the last day of the holiday six of us decided to go on a coach trip to a place called Guadalesk—the blue lagoon—high in the hills above Benidorm. Craig didn't want to come and we left him in the hotel with Steven, his girlfriend Sharon and their friends.

The view from the top of the old stone steps at Guadalesk was wonderful. Ernie had rented a video camera for the holiday and he'd filmed just about everything that happened that week. Every disco evening. Every trip to the freezing cold beach . . . I made him sweep the video round the whole view at Guadalesk. "Isn't that absolutely magnificent, Ern?" I pointed down to the brilliant blue lake below us. This was the only bit of Spain that had impressed me so far. The beach at Benidorm might as well have been in Siberia, and the hotels looked like concrete boxes. But this was more like it. I was fooling around and waving to the camera, happy because we were going home soon. The holiday had done its job. My blues were gone. I felt ready to face life again. After the weather this week I even felt ready for the British winter. *"Adios amigos,"* I shouted.

At the top of the steps there was an old cemetery with a high stone wall around it and inside there were long walls of family vaults piled one on top of another. On the wall surrounding the cemetery I noticed a plaque with some engraved lettering and I walked over to read it. The inscription was in Spanish and English. I read it aloud to Ernie.

"Wanderer stop awhile and think of the marvelous works of God and of your short passage on earth."

It was as if a bubble had burst. That plaque brought it all back to me. How much I missed my mum. How I'd never ever see her again . . . I called Ernie over to film the inscription. It touched something deep inside me and I wanted to remember it. "It's very true that, isn't it, Ern?" I said. Ernie nodded. He could see I was down. I shivered. Suddenly all I wanted was to get back to the hotel and to Craig.

"Come on," I said. "Let's go," And Ernie put the camera down, tucked his arm through mine and we walked back to the bus.

Chapter 2

—∞—

IT STARTED in the plane on the way home from Benidorm.

"Oh Mum, my ears hurt," Craig complained a couple of minutes after we took off. The change in air pressure had never bothered him when we'd flown before but a couple of babies in the front of the plane were crying so I thought maybe that had put the idea in his head. The plane leveled out and the babies stopped crying, but Craig's earache didn't go away. He started to moan and hold his head. I was puzzled. Craig wasn't a whiner—this wasn't like him . . .

People were turning round to look. I asked the stewardess if she had anything I could give him. "Maybe his sinuses are blocked," she suggested. She found some inhaling capsules in the first-aid box. "Here, try these. They often do the trick."

I broke the capsules on to a handkerchief and held them to Craig's nose and after a while he stopped crying and dozed off. As we were coming in to land he woke up again and whimpered but the stewardess brought me some paper cups to hold over his ears and it seemed to help.

Back home the next morning Ernie left for work as usual at six-thirty and an hour later Craig came in to winkle me out of bed. I opened my eyes and saw him hovering by the door, his face all screwed up with pain. "Oh Mum, my ear does hurt," he said.

13

"All right, darling, you can stay off school today," I said, still half asleep. "Come on, climb into bed and have a cuddle." Craig didn't need asking twice. He was always ready for a cuddle.

When the earache hadn't gone away by the afternoon I took him up to the local surgery. The doctor thought the flying had probably upset the pressure inside Craig's ears. "It should settle down in a day or two. Give him a couple of paracetamol if it gets any worse," he said. He didn't seem too bothered, and I wasn't terribly worried myself. Craig had been bound to get earache sooner or later—he'd had just about every other childhood illness.

I kept him at home for two days. By the third day the pain had eased off and Craig was nagging me to let him go back to school. In the end I gave in, although I still didn't think he looked a hundred percent. He was screwing up his eyes and blinking a lot, and I thought he needed to catch up on his sleep. But he was desperate to tell his mates all about Benidorm.

Over the next few days the pain kept coming and going and Craig started to look very pale. I suspected he was going down with a virus. "Stay off school, darling," I persuaded. "There's only a couple of weeks to go before you break up—you won't miss much." But he was set on going. "We've got the play. And I'm King Herod. I must go, Mum."

For a week the earache came, went and came again until after another sleepless night I took Craig back to see the doctor. After he checked Craig's ears he patted him on the head and said, "Would you go and sit in the waiting-room, Craig. I'd like a little word with your mother."

"There's no infection at all in Craig's ears," he told me when we were on our own. "I'm not saying the pain isn't real but I'm wondering if it could have been brought on by stress. It could be a delayed reaction to his grandmother's death. He was very close to your mum, wasn't he?"

I was a bit taken aback. But he was right—Craig *had* been terribly close to his nan. He'd idolized her. He used to tease me sometimes that he was going to leave home and live with her because she was a better cook than I was. "No one in the world can cook skate like my nan," he'd say. "Yours doesn't taste half as good." But he hadn't cried at all when she died—not in front of me anyway. Maybe the doctor was right, I thought. Maybe Craig had bottled all his grief up inside himself and now it was coming out in physical symptoms.

"Can you give him anything for it?" I asked.

He shrugged. "It should get better with time. Give him painkillers if it gets too bad, and try not to worry about it."

I decided to take his advice. Earache wasn't that serious, I told myself. I used to have a lot of earache myself when I was Craig's age.

I had something else to worry about now anyway—Steven had just informed us that Sharon was having a baby and that they were going to get married. Compared with that bombshell Craig's earache seemed a minor problem. I liked Sharon but I was furious at the pair of them for being so stupid. "Haven't they heard of birth control?" I stormed at Ernie. "Steven wants to be a fireman. How's he going to do his training with a wife and baby to support?"

As usual Ernie calmed me down. "They'll manage, Mal," he said. "They do love each other. That's the important thing . . . "

By the afternoon of the school nativity play life had settled down again. I was beginning to get used to the idea of being a grandmother and, as the doctor had predicted, Craig's earache seemed to be getting better. I went along to the school to see his acting debut. It wasn't a star role but he made the most of it. He swaggered on stage wearing his shiny tinfoil crown and gold epaulettes, strode around looking important, and said his few lines loud and clear. He really enjoyed playing the villain, you could tell. The next day school broke up and we started to get ready for Christmas.

I'm always very silly at Christmas. It's like Selfridges in our house—you can't get another decoration up on the walls and I always make a sack for everyone, even for Ernie. This year Steven had been invited to Sharon's mother's house for Christmas lunch and after he left on Christmas morning Craig brought his sack downstairs to open his presents in front of the telly. But he didn't seem very interested in them. After he'd opened them he put them straight down on the floor. Then he said, "Thanks, Mum," in a little voice and curled up in the armchair to watch the telly. I felt disappointed. Usually Craig was so pleased with his Christmas sack. Maybe I should have asked him what he'd like instead of just guessing, I thought. Kids started to know what they wanted when they were nine.

His big present from Ernie and me was a new bright-yellow BMX bike. "Do you want to go out after breakfast and have a ride up the road on it?" Ernie asked him. "I'll come with you."

Craig gave a little sigh. "I don't think so, Dad. I think I'll just sit here and watch telly for a bit." Ernie looked at me and raised his eyebrows. I shrugged. Craig's behavior puzzled me as much as him.

There was a cartoon on telly and Craig sank into his chair and started to watch it. I sat down near the window and began to fold up the crumpled wrapping paper from his presents, watching him out of the corner of my eye. He was still blinking a lot, I noticed, and screwing up his eyes as he stared at the screen. Maybe he was just tired. Too many late nights. Craig did stay up late when we had people round—he hated to miss anything. And there'd been lots of people round over the holidays. Every night had been a party. "Perhaps we ought to be stricter about his bedtime," I said to Ernie that night.

Over the next few days I made sure that Craig caught up on his sleep so that he'd be able to enjoy New Year's Eve. We always had a big "do" to see the New Year in and Craig loved helping to carry the food and drinks round.

And then, the day before the party, I woke up with earache myself. I couldn't believe it. The pain was so bad I could hardly speak. I dragged myself to the doctor who shone a light in my ears. "Well, there's no mystery about *your* trouble anyway," he said. "You've got a really bad infection in both ears. I'll give you some antibiotics."

It got worse. By New Year's Eve I was in absolute agony. The only way I could make it bearable was to let my jaw hang open the whole time. I looked half-witted but I was past caring. I'd never had an earache like it. "Come on, Mal, let's call the party off," Ernie said. "Everyone'll understand." But I couldn't face letting people down at the last minute. I doped myself up with painkillers and spent the day making sausage-rolls with my eyes half-shut and my jaw hanging open. Ernie moved the dining table into the kitchen and pushed back the furniture and at eight o'clock the house started filling up. There was my old dad, wearing a brave face for his first new year without my mum, Steven and Sharon, Ernie's brother Fred and his wife Joyce, Craig's godparents John and Sandra, my sister Kate and her husband Jimmy, and dozens of aunts, uncles and friends.

Craig really seemed to be back to his old self and was doing his bit to help. I stayed in the kitchen carving turkey, pouring drinks and nursing my ear, but I kept catching glimpses of him in the other room offering plates of prawns and cockles around. My party tapes were playing and everyone was dancing but there was no way I could join in. Even keeping my smile fixed in place took a real effort. It felt as though there was a road drill going in my head.

I was washing glasses when Steven came into the kitchen at about ten o'clock. "Where's Craig, Mum?" he asked. "I haven't seen him for a bit."

It doesn't take long to search a house the size of ours. We found him in his bedroom—curled up tight under his blue Chelsea comforter with just the top of his head showing.

"Craig?" I said. "Are you all right?"

The comforter twitched and a little voice said, "Yes, Mum."

"Aren't you coming down to see the New Year in?"

Craig peered out at me. "No. I'll say Happy New Year tomorrow. I'm very tired." And his head disappeared again under the comforter.

It was strange. Craig always loved New Year—I closed his door and walked slowly downstairs. The way this ear business seemed to be draining all his energy was beginning to bother me. Maybe I ought to ask the doctor for a tonic for him.

Then at midnight when all the poppers were going off and everyone was singing "Auld Lang Syne," a pair of bare feet appeared at the top of the stairs. "Can I have a popper, Mum?" a little voice asked. A couple of minutes later he was away—laughing, popping poppers at Steven and wiping kisses off his face. Ernie nudged me. "Look at him—there's not much wrong with him now." For some reason when he said that I burst into tears and he put his arm round me. "Come on, cheer up. It's been a bad year. It's 1989 now—things have got to start getting better."

He was too optimistic. Over the next few days, although Craig did seem more like his old self, my earache got steadily worse. The antibiotics didn't seem to be doing me any good at all. Then, two weeks into the New Year I woke up one Sunday morning to find Craig standing by our bedroom door holding his hand over his ear and sobbing. I knew that what I'd been dreading had happened. I'd given Craig my ear infection.

The surgery wasn't open until the next day and by the time we got there Craig was huddled into a ball, rocking backward and forward with the pain. The strange thing was, my own earache had gone. The doctor took one look in Craig's ear and confirmed my fears. "Yes, he has an infection," he said. "But it's not too bad. I think we've caught it early." He scribbled on his prescription pad. "I'll give him some antibiotics. It should start to improve in a day or two."

Once more I kept Craig off school, but after two days he was getting worse rather than better. I gave him as many paracetamols as I dared but he spent all day clutching his head. "I can feel water in my ears, Mum," he kept saying. Yet again I picked up the telephone to make an appointment with our GP.

I felt a bit uncomfortable sitting in the waiting room this time. I was sure the receptionist was beginning to think we were a family of hypochondriacs.

"It's not very inflamed," the doctor said, shining a light in Craig's ear. "I can't understand why he's in so much pain. It's not nearly as bad an infection as you had."

He gave Craig a puzzled look. "Have you been sick?"

Craig shook his head. "No. But I feel a bit sick."

The doctor picked up his pen. "I'll write a prescription for something to help that. This is a medicine that your mother can drop by syringe on to the back of your throat, Craig. It should take the nausea away."

As I opened the door to go out I remembered something and turned back. "Doctor, he says there's water in his ears."

The doctor nodded. "It can sometimes feel like that if there's an infection. It should clear up by the time he finishes the antibiotics."

I didn't feel at all reassured. Craig slumped in the seat beside me as I drove to the chemist to pick up the prescription. He was trying to be brave but I could tell his ears were hurting again. His eyes were very wide and every time we went over a bump in the road he was flinching with pain. I was sure the doctor had made a mistake. I knew my Craig wasn't a crybaby. When he grazed his knees or bumped his head messing about on his skateboard he never made a big fuss about it. Even when he'd been ill with whooping cough he hadn't cried the way he'd been doing this week. But then my own earache had been so bad I'd felt like screaming. Maybe the infection was much worse than it looked. After all, I thought, that instrument the doctor used couldn't see all the way into his ears.

The chemist on our estate is on "the circle," which is a roundabout surrounded by shops. The pharmacist was a little Chinese man who could only speak broken English but was always very friendly. He'd been making up medicines for me for nearly two months now so he was getting to know my face. I gave him the prescription and saw him frown at Craig before he disappeared out the back. A couple of minutes later he hurried back holding the packet with Craig's medicine inside. But instead of just handing it over the counter he came out into the shop and bent over and stared into Craig's eyes. Then he looked up at me and his face was worried. "I no like! I no like!" he said.

I felt scared. "What do you mean, you don't like?"

He shook his head and waved his hands about excitedly. "No good, no good. Me no happy with your son. Hospital! hospital!"

It was all I needed. Suddenly I was filled with energy. "Right," I said. "Thank you very much." I bundled Craig back into the car. "We're going to hospital, Craig," I said.

"We'll see if *they* can find out what's wrong with you." I
don't know if he heard me. He seemed to be in another
world. I decided to take him to Queen Mary's, the big
children's hospital in Carshalton which was only about a
mile away. I thought he'd be seen more quickly there than
in a general hospital. But I was wrong. The casualty department was like a madhouse, with queues of children
waiting for attention. Every kid in Carshalton seemed to
have chosen that day to fall off his bike or get bitten by
the dog.

It was two hours before we were seen. Craig had gone
drowsy again and was lying across my knee by the time a
nurse bustled up. "Now, what's the problem here?" she
asked. I told her about the earache and she nodded, stuck
a thermometer in his mouth and disappeared. Twenty minutes later I laid Craig down, and went looking for her. I
found her staring at an X-ray.

"That thermometer'll have gone hot and cold again by
now," I said.

She jumped. "I'm ever so sorry," she said, "but we're
so busy . . . "

Craig's temperature was normal. But the nurse said she
would ask a doctor to have a look at him "just in case"
and led us into a cubicle. It was a lady doctor, and I
guessed she'd been on duty a long time, because she
looked as tired as I felt. She listened as I told her the
whole story and then she shone a flashlight in Craig's ears
and tapped his cheekbones. He winced.

"He seems to have blocked sinuses," she said. "I think
we'll change his antibiotic to a stronger one." She wrote
out a prescription and handed it to me. "You can collect
that from the dispensary here. And I'd like you to get
some inhaling crystals for him—you can buy those from
any chemist. Once his sinuses start to clear it should relieve the pain." She scribbled something on a notepad.
"I'll ask the ENT department to make an appointment for
him to see the ear specialist next week. They'll send you
a card to let you know what day." She moved on to deal
with a little girl with a cut hand in the next cubicle.

She had seemed very sure of her diagnosis and I left the
hospital feeling much calmer than when I'd gone in. I'd

suffered from sinus trouble myself from time to time and I wanted to believe that's all it was. Sinuses weren't too serious—I was pretty certain of that.

Ten minutes later I was back at the chemist on the circle. I'd given a lift to Theresa, my Irish next-door neighbor, and I left Craig outside in the car with her. He was dozing and there didn't seem any point in waking him up.

I smiled at the little Chinese pharmacist. "I've been to the hospital," I told him.

"Oh good, good." He rubbed his hands together. "What have they told you?"

"They said to get some inhaling crystals."

His face changed. "This is for you?"

"No—for Craig."

"For Craig? No! No!" He shook his head as if I'd told him to hand me the money out of his till. He did fetch a packet down off the shelf but he wasn't happy about it. Even as he put them in a bag for me he was still muttering "No! No! No!" to himself.

I paid for the crystals and he followed me out of the shop. As I got into the driver's seat he bent down and peered through the car window. Craig half-woke up and stared back at him. "No like. No like!" the pharmacist said to me again. Then he turned and walked back into the shop, shaking his head from side to side.

It really did frighten me. As I drove home, his words kept running through my head. I knew Chinese people understood a lot about medicine—things that couldn't be properly explained by Western doctors, like acupuncture and herbal treatments. What if that little Chinese man had seen something in Craig that English doctors couldn't see?

Ernie pooh-poohed the idea when I mentioned it that evening. "He's not a doctor, is he?" he said. "You don't want to go listening to people like that. Craig'll be all right. You're just scaring yourself for nothing. Give the new medicine a chance." So that night after Craig had taken a spoonful of his new antibiotic, I dissolved the inhaling crystals in hot water and made him sit over a basin with a towel over his head. He hated it and kept saying he was going to be sick, so in the end I gave up and fetched my own box of inhaling capsules. I broke one open, spread the liquid on a handkerchief and laid it on his pillow hoping it would do the same job as the crystals.

The next morning when I tiptoed into his bedroom Craig was sleeping peacefully and his breathing sounded easier. I told Ernie the medicine seemed to be working. Ernie left for work and I was clearing up his breakfast things when Craig came downstairs, rubbing his eyes. "Hello, Mum," he smiled.

"Hello, darling," I said. "How are you this morning?"

"I'm unbelievably tired," he said slowly. Then he gave me a cheeky grin. "I am hungry though."

I felt like giving three cheers. Craig hadn't been interested in food for days.

"What would you like then? Rice Krispies? Weetabix?" I ran through the list of cereals in the cupboard and after a long think he decided that what he really fancied was a bowl of Shreddies in hot milk. Thank God, I thought. The old Craig's back. I was humming to myself as I warmed up the milk in the kitchen.

Craig sat down at the corner of the dining table so he could watch telly while he ate and I put the bowl of Shreddies in front of him. "There you are, darling." I sat down on the chair in the corner and watched him wolf it down. Typical, I thought. After all my worrying. All he'd needed was a change of antibiotic. What had I been getting myself in such a state about? Thank God I'd taken him to the hospital and got a second opinion. You couldn't beat a mother's instinct. I sat there feeling really pleased with myself as Craig polished off the whole bowl of cereal. "Delicious," he grinned and pushed his chair back from the table and walked over to the settee.

And then, without any warning at all, it happened. As he sat down on the settee, he vomited. Only when I say vomited—the word doesn't really describe it. What happened was more like an explosion. Craig's breakfast shot back out of his mouth and across the room and hit the wall so hard it splattered in all directions. There were Shreddies and milk everywhere.

For a moment I stood rooted to the spot. Then I screamed, "Theresa! Theresa!" I kept yelling my neighbor's name like a mad thing until she rushed in from next door.

"What's the matter, Marion? What's happened?"

I pointed at the walls. "Craig's been sick."

Theresa let out her breath. "Oh Bejasus," she said in her Irish brogue. "Is that all? I thought someone was being murdered. Sure he'll be fine now all the muck's come up. It's just what he needed."

"Don't be so stupid." I was beside myself. "He's not *fine!* You don't know what it was like. Just look at him."

Craig wasn't with us. He lay on the sofa, his eyes open, staring into the distance.

"Theresa, please." I grabbed her shoulder. "Stay here with him—just watch him while I phone the hospital. I'm afraid to leave him." Theresa stared at me as if I was mad, but she stood obediently in the living room while I ran up the stairs to the landing and picked up the phone.

The telephone directory was on the chair next to the phone. I flicked through the pages till I found the number of Queen Mary's Hospital but my fingers were shaking so much I could hardly dial. The operator answered and I asked to be connected to the Ear, Nose and Throat department.

The phone seemed to ring for an age before it was picked up.

"Can I help you?" a bored voice asked. I tried to stay calm. "This is Marion Shergold speaking. My son Craig has an appointment some time next week, but he has just been very, very sick. I want to change the appointment to today."

There was a pause and the sound of pages being turned.

"I'm sorry, Mrs. Shergold, but all the available appointments are taken today. Your son has an appointment on Thursday."

Something told me I was fighting for more than a place in the queue now and I clenched my teeth. "Listen, lady," I spat, "if you don't let me come to see you today I shall go to every bloody hospital in the country. My little boy is not a whiner. I'm telling you he is ill. This sickness was like a *bomb!*"

There was another long pause at the other end. Then a

heavy sigh. "Well, I can't promise you anything, Mrs. Shergold, but I'll see what I can do. Leave me your telephone number and I'll ring you back."

I hovered anxiously by the phone until, five minutes later, it rang again. "I have an appointment for you at three o'clock." The woman sounded put out. "I'm afraid that's the best I can do."

I looked at my watch. Five past nine. How on earth was I going to fill in the next six hours? I ran downstairs. Theresa went back next door promising she'd return if I called and I sat down next to Craig on the settee. He looked up at me. "Oh Mummy," he said, "I'm so tired." Craig didn't often call me Mummy now. Since he'd been at school it had been Mum. It was as though he'd gone back to babyhood. He even looked like a baby lying there, with his eyes all big and dark against his white face. "Would you like to go on Mummy's bed, Craig?" I asked and he nodded. I cleaned him up as best I could and then I half-led, half-carried him upstairs to our bedroom. "I'll make you a boat of pillows, shall I? Like I used to do when you were little?" He nodded again. I put pillows all around him and sat by the bed until he fell asleep. Then I covered him up with our comforter and came downstairs.

It took me nearly an hour to clear up all the mess and disinfect the carpet and walls. The sick had got everywhere. I couldn't believe how far it had spread. Afterward I washed the dishes and peeled the vegetables ready for Ernie's and Steve's dinner that night. Then I got the Hoover out—anything to fill in time. Every ten minutes I broke off what I was doing and ran upstairs but Craig didn't stir all morning from the position I'd left him in. He was in a very deep sleep, his breathing slow and regular. He was even sleeping like a baby. "While they're sleeping, they're getting better," my old mum used to say when kids were ill. I just hoped she was right.

At a quarter past two I put the kettle on for a pot of tea. Suddenly I heard a noise and I ran out of the kitchen to see Craig standing on the stairs. "Mum," he said, and I knew from his voice that the tears weren't far away, "my ears are hurting again. Please take me to the hospital now."

I went over and hugged him to me. "Try and hang on a bit longer, darling. Our appointment's not until three. It'll only mean sitting in the hospital waiting room. If we wait half an hour we can go straight in."

"Oh Mum, I can't wait. I just can't wait."

"Yes you can," I coaxed. "Do you want something to eat?"

He pulled a face. "Oh no! No! No!"

He sat down on the settee and put his head in his hands. I watched him for five minutes then I couldn't stand it any longer. "Come on then, Craig," I said. "Let's go."

Queen Mary's is a big hospital made up of lots of single-story red-brick units separated by neat lawns. The ENT unit was in a building just around the corner from the casualty department we'd visited the day before. I parked the car next to the entrance and steered Craig inside. Everything was quiet. A receptionist was peering at us through a little cubby hole in the waiting room. I told her Craig's name and we sat down. "There's no one else here, Craig," I whispered. "We should be first in." But I spoke too soon. After a few minutes the door swung open and a little boy came in with his mother. Seconds later three more kids came in with their parents. Before long the tiny room was packed, not just with patients but their brothers and sisters too. A lot of the children seemed to be deaf and had no idea how much noise they were making. There was a box of toys in the corner and some of the kids started pulling out toy drums and xylophones and having a real go at them. The din was terrible. Craig was flinching at every sound. Then one by one the kids who'd arrived after us were called in to see the doctor. I could feel my blood rising. I went over to the receptionist. "How much longer will it be, do you think?" She looked at the book. "Oh, I shouldn't think it'll be too long now, Mrs. Shergold." She gave me a serene smile. By a quarter to four Craig was looking green. "Oh Mum, the noise," he moaned. Every time a child banged on a drum his whole body recoiled as though someone had hit him.

And then, suddenly, his face changed and I moved like lightning. I'd brought a carrier bag with me in case he was

sick again and I just got it in position in time, but the force
and the quantity caught me by surprise. The bag just filled
up and overflowed in seconds and Craig continued to
throw up all over the floor—it was like a hose-pipe gushing out.

No room ever cleared so fast. All the parents just swept
their kids under their arms and dashed out and within seconds we were on our own. Craig stopped vomiting at last
and began to cry. The receptionist must have called for
help because a nurse in a blue uniform—I guessed she
must be a sister—appeared and bent over Craig. "All right,
sweetheart," she comforted him. "It's all right. Don't cry."

"I couldn't help it," Craig sobbed. "I didn't mean to.
I'm ever so sorry." He was really upset about making such
a mess.

"Don't worry about that. We can soon clean it up." The
sister was looking into his eyes as she spoke and all at
once I saw her expression alter. Reaching into her breast
pocket she pulled out a small black flashlight and flicked
it on. Then she bent over and shone the flashlight into
Craig's eyes. First one, then the other. I knelt beside Craig
and watched her, puzzled. It was the first time since Craig
had been ill that anyone, apart from that Chinese pharmacist, had looked into his eyes. She stared hard for a long
time, then slowly she stood up and put the flashlight away.
I felt her hand touch my shoulder and when I looked up
her face was full of pity.

"Mother," she said gently, "your son is very, very ill. I
am so sorry."

I stared at her in horror, then I burst into tears. "I knew
he was ill," I sobbed. "I kept saying he was ill. Why
wouldn't anyone believe me?"

Chapter 3

—⚮—

SUDDENLY CRAIG was the center of attention. An Indian lady doctor wearing a sari hurried into the waiting area and led us out into a consulting room.

"Sit down here, Craig," she pointed to a chair and picked up a headset.

I thought the sister was going to explode. "You're surely not going to do a hearing test now?" she said, and they started to argue. The sister wanted Craig to go straight down to see the pediatrician, but the ear doctor disagreed. They both seemed to be in a state of panic. Luckily Craig didn't realize the row had anything to do with him. He was far away again, his eyes almost shut. Oh God help me, I thought. I want Ernie with me. I can't cope with this on my own . . .

The squabbling went on. Then, just when I thought the two women were going to come to blows the consulting room door swung open and a man in a white coat came in. He turned out to be the senior registrar—someone had rung him to say there was an emergency. He took charge of the situation and before I knew what was happening Craig had been bundled into a wheelchair and the sister was pushing him hell for leather out of the ENT unit.

The lawns outside were criss-crossed with tarmac paths linking the hospital units to one another but the sister ignored them and pushed the wheelchair straight across the grass with the registrar and me running alongside to keep up. I hadn't a clue where we were going but when we turned into a familiar room packed with kids and adults sitting on benches, my heart sank. Not the casualty ward again, I thought. They hadn't been able to find out what was wrong here yesterday. But the sister carried on straight through casualty. She seemed to be following a red line on the floor and it led us into a glass-sided cubicle with a bed in it. Carefully the sister lifted Craig out of the wheelchair on to the bed.

"Please sit down, Mrs. Shergold," the registrar waved me toward a chair. "Now, Craig, I'd like you to do a few tests for me. Do you think you can manage to do that?"

Craig nodded.

The panic seemed to be over. The sister went back to the ENT ward. Then, for what seemed like hours, the doctor held up his fingers and asked Craig to count them. He made him touch his nose with his forefinger. He got him to walk along lines on the floor. I sat watching, afraid to ask questions, just thankful that they were really checking him out at last.

Craig wasn't very good at any of the tests—he got the numbers wrong, he kept missing his nose and he wobbled like a drunk when he walked the line. After half an hour I started to get impatient. How could Craig do tests properly when he was feeling so ill and tired? Why didn't they give him some treatment first? Surely they could do all this later?

By the time the registrar finished Craig was absolutely exhausted. We helped him up gently on to the narrow bed and he lay back. Then he turned his head to look at me and I saw his face was beaded with sweat. "Mum," he said, "there's water in my ears."

"He keeps saying that," I said. "Everyone seems to think he's imagining it but he *keeps* saying it. I'm sure he's right."

The registrar nodded. I wasn't sure he'd heard me. He was busy writing something at his desk. "We're going to admit Craig into hospital, Mrs. Shergold," he said.

I'd been expecting it ever since the sister had looked in his eyes with her flashlight but hearing him say it out loud still came as a shock. All I could think was, I have to ring Ernie. He'd be back from work now and he still didn't know anything about this. He wouldn't have a clue where Craig and I were because in my panic I hadn't thought to tell Theresa that I'd changed Craig's hospital appointment. "Mummy'll be back in a minute, darling," I told Craig. I stumbled out of the office and wandered down the corridor until I found a pay-phone. I took out my purse. There was a twenty-pound note inside—nothing else. I fumbled about in the bottom of my bag for some change, but I didn't have a penny. Sod's law, I thought. Usually my bag has a ton of loose change that's fallen out of my purse and been left. Never mind, I'd just have to reverse the charges. I picked up the receiver and my mind went completely blank. How on earth did you make a transfer charge call? I tried to think, but it was no good. I was in a total panic.

It wasn't like me at all. Normally in a crisis I've always been very good—if a customer in the restaurant ever got taken ill, it would always be me who took charge of the situation—but now I just couldn't think straight. I didn't even have the sense to ask one of the nurses if I could use the hospital phone. Instead I put the receiver down and ran back to Craig.

A new nurse was waiting with him. She told me he was to be admitted to Ward B1 which was in another unit in a different part of the hospital. But this time, instead of being pushed across the lawn, he was put on a stretcher and lifted into one of the hospital's small blue ambulances for the two-hundred-yard journey.

Less than ten minutes after being put into a hospital gown and tucked up in bed in a corner of Ward B1 Craig had fallen fast asleep. I sat on the bottom of his bed, hugging myself for comfort. I couldn't believe this was happening. I thought of the thousands of times I'd sat on Craig's bed in the past watching him sleep like this, hurting inside with loving him so much. But I'd never ever hurt the way I was hurting now. Someone touched my arm. It was a nurse I hadn't seen before. She stood next to me for a moment without speaking, then, like the sister in the ENT department, she put a hand gently on my shoulder. "You do know that Craig is very ill, don't you?" she asked. I nodded. In my heart I think I'd always known.

Craig continued to sleep and I sat there in a sort of trance watching him. I knew I should let Ernie know but I couldn't think how to do it. My mind was paralyzed. Then at eight o'clock the ward door swung open and Ernie hurried in followed by Mitchell, my brother Kevin's son. I was so relieved to see them. All I could think was, Thank God it's not all in my hands any longer. Somehow I expected poor Ernie to magically make everything all right.

He put his arms around me. "Oh love, I've been looking everywhere for you. Why didn't you leave me a note?" Then his eyes moved to the bed and I felt him go rigid. "Oh Mal . . ."

I started to gabble. "I had to get him here, Ernie. He's very ill. They've said he's ever so poorly."

Craig must have heard Ernie's voice and his eyelids fluttered open. "Hello, Dad," he said and he gave Ernie a lovely big smile.

"Hello, son," Ernie said in a choked voice. He was struggling to hold back the tears. "What's all this then? You're going to be all right, aren't you?"

"Yeh," Craig said, as breezy as anything. " 'Course I'll be all right!"

"Craig looks better than you do, Marion," said Mitchell, trying to lighten the atmosphere. But it didn't work. Ernie was shaking now. I was too.

"Go on, Mitchell, you go home," Ernie said. "We'll be all right. Thanks for the lift."

We sat beside Craig's bed and I started to tell Ernie everything that had happened, keeping my voice down so as not to wake the other kids. There were about ten beds in the ward, all with little shapes snuggling under the blankets. It was getting late and the lights had been dimmed for the night.

Suddenly the ward doors opened and someone in a white coat walked up to Craig's bed. It was the registrar. "I've arranged for Craig to go to St. Helier Hospital for a brain scan," he said quietly. "The ambulance should be here in a few minutes."

"What? Tonight?" Ernie looked at his watch. It was gone nine o'clock.

The registrar nodded. "I don't want to delay it until to-morrow. The sooner we get a picture of what's happening inside Craig's head the sooner we can start treatment."

Twenty minutes later we found ourselves sitting in the ambulance beside Craig for the short journey to St. Helier. Craig was wide-awake again and he'd cheered up since Ernie arrived. I wasn't exactly on top form, but I was calmer. At least things were moving along now, I thought.

But when the two young female radiographers met us at the door to the scanner-room I knew there was something very wrong. These women had too much make-up on. They were wearing the usual white coats but underneath they were dressed up to the nines. They were both wearing high-heeled dance shoes and one of them had sparkly stockings with a rhinestone butterfly on the ankle. I nudged Ernie. "They've come in specially," I said. "They've come in just for our Craig."

"No," Ernie shook his head. " 'Course they haven't. They'll be working an evening shift." Ernie didn't know. He didn't want to know. But I knew these two weren't dressed to do a night-shift in hospital.

"Were you on your way out tonight, then? Have we messed up your evening?" I asked.

"No, no," they said. They were busy arranging Craig on the trolley and they wouldn't look at me properly.

I kept on. "You've come in specially for my Craig, haven't you?"

"No—really we haven't." One of them gave me a bright smile.

I shook my head. "It's no good. You can't fool me, love. I've been a waitress all my life and I know when someone's dressed for a dinner and dance." They looked at each other. Then one of the girls shrugged and said, "Yes, we have come in specially but please don't worry about it. He'll be all right. We're going to look after him."

They wheeled Craig into the scanner-room then and the door closed behind them. I looked at Ernie. "They don't call people away from a dinner and dance on a Friday night for nothing," I said. "There's something seriously wrong, Ernie. He's really ill." And suddenly like a bolt from the blue it came to me what must be wrong with Craig. The papers had been full of it recently—there was an epidemic among school-kids up North.

"You know what I think, Ernie?" I said slowly. "I think he's got meningitis."

Ernie glared at me. "Shut up, Marion," he said.

But I couldn't let it rest. "I'm sure I'm right, Ernie."

He shook his head. "No way! Don't you start all that! Just don't you start thinking like that!" Then suddenly his face cracked and he stood up and ran out of the room. I heard his footsteps going down the corridor and a door banging and then it was quiet again. I sat there torn in two, wanting to follow him but not daring to in case Craig came out from the scanner.

I felt so guilty. Me and my big mouth. Poor Ernie. He was still in shock from finding Craig in hospital. I should have kept my thoughts to myself. After all I'd seen Craig being sick this morning. I'd had a whole day to get used to the idea of how ill he was. But Ernie, right up until he got home from work, hadn't had any idea. It wasn't surprising he couldn't handle it. But I was right. I knew I was right. It had to be meningitis. I'd read an article about it in some women's magazine. All the symptoms it described fitted Craig. Headache, tiredness, sickness. Why hadn't I thought of it before? Oh God, please let them have caught it in time, I thought. Meningitis could kill kids if you didn't treat it early enough, I knew that much.

Ernie came back, his eyes all red and swollen. "I'm sorry, love." He sat down beside me and took hold of my hand and I put my arm around him. "Hasn't he come out yet?" he asked. I shook my head.

"You've got to be wrong, Mal," he said after a bit. "He *can't* have meningitis."

But I'd almost accepted it by now. "Be sensible, Ernie love—it's got to be something really bad. Those two girls wouldn't have come out for him otherwise." I tried to look on the bright side. "At least he's been on antibiotics. Maybe that'll help him fight it."

The doors opened at last and the radiographers wheeled

Craig out. He was asleep again. I went up to the trolley and held his hand.

"All right. We've finished with him now," the girl with the sparkly stockings said.

"Has he got meningitis?" I knew the radiographers weren't supposed to tell you what they'd seen—the leaflets in the waiting-room told you not to ask them—but I couldn't help myself.

Her smile was bright. "No, no he hasn't got meningitis," she said. "Don't worry. I'm sure he'll be all right."

"Oh!" I wanted to kiss her. "Thank heavens for that! Thanks ever so much."

Ernie breathed a sigh of relief. "See?" he said.

A nurse took us downstairs to the foyer to wait for the ambulance to take us back to Queen Mary's. Craig's forehead was beading with sweat again. The ambulance took ages to arrive. When it did come Ernie and I sat opposite each other, both watching Craig as he made little whimpering noises in his sleep. Ernie looked frightened again and I knew he must be thinking the same thing as me. "If it isn't meningitis then what the hell is it?"

"Maybe it's just a virus," he said suddenly. "Like he had that time when he was four and had to go into hospital."

"Yes." I nodded. "He was better in a few days then wasn't he?" But I knew deep down neither of us believed it.

Outside it was bucketing down and the rain was belting against the sides of the ambulance. I could hear the windshield wipers going and I suddenly remembered a scene from an old black-and-white film I'd seen years ago, where the hero and heroine were escaping into Mexico in a rainstorm. "Listen to the windshield wipers," the hero had said to his girl. "Do you hear what they're saying? 'Together. Together. Together.'"

I listened to the ambulance's windshield wipers imagining I could hear them saying it, and I prayed, "Oh dear God, please let us always be together. Please don't take our little boy away from us. Please, please, dear God, get him well . . ."

It was past midnight when we got back to Queen

Mary's. The ambulance drivers wheeled Craig back into the ward and put him in the same corner bed next to the sister's office. Ernie and I sat by the bed watching him, not speaking, our arms around each other. Some time later I heard a noise and when I looked up I saw the senior registrar talking to the ward sister.

The sister looked over and caught my eye. "Mrs. Shergold? Will you and your husband come into the office for a moment. Would you like a cup of tea?"

I jumped to my feet as though I'd been stung. "What?"

She walked over to me. "Would you like a—"

But I wouldn't let her finish. "No. I don't want a cup of tea. When you give people a cup of tea you're telling them bad news. I watch enough telly . . . I know!"

She reached out to take my arm. "Look, my dear, come into the office so we don't wake Craig up."

That worked. "All right," I took Ernie's hand and walked toward the door. "All right but I don't want tea. I'm not having your tea."

We followed the sister into her office. The registrar had gone ahead and was standing in the corner.

"Please sit down," the sister said.

I shook my head.

My poor Ernie stood beside me not saying a word.

The sister and doctor looked at one another as if they were each waiting for the other one to speak.

"What is it then?" I asked.

The registrar cleared his throat. "Mr. and Mrs. Shergold, I'm very sorry to have to tell you this, but I'm afraid that the scan has revealed that Craig has a brain tumor."

For a long, long moment I felt numb. I'd heard the doctor's words but somehow they hadn't sunk in. A brain tumor. A *brain* tumor!

"Is he going to die?" I heard myself asking.

The registrar looked at me and his eyes were sad and very tired.

"I'm afraid it's a possibility," he said.

Chapter 4

—∞—

THE WORLD *has gone black. Far away I can hear a voice screaming. "No! No! No! No! No! No!" and I know it's my voice. The doctor's wrong, I think. Not my little boy. Brain tumors happen to other people. You read about them in the newspapers. It can't happen to us. It just can't ... I'm trembling all over and I can feel Ernie's arm tight around me trying to calm me down. His face is shiny with tears. "Hush, Mal love. Hush!" he's saying. "You'll wake Craig." But I can't hush. I'm beside myself. Completely gone ... Then, all at once, I start to feel angry. The doctor's a fool, I think. All doctors are fools. They've been getting it wrong for the last six weeks. They've got it wrong again, that's all. How dare he say such a thing about my lovely son? How dare he?*

I push Ernie away and run back into the ward and bend over Craig's bed. He's still asleep. He looks so lovely. So perfect. How can he possibly have a brain tumor? There's a pain like a knife in my chest and I can hardly breathe. I stand by the bed taking deep breaths, then I go back into the office. "You're wrong," I say. "You're all wrong, He's in a lovely sleep." I glare at them, and then suddenly I double over in sobs because deep inside me I know that they're not wrong and that my happy, jokey, lovely little boy is going to die.

35

* * *

"Won't you sit down, Mrs. Shergold?" The registrar was looking uncomfortable. Somehow the sister and a nurse got me on to a chair and Ernie stood behind me and gripped my shoulders tight. I could feel his sobs shaking through me. The registrar sat down facing us and clasped his hands together. "I'm afraid there's no way I can make this any easier for you," he said. "What the scan has revealed is a very large tumor in Craig's mid-brain. It's about the size of an orange and it has an unusual appearance. It doesn't resemble any of the brain tumors I've come across before. At the moment that's all we know. There's no one in this hospital who's qualified to interpret the scans in any more depth. What Craig needs now is specialist neurological care and I've arranged to have him transferred to Great Ormond Street Hospital—they're much better equipped to deal with this sort of problem." He stood up. "Craig has to be there by seven o'clock in the morning. Sister will tell you about the practical arrangements." He hesitated, "I really am very sorry." He closed the door quietly behind him.

I turned to the sister. She looked as if she was about to cry too.

"I haven't even got any cigarettes," I wailed and I gave a hysterical giggle—what a ridiculous thing to say at a moment like this, I thought. I was crying and laughing all at the same time. I didn't know what I was doing. I felt as though I'd been mugged. The sister came over and put her arm around me. "Come on, darling," she said, "I've got some cigarettes. Come with me." She half-carried me down the corridor, with Ernie following behind, and led us into a small room with a bed and a sofa and a TV. Then she brought out a packet of Rothmans and lit one for me, and Ernie sat down on the bed next to me and we cuddled up to each other again. I'd never needed Ernie's arms around me like I did then.

The sister was a perfect angel. "Come on, you two," she said. "Don't give up hope. Craig knows you love him and that's important. He'll fight it. Come along. Chin up. I'll fetch you a cup of tea from the machine." She went out and I buried my face in Ernie's chest. His shirt was soaking wet from our tears. "Oh Ern, please don't let him die," I begged. "I love him so much."

"So do I, love," said Ern. "He won't die. God won't let him die. Hold on, Mal. We've got to be strong for Craig."

The sister came back with the tea. "Here, drink this." She sat down on the sofa opposite us while I cradled the blue plastic up in my hands and sipped the tea. "Thank you for being so kind," I kept saying. "Thanks for the cigarettes." She waited until I'd finished my tea, then she said gently, "We've just had a call to confirm that they're waiting for Craig at Great Ormond Street. Why don't you go home and throw a few things into a bag? You'll probably have to stay with him in the hospital so you'll need sponge-bags and a change of clothes for yourselves as well as for Craig." She peeped at her watch. "If you get back here by six o'clock you'll be able to travel over with him in the ambulance."

"Can we just go and see him first?" I asked.

She walked back to the ward with us. It was very dark now, with just a couple of sidelights on. All the children in the other beds were sleeping peacefully. Two nurses sat at a round table near Craig's bed and as we came in they both gave us sympathetic smiles.

Craig looked so peaceful. So lovely. It was impossible to believe there was a tumor inside his beautiful head. The size of an orange, the registrar had said. I tried to imagine it and my eyes filled up again. "I can't leave him. I want to stay," I sobbed. But Ernie took charge. "Come on, love. Let's do what they say. Don't forget we've got to tell Steven." I was choked with guilt. How could I have forgotten about Steven? Steven, who idolized his baby brother.

"Promise you'll ring me if he gets worse," I said to the nurses and they nodded reassuringly.

It was a quarter to two. Outside in the hospital parking lot the flood-lights had gone out long ago and the rain was still sheeting down. As we stumbled across the tarmac it felt as though we were the only two people left in the world. In the distance I could see the illuminated cross of the hospital chapel. "Ernie," I pointed. "Can we just go in there for a minute?"

We crept inside, dripping water all over the tiled floor and I fell to my knees in front of the altar. Ernie has never been a religious man, but he knelt beside me and for five minutes we both prayed as we'd never prayed before. Then Ernie touched my shoulder. "We'd better go, Mal. Steve'll be waiting."

By the time we climbed into the car we were both soaked to the skin. Ernie switched on the headlights and reversed out of the parking space. The wind was blowing papers and leaves all across the parking lot and a small bare branch of a tree hit the hood of the car and blew away into the darkness. "For God's sake, Ernie, drive carefully," I begged. The rain was coming down so fast the windshield looked like frosted glass—the wipers just couldn't cope with it. Between that and Ernie's tears I don't know how we got home safely that night.

As we turned the corner into Selby Road I saw Theresa's porch door standing open with the light streaming out on to the garden. Steven must have heard the car. Even before we'd opened the gate he was at the door. "Mum, Mum, is he all right?" He looked terrified.

"Come inside, Steve," said Ernie quietly and pushed him gently back into Theresa's hallway. The door into her front room was open and I could see my brother Kevin and his wife Carole sitting on the settee. They looked just like the last time I'd seen them. I felt somehow that they ought to look different. Our whole world had turned upside down. Why did everything still seem so normal?

"Mum. Please tell me what's up. What's wrong?"

"Steve . . ." I began, then I broke down. How on earth could I tell him?

His eyes were wide with fear and I tried desperately to pull myself together. After all Steve was my son too. I had to be strong for him. I took a deep breath. "Steve, I'm afraid it's very bad. Craig has got a brain tumor."

Steve's face twisted in pain. I tried to throw my arms around him—my dear shy Steve—but he wouldn't let me. "No, Mum! No, Mum! No!" he yelled over and over again. "No! He can't have! Not my brother!" Tears streamed down his cheeks. He turned toward Ernie. "God has got the wrong house. We've never hurt anyone. We don't cheat. We don't tell lies. Why does it have to be us? What have we done wrong? Suddenly he raised his fist and punched Theresa's door so hard that I heard the wood splinter. "He's taken my Nan," he cried. "No more!" and he ran out into the night.

"Ern, get him back. Please get him back," I screamed.

"No. I'll go," Kevin pushed past me. "You two get inside and get dry." Everyone in the house was crying now—Theresa, Carole, Ernie, me . . . "We had no idea he was so ill," Carole said as I sat down on Theresa's settee. "Mitchell told us he thought Craig would be all right. He was more worried about the state you were in."

Theresa tried to give me a brandy but I didn't want one. She tried to tell me about people who'd had brain tumors and got better but I didn't believe a word of it. Suddenly I heard Kevin calling and I rushed outside. Steven was standing with Kevin in our front garden. He was soaked through and his face was all puffed up from crying. "Oh, Mum, Mum," he kept saying. I put my arm around him and tried to get him in out of the rain. "I'm sorry, Mum," he sobbed, "but I can't take it. I love Craig. He's the best kid in the world."

He let me cuddle him. "Come on, Steve, let's go indoors," I said. "God'll get him better." It did me good to look after my poor Steve. It took my mind off my own pain.

Kevin and Carole decided to drive to my sister Kate's house to tell her the news and they set off, promising to be back by five. We said good night to Theresa and went inside. Our house felt cold and miserable. It was only hours since Craig had been here but already it seemed empty, as though he'd gone forever.

"Come on, mate," I said to Steven. "You'd better get some sleep. It's nearly three o'clock."

Steve shook his head. "No, don't make me go upstairs, Mum. I couldn't sleep on that bunk-bed knowing Craig wasn't there."

"All right then lie on the settee," I said. He fell on to it, with a little groan. I knew he was hurting just the same as Ernie and me. We went upstairs and lay on our bed and held each other close. Every so often Ernie tried to reassure me, but in the next breath he was casting doubts and I had to try to comfort him.

I kept seeing that image of Craig in a coffin surrounded by white lace. I couldn't get it out of my head. "That nightmare's coming true," I told Ernie. "Maybe I dreamed the future."

"No." He sat up. "Don't even think it."

I started to pray out loud. "Please God, don't let him die. Please, please don't let him die."

A tumor, they'd said. Memories came flooding back. I remembered Mum lying terrified on the bed, her fingers crossed, waiting for the results of her breast biopsy. And the young doctor's brisk voice as he announced, "Mrs. Blyde, you have a malignant tumor." And I remembered his astonished look as she cried in relief, "Oh God bless you, doctor! Thank you! Thank you!" because she hadn't known he meant cancer ... Did they mean cancer this time too?

Ernie got up and stuffed Craig's pajamas and some clean underpants into a plastic carrier, then went into the bathroom for his sponge-bag. When he came back he sat on the edge of the bed and put his head in his hands. Neither of us could keep still. All we wanted to do was to get back to the hospital. I stared at the alarm clock on my bedside table—the hands didn't seem to be moving. Every twenty minutes I said, "Go on, Ernie, phone the hospital," and poor Ernie jumped up to obey. The nurses were so patient with us. "He's still asleep," Ernie kept reporting back. "They say there's been no change."

At five, Kevin and Carole returned and I made us all a cup of tea before we left. Ernie and Steven sat with me in the back of Kevin's car as he drove to the hospital. Steven, tears quietly running down his face, held my hand the whole way. It comforted me. We all needed each other so much.

It was still pouring with rain as we pulled into the hospital grounds. After a night of crying I felt numb, but suddenly I was filled with fresh terror. "Please don't be dead, Craig. Please don't be dead," I prayed, and without waiting for the others I leaped out of the car and raced into the ward.

Craig was lying in the same position as when we left him. He looked like a china doll, his long eyelashes dark against his white cheeks. The young nurse sitting with him put her hand softly on my shoulder. "I've not left him for a second," she said. "He hasn't woken up at all."

She went out for a moment and when she came back she had a navy-and-red cape over her shoulders. "I'm coming with you to Great Ormond Street," she told us. "The ambulance should be arriving any minute now."

I sat on Craig's bed pressing my arms to my chest, aching to hug and kiss him, but afraid to disturb him.

At last a voice said, "The ambulance is here. You can wake Craig up now" and I touched his cheek gently with my hand.

"Hello, Craig," I whispered. "Mum's here." His eyelashes fluttered and he opened his eyes.

"I know," he said quietly. I kissed him and he smiled. "I love you, Mum," he said. His voice sounded strange and slurred. "I'm sorry I'm ill."

Before we'd set off from home I'd promised myself I wouldn't cry in front of Craig, but now I couldn't stop the sobs. They came from my boots. I bent over him trying to hide my tears and his hands came up and cradled my head. "Don't cry, Mum," he said. "I'll be all right." He looked across at Steven and gave him a sleepy smile. "Hello, Ugly," he said. "Have you been crying over me too?" Poor Steve broke down again. Craig was the only one in control. "Steve," he said, "you're the best brother in the world. I'll be all right." He closed his eyes.

By the time they got Craig into the ambulance he was drifting in and out of sleep. Steve and Carole climbed up the ambulance steps after me while Ernie traveled in the car with Kevin.

It was the longest, most horrible journey I've ever made. At every bump in the road Craig jumped as though someone had hit him. And every time I spoke he went "Sh-sh-sh" and put his fingers to his lips. The ambulance team was very good. Once, while Craig was sleeping, the driver's mate told me that he'd had a brain tumor when he was a kid but they'd operated to remove it. "And look at me now," he grinned. But I was sure he was just trying to make me feel better. It was part of his job.

The ambulance crawled. I knew they were trying to give Craig as smooth a journey as possible and I tried not to be impatient but I was terrified he was going to die before we reached Great Ormond Street.

For most of the journey I hadn't a clue where we were. I was born and bred in London but I felt like an alien. Outside it was still pitch dark and for mile after mile all I could see from the ambulance windows was the reflection of streetlights on shiny wet pavements. The rain was still pouring down. Every time we stopped at traffic lights I could see it hitting the puddles and hear it drumming on the side of the ambulance.

Now and then Craig's eyes flickered open. "I've got water in my ears, Mum," he kept saying. I rocked backward and forward. I'd never felt so frightened in my life. Outside, the streetlights went out suddenly. I hadn't even noticed it getting lighter. I stood up and pressed my face against the ambulance window, trying to get my bearings. We were passing an underground station and I peered at the sign. Clapham Common. How much further? We seemed to have been traveling for hours. Only a few weeks ago I'd driven down this road heading for East Lane Market to buy Christmas presents. It could have been in another lifetime.

Finally the ambulance stopped and the driver switched off the engine. "Here we are then." The driver's mate opened the door and Steve and Carole and I stepped down and stood out of the way as they maneuvered Craig's stretcher out of the ambulance. I looked up and saw a dingy building with crumbling concrete balconies. The Great Ormond Street Hospital for Sick Children. Everyone had heard of it—it was one of the best hospitals in the country—but it didn't look too inspiring to me that morning.

Ernie and Kevin joined us as we followed Craig's stretcher through the main doors of the hospital into the entrance lobby. It was like walking into Waterloo Station. There were people everywhere and a great roar of noise. Luckily Craig had dozed off again. Two nurses came up and said they'd been waiting for us. "Craig is being admitted to the Punch and Judy ward," one smiled. They led us to a small elevator and Ernie and I piled in after Craig's stretcher.

We got out on the first floor and the nurses guided us into a small bright room filled with toys. "If you'll just wait in the playroom I'll tell Sister you're here," one nurse said. Steven, Kevin and Carole joined us. The ambulance drivers were still cracking jokes, trying to keep our spirits up but Ernie and I couldn't pretend to smile anymore. We only had eyes and ears for Craig.

The ward sister came in to fetch us. "Sorry," she held up her hand to the others, "Mum and Dad only."

Ernie and I followed the ambulance drivers as they pushed Craig's trolley ahead of us. I was taken aback when I saw the ward. All the hospital wards I'd ever seen had been orderly with neat rows of beds on either side. But the Punch and Judy Ward was packed with beds laid higgledy-piggledy in all directions so that we had to walk through a sort of maze to reach Craig's bed in the far corner.

Gently the ambulance drivers and the pretty nurse who'd traveled with us transferred Craig from the gurney to the bed and pulled the metal sides up to stop him falling out. Then, with a cheerful "All the best, Craig" they left to return to Queen Mary's. While Craig's new nurses took his temperature and blood pressure I unpacked the plastic carrier and put his things into the small locker beside his bed.

There were strange noises coming from further down the ward. I looked over and saw a young boy sitting in a chair. One side of his head was shaved bare showing a long operation scar on his scalp. He was dribbling and he didn't seem able to hold his head up properly. A woman was sitting next to him talking, and he was answering her with long moans like an animal. My God, was this what a brain tumor did to you? I stared in horror. The woman caught my eye and I looked away quickly but I knew she'd seen the look on my face. She stood up and came over. For a moment I was afraid she was going to have a go at me but instead she put her arm around my shoulders.

"Please don't be afraid," she said quietly. "My son was born like that."

"Hasn't he got a brain tumor?" I asked.

"No, it's a different sort of problem," she said. I felt so ashamed of myself and a bit stupid. Why had I imagined this would be a special ward for brain tumors? There were obviously kids with all sorts of brain problems here.

I tried not to stare after that but it was hard not to. Nearly every child on the ward seemed to have had a brain operation. In the cot opposite Craig's bed a baby was crying. He had a row of metal clips right round the front of his head—I shuddered and turned back to Craig.

He was complaining again to Ernie that there was water in his ears. "Mum, help me," he said. "They feel like they're going to break." The nurses had moved to the next bed and I called one of them back. "Do you think you could look in his ears?" I begged. "I'm sure he's not imagining it." The nurse fetched some swabs and probed his ears gently. When she pulled the swabs out they were damp.

"I'll just go and make a phone call." She hurried off. Very quickly a doctor arrived at his bedside, took more swabs and sent them off for testing. I felt really upset. Why hadn't anyone listened to him till now?

All morning the tests continued. Blood tests, hearing tests, mobility tests, tests I'd never heard of. It seemed as if every specialist in the hospital was looking into Craig's ears, or checking his balance. Every twenty minutes a nurse shone a flashlight in his eyes. Three times he was put on a gurney and wheeled away for X-rays, brain scans, and sight tests. By the end of the morning he was exhausted and fell into a deep sleep. What frightened me was that in a few hours his appearance had changed before our eyes. Craig was a stocky little boy but he'd never carried any spare flesh. Suddenly his whole face and body were swollen. The sweet baby look of the day before had gone. Anyone could see Craig was a very sick child. I hadn't thought there were any more tears left in me but I was wrong. They started rolling down my cheeks again and nothing I could do would make them stop.

I went out into the corridor and walked up and down

trying to pull myself together. Two cubicles opened on to the passageway and in one of them a boy of about thirteen was sitting up in bed playing an electric organ. I stopped in the doorway. "Hello. You're clever. What's your name?"

"Simon," he smiled.

"Is that your organ, Simon?"

"No," he said. "I wish it was. It belongs to the hospital."

"Have you been ill?"

He nodded. "Yes, I've had a brain tumor."

My eyes popped. "How do you feel now?"

He gave a careless shrug, "I'm fine."

He sounded fine. When I walked back to the ward I was in control of myself again. Perhaps after all a brain tumor wasn't the end of the world.

At midday the sister told us the ward phone had been red hot with friends and relatives ringing up asking about Craig. She said they were going to arrange a special line for us in the hall to keep the ward line clear. "That's VIP treatment. You're honored!" she smiled. Because there was only one chair beside the bed Ernie, Steve and I took it in turns to sit with Craig. Every time I went out to the visitors' room someone else had turned up. I remembered a hazy blur of people. My dad, not able to say a word, shaking his head backward and forward. My sister Kate, her face white, clinging to me, both of us crying. My best friend Carol. Craig's godparents John and Sandra. Ernie's brother, Fred ... By midday more than twenty people were waiting their turn to spend a couple of minutes at Craig's bedside. I was touched by all the support and love. Kevin and Carole too were still waiting patiently. When the tests were over and they were finally allowed into the ward Carole handed Craig a big poster of Kylie Minogue which she'd popped out to buy during the morning. Craig's face lit up. Kylie was still his idol—he had all her records and he watched *Neighbors* on TV every day. Then Kevin changed places with Carole and handed Craig an envelope. Craig had trouble opening it. He couldn't seem to get his hands working together but he wouldn't let me help him and in the end he managed it. It was his very first get-well card. It had a clown's face on the front and when you pulled the tab at the bottom the clown poked his tongue out and on his tongue it said "Get Well." Craig beamed. I stuck the card up on the wall behind the bed. "That's the first of many—you wait and see," I said.

At two o'clock a nurse came over and asked Ernie and me to go to an office up the corridor. She promised to stay at Craig's bedside until we got back. As we went out into the corridor I noticed a board on the wall with pictures of all the ward staff and I stopped to have a good look. At the top were photographs of the Great Ormond Street neurosurgeons. One surgeon really caught my eye. He was handsome and distinguished looking, with lovely kind eyes and dark hair turning silver at the temples. As I looked at his face a strange calm came over me. I read the name underneath the photo. Dr. Richard Hayward. I turned to Craig. "That man is going to save Craig's life," I said. I'd never felt so sure of anything.

"Come on now, don't start," said Ernie. "You won't have any choice."

"I will," I said. "That's the man I want to do the operation."

We knocked on the office door and a voice told us to come in. We stepped into a bright modern office—nothing like the old-fashioned ward we had just left. Sitting behind the desk sat the man in the picture.

"Well that's my first prayer answered," I said.

Richard Hayward smiled and raised an eyebrow. "Oh? What's that?" he asked.

"I saw your picture," I said. "I want you to do my Craig's operation."

He had a twinkle in his eye. "I'm flattered. But why?"

"Because you've got children of your own, haven't you?"

"Yes I have—how do you know?"

"I could just tell by your face," I said.

He smiled. Then he asked us to sit down and the twinkle in his eye disappeared.

"You must have realized by now that Craig is very ill," he said gently. "The scans have shown us that he has a very large tumor in the region of the mid-brain."

"Is it cancer, doctor?" I had to know.

"We don't know yet. It has an unusual appearance. But it's far too dangerous to try and do a biopsy. We won't know if it's malignant until we try to remove it. What we're most concerned about at the moment is that the tumor is causing fluid to build up in Craig's brain. That's the reason he's experiencing such severe earache."

"Is that why he's got water in his ears?" I asked.

"That's right," Dr. Hayward nodded. "If we don't relieve the pressure soon, the cavity walls will break down, so dealing with that has to be our priority. We've started treating the problem with drugs and the day after tomorrow we plan to put a small plastic device called a shunt into Craig's brain to drain away the fluid. Once the pressure's relieved we'll be in a better position to try and remove the tumor."

"He will be all right though, won't he?" I interrupted. "You will be able to take it out?"

Dr. Hayward stood up and came around to our side of the desk. "Mr. and Mrs. Shergold, I'm not going to mislead you. Craig is a very sick little boy. You can thank God that you got him here today. If you hadn't, he might well have been dead by tomorrow. Even being optimistic I don't think he would have survived beyond Thursday at the latest."

I struggled to take it in. Craig had been literally dying all last week and yet nobody had realized it. How was it possible in this day and age?

"Now that he's here with us he has a chance, but his condition is still very, very serious," Dr. Hayward went on. He clasped his hands together and looked from Ernie to me. "Craig could die before we're able to operate. Or he could die on the operating table. Even if he comes through the operation, removing the tumor could cause permanent damage. It's in an area of the brain which controls a lot of important functions. There's a possibility that the surgery could leave him blind or paralyzed . . ."

I held up my hand. "Don't tell me any more." I had such faith this doctor could save Craig. How could I make him share that faith? Suddenly instinct took over. I took hold of Dr. Hayward's hands and pressed my own hands around them. Then, holding them tight I willed every bit of power in my body into his hands. "You can do it, Dr. Hayward," I said. I could see Ernie giving me a funny look. He didn't have a clue what I was doing. But Dr. Hayward knew. He probably thought I was a nutty old cockney mum but he didn't try to take his hands away and I was grateful for that. He smiled. "I'm glad you've so much faith, Mother," he said gently. "But please—not too much."

I shook my head. "God will bless your hands." I told him. "Craig is not going to die. He is not going to be blind. Because you are going to get him well."

While we were in Dr. Hayward's office Ernie and I had managed to stay quite composed. But the minute we left we broke down and had to dive into the empty waiting-room to recover. It was a few minutes before we were able to face walking back into the ward. To our relief we found Craig had been given some painkillers which had sent him to sleep.

Ernie went back to see our family while I sat beside Craig's bed holding his hand, struggling to come to terms with what Dr. Hayward had told us. I thought back to all the moments of joy Craig had brought us, remembering his birth, reliving every birthday and every Christmas. I re-called his little caring actions—the times he'd massage my feet when I came in tired after work, the way he'd learned sign language to speak to the deaf children at school. Why should this terrible thing happen to my little boy? He didn't deserve it.

I searched my memory for signs that should have warned me. Maybe if I'd been more alert, I thought, if I'd taken him to see the doctor sooner, he'd have stood a bet-ter chance. They said the tumor was the size of an orange. A tumor that size didn't just appear overnight. It must have been growing for months. I remembered Ernie com-ing home after football practice a few months before and telling me that Ken, Craig's football coach, had said some-thing was the matter with Craig—he was going sideways when he went after the ball. I'd been really cross. "Who does that Ken think he is? Bobby Robson?" I'd said. "There's nothing wrong with my Craig."

If only I'd listen to him.

There was a shelf above Craig's bed and someone had left a big furry green elephant on it. Elephants were my mother's lucky mascots. I felt a strong sense that she was here with us. A couple of weeks before she died Mum had called us in to see her—Kevin and Kate, Ernie and me. "I'll always be with you," she'd promised then. "I'll be watching over all of you. I'll never leave you." I stared at the elephant. "Mum," I prayed, "if you're there, please ask God and the angels to keep him safe and get him well."

Craig stirred and opened his eyes. I guessed the noise in the ward had woken him. It was nearly driving *me* crazy. There was a television at the far end of the ward and some of the kids were out of bed watching it. Two beds away a boy was playing a computer game—bip! bip! bip! bip! Opposite us a little girl had a cassette player going full blast. And as if that wasn't enough there were builders hammering and sawing in a closed-off ward next door.

"Everyone knows noise makes a headache worse," I complained when Ernie came back from the waiting-room. "Why can't they put him somewhere quiet?"

"They're short of space with all the building work, love," said Ernie. "You can't blame them." But I did blame them. I felt a sudden urge to wrap Craig in a blanket and run—to carry him away from this crazy, noisy place. I fought it back and picked up the cold compress a nurse had left on his locker and held it to his head.

"Mum?" Craig was looking at me and his eyes were huge. "Mum?" he said again. For the first time since he'd been here he seemed really wide awake. He stared at the other kids on the ward, frowning at their bald heads and operation scars. My heart sank. In a minute I knew he was going to ask me what he was doing here. What would I tell him?

Craig trusted me. I'd never lied to him, not even about Father Christmas, so I knew I had to be honest with him now. I decided to tell him before he asked me. I took hold of his hand. "Craig," I said softly, "you do know you're very ill, don't you?"

He stopped me. "I know, Mum. I've got a brain tumor."

My jaw dropped. So did Ernie's. We'd been so careful

not to mention it in front of him. "How do you know that, Craig," Ernie asked.

"I just guessed," he smiled. "Lucy in *Neighbors* has got a brain tumor."

"Oh Craig." For the first time that day I was laughing. Thank heaven for *Neighbors*.

Craig's eyes were fixed on my face.

"Lucy's getting better, Mum," he said.

"I know she is, Craig. And so are you." I squeezed his hand tightly. "Just you remember that."

Chapter 5

—⁓—

BY SUNDAY morning the smell of canteen food and the hum of the generator outside the waiting-room window had become part of our lives. Ernie and I had spent Saturday night dozing on two reclining chairs in the waiting-room. One of the nurses found a couple of blankets for us but even so I woke up feeling stiff and numb. Ernie had woken before me and he'd already been into the ward to check on Craig.

"They've put him on a drip," he reported. I sprang up out of the chair in panic but he shook his head. "Calm down. The sister said not to worry. It's only because he's dehydrated from being sick and they want to get some fluid into him. She said he's had a peaceful night." Ernie had found a plastic bowl somewhere and filled it with water. He put it on the coffee table. "Here, have a wash before you go in to him. You'll feel better." I splashed some water on my face then fished in my handbag for my compact. I was shocked by my reflection. I looked about a hundred years old—my eyes were all red and swollen from crying and my hair was standing on end. I rubbed some foundation on and dragged a comb through my hair. It wouldn't help Craig to have his mum looking like something out of a horror film.

Craig squinted up at me as I arrived at his bedside. "Hello, Mum," he said. Then he shut his eyes again quickly.

The ward lights were very bright and they seemed to hurt his eyes. For most of the morning I sat with him while he drifted in and out of sleep. The painkillers weren't working as well as they had yesterday, and the noise of the ward was bothering him more—even the sound of my voice when I spoke to Ernie made him flinch in his sleep. When he woke, the slightest movement caused him pain—he could hardly bear to lift his head off the pillow. The little girl with the tape recorder was playing his favorite Kylie Minogue hit, "I Should Be So Lucky," at full volume. "Mum, please make her stop," Craig begged. The nurses gave me more cold compresses to hold against his head but they didn't seem to help much.

By the middle of the day his speech had slowed right down and he was having to search for every word. A doctor who'd arrived to do more tests explained that Craig's speech center was being affected by the pressure from the tumor. By the time my friends Carol and Peg came in to see him he'd given up trying to speak and was using sign language. "I love you," he signed to me. Carol turned her head away and I bit my lip. Don't cry, I told myself. He mustn't see you cry anymore ... Dear Peg hugged me tight. "Marion, he'll be fine," she whispered fiercely. "You two are one. Keep fighting."

A new doctor came to check him and to my relief he increased Craig's painkillers. Halfway through the afternoon, while Craig was sleeping, a pretty dark-haired nurse came up to us, holding something in her hand. "Hello, I'm Sally," she said. "I've come to show you what a shunt looks like so you'll understand a bit more about the operation tomorrow." She handed me a little plastic thing—it reminded me of the sherbert "flying saucer" sweets I used to buy when I was a kid. Attached to it was a long piece of fine tubing. "The tube will run down a vein inside Craig's neck so all the excess fluid in his brain drains into his blood system," Sally explained. "As soon as the pressure inside his head gets less his earache should improve."

Far from reassuring me, seeing the shunt frightened me even more. It looked such a big thing to put inside a little boy's head. Sally patted my arm. "Try not to worry about it. It really is quite a routine operation. Most of the kids in this ward have got a shunt. I'm sure he'll be all right." Suddenly she put both her arms around me and gave me a big hug. "Why don't you go and have a cup of tea?" she said. "You both look as though you need a break."

I knew she was right. Ernie's face was turning gray with worry and I'd felt sick ever since I woke up. I couldn't face tea but we decided to go out for a bit of fresh air. We sat outside the hospital entrance on a wooden bench and I lit a cigarette. There was a light drizzle of rain still coming down—it seemed to have been raining non-stop for the past two days. On the other side of the entrance from where we were sitting there was a big model of a wishing-well. I guessed it was publicizing the Wishing Well Appeal. I'd read about it recently—it was raising funds to modernize Great Ormond Street. Not before time, I thought.

We went over and threw some money in, made silent wishes and walked slowly back toward the hospital entrance. As we passed through the reception area I noticed a sign saying "CHAPEL." Underneath it was a big arrow, pointing up a ramp laid over some worn stone steps. I caught Ernie's arm. "Ern, I want to go in there," I said.

I'd been brought up to go to church. When I was a kid I was sent twice every Sunday and my first school was a Protestant convent school in South London, where I was taught by nuns. I'd stopped going since I'd grown up, but I still said my prayers every single night and somehow now it felt as though this chapel was calling me. I walked up the ramp, pulling poor Ernie after me. We found ourselves in a very old part of the building, much older even than the wards in Craig's wing. It was quiet and a bit eerie after all the noise in the main hospital. Ahead of us a door stood half-open and we tiptoed in. On a table just inside the door piles of Bibles and books were displayed for sale. Beyond, another door led into the chapel. As I pushed it open I stopped astonished. It was beautiful. Most of the hospital needed a lick of paint but not this chapel. The lighted candles reflected off gilt paint and polished brass. Ten dark wooden pews faced the altar and we sat down in one of them. There was an arch over the altar and on the wall above it was a large painting. I stared up at it. The painting showed Jesus with two children, one on his lap, and one by his side. Next to him stood a sheep and a goat and above his head in gold lettering were the words, "Suffer the little children to come unto me."

As I read the familiar verse I felt anger growing inside me. I'd always thought that was such a beautiful text—I remembered the nuns teaching it to me at school. But it meant something different to me now. It seemed to be telling me that Craig had to suffer to go to Jesus, and the idea made me see red. Oh no, I thought, why should he suffer? Craig isn't going to Jesus. I want him here with me. I started to cry, then I prayed, then I cried again. Ernie sat beside me, his arm around me, waiting patiently.

On the way out we passed a table with a visitors' book and a pen on it. I stopped and read the last message in the book. Straight away I recognized Steven's handwriting. "Please don't let Craig die," he'd scribbled. Above that, my niece Sue had written, "Please God, let my cousin Craig live." Higher up the page was a message from Carol . . . Almost everyone who'd visited Craig in the hospital yesterday had written a few words. I picked up the pen and started a fresh line. "Dear God," I wrote, "I love Craig so much. I couldn't live without him. Please don't make him suffer. Please don't take him from me. Take me instead."

Craig was just waking up when we got back to the ward. A great crowd of visitors was waiting to see us and they were allowed in, one at a time. Some of Ernie's brothers and sisters had traveled from Hemel Hempstead and Nottingham just for those two minutes at his bedside. They'd all brought furry toys and get-well cards and I stuck the cards up on the wall next to Carol's and Kevin's card. Steven had spent the night at Sharon's mum's house and Sharon had come in with him to see Craig this morning. "You know Sharon is having a baby, Craig?" Steven said. Craig nodded slowly. "Well we know it's going to be a girl and we've decided to call her Kylie because she's your favorite." Craig put his thumbs up and mouthed, "Thanks, Sharon. I love you." It was too much for Sharon and Steven had to take her outside to recover.

I was deeply touched by the love everyone was showing us and I really did feel strengthened by it, but there was a

real, physical pain gnawing into my body now. I told Carol
about it. "You've got to eat," she said. "You'll be no use
to Craig if you end up ill as well."

We'd discovered a canteen where you could get a cup of
tea and a bite to eat and Ernie and I took turns to go there
with our visitors. I didn't feel a bit like food but I knew
that Carol was right and next time I went I forced a sand-
wich down and had a cup of tea. I was gasping for a cigarette as well but you weren't allowed to smoke in the
canteen or anywhere in the hospital as far as I could see.
There were "no smoking" signs everywhere. "And quite
right too," Ernie said when I complained—it was all right
for him. So after I finished my tea I went out through the
main hospital door again and sat on the bench in the drizzle to have a cigarette. While I smoked I stared up at the
window of Craig's ward on the first floor. I could just
make out the shadow of Ernie's back through the glass.

Parts of the front of the hospital seemed to be crumbling
away and I couldn't stop myself worrying as I looked up
at it. I'd come here believing that Great Ormond Street
was the best hospital there was but the shabbiness of all
the wards was making me feel very uneasy. I was on to
my second cigarette when a young woman came up.
"Have you got a kid in the hospital?" she asked. I nodded.

"Come with me. I know a place where you can have a
cig in the dry."

The rain was the least of my worries, but she insisted
and took me up in the elevator to the fifth floor of the hospital. "Here," she opened a door. "We call this the smoking
room, though I don't suppose *Blue Peter* would like it!"

She explained that the *Blue Peter* TV program had paid
for the room so the parents of sick children could have a
break from sitting in the ward all day. Its proper name was
the family-room. But you could see why it was called the
smoking room. Three women and a man sat in comfortable armchairs drinking coffee and smoking. The room
was bright and warm and it felt welcoming, not a bit like
the dingy visitors' room downstairs where Ernie and I had
spent the night.

I sat down and started chatting, and after twenty minutes my faith in the hospital was restored. The mums and

dads in that room had children suffering from all kinds of diseases. But they'd all come to Great Ormond Street for the same reason—it offered them their last chance. "You don't want to worry about the state of the place," one girl said. "They're too short of money to keep up appearances. It's the staff that count. The surgeons here are the best there are. Believe me. My kid wouldn't be alive without them." It turned out she was a soldier's wife from Germany whose son had been born with his bowel outside his body. For three years she'd been flying him over for regular treatment. She seemed to know everybody else in the room. And there was absolutely nothing she didn't know about GOSH—as she called Great Ormond Street. "You'll get the best medical treatment in the country here. Don't worry about that." She smiled. Other mothers chipped in to back her up. Most of them were old hands, and they did everything they could to make me feel at home. They told me how to get a parking permit for our car and where to shop and how to fit in with the hospital routine. Some of them had been sleeping in the hospital for days and looked as rough as I did. Meeting them did me good. Afterward I didn't feel quite so much on my own.

Back downstairs I tried to persuade Ernie to visit the family-room. But he wasn't keen.

"Please, Ernie, just go up and listen," I coaxed. I was sure it would boost Ernie's confidence for tomorrow to hear some success stories. In the end, to keep the peace, he did go but he was back down again in ten minutes. I was disappointed but I wasn't really surprised. Ernie's always been a bit of a loner and I should have guessed he'd hate the smoky atmosphere. But for me knowing I had a bolt-hole to run to was a big comfort.

On Sunday evening John and Sandra—Craig's godparents—turned up with a bottle of brandy and John insisted I drink a little. It did seem to help, but it didn't take away my fear of the next day. Nothing could do that. The shunt operation hung over us all like a black cloud.

The nurses were very kind. They obviously knew how we were feeling and nothing was too much trouble for them. That evening there was a new nurse on duty called Jo. She was slim, blonde and bubbly and every so often she would put her arms around me and give me a comforting hug. It really helped. I felt like asking her to hug Ernie too ... Poor Ernie. He'd been an absolute rock to me these last two days but the strain was telling on him. He was growing old in front of my eyes. I knew that, like me, he was worried that time was against us, afraid that the cavity wall might break down before Craig had the operation. I didn't even know what the cavity wall was. I pictured the tumor bursting like a balloon. Oh God, I prayed, please let tomorrow come quickly.

The ward lights had been dimmed for a long time and most of the children on the ward were asleep when a nurse came over and whispered, "There's a telephone call for you, Mrs. Shergold. You can take it in the family-room."

It was my old boss Joan Spears. Years ago I'd organized garden and dinner parties and charity functions for her and she'd remained a very dear friend.

"Marion, I've just heard the news," she said. "Please be brave. Don't lose your faith."

I started to reply but the sympathy in her voice was too much for me and I broke down.

Her voice was firm as she listened to my sobs. "Marion, please, I want you to listen to something," and she began to read me a story. I recognized it straight away. It was the tale of the suffering man who looks behind him and when he sees only one set of footprints in the sand thinks God has deserted him. But in fact the reason is quite different—God has been carrying him through his time of trouble ... I knew *Footprints* word for word. I'd always thought it was beautiful but it had never touched me as it did then listening to Joan read it over the telephone.

When she'd finished neither of us said anything for a moment. Then Joan said quietly, "Marion, Craig will be fine tomorrow. God is with you. And He will carry you too. Never forget that ..."

I walked slowly back to the ward. I'd always believed that friendship and love were the most important things in life. After Joan's call I was more certain of it than ever.

At six in the morning after a quick wash and brush up in the visitors' room we headed back to the ward. For us it had been another uncomfortable night. Ernie had traipsed backward and forward to check on Craig half a dozen times and he looked really washed out. Halfway through the night he'd sat up suddenly in his chair and put his head in his hands and cried, "Please don't let him die, Mal, please don't let him die." I'd begged him to get down on his knees with me and pray, and he had.

Our prayers had been answered. Craig hadn't died during the night, but he looked dreadful. His body was even more bloated and his skin had turned an ugly yellow color. We sat with him until eleven when the ward door opened and an orderly pushed a gurney in. Craig hardly seemed to be conscious as the orderly and a nurse lifted him on to it. "We'll see you back here soon," the nurse said.

We waited in the playroom. They hadn't told us how long the operation might take. An hour went by. The room was crowded with anxious family and friends and I slipped away and went back to the chapel, wanting to be on my own. I threw my whole heart into my prayers this time. I couldn't keep still. It felt as if an electric current was running through my body. I knelt in the pews. I knelt on the steps. I knelt in front of the altar and kissed the cloth. And every time I knelt I begged God to spare Craig's life. Then, feeling calmer, I went back upstairs.

It was half-past three when the waiting-room door opened and Sister Lindy the day sister came in. She was smiling. "Craig's all right," she said. "You can come back into the ward to see him now."

He was asleep, his head propped high on pillows to help the shunt drain the fluid from his brain. One side of his head was shaved bare and there was a crescent-shaped incision where the shunt had gone in. His face and body were still swollen but in other ways I could really see a definite improvement. His sleep was more restful—he wasn't twitching and jerking the way he had been yesterday. His breathing was easier too. He even seemed to be a slightly better color. While Ernie sat and held Craig's hand I slipped back once more to the chapel. This time the message I wrote in the visitors' book was short. "Thank you God."

Craig slept for the rest of the afternoon while Ernie and I sat beside him chatting quietly. There was a pile of envelopes on his locker. "What's that, Ernie?" I asked. Ernie peered.

"It looks like get-well cards. Dozens of them. They must have arrived while he was in surgery." He leaned over Craig's bed and passed them to me. "Do you want to open them?"

I hesitated. "I don't know. He might want to open them himself tomorrow."

"He'll have some more by tomorrow," Ernie said. "I reckon it'll cheer him up if he can see them when he wakes up." He squeezed round the bed to Craig's locker and took out the packet of tape Kevin had brought in. "Come on. It'll give us something to do."

The cards were from relatives, friends and almost every one of our neighbors in Selby Road. "How do they all know?" Ernie asked.

"Bad news travels fast," I said. There were seventy-four cards, most of them with a long handwritten message for Craig. I decided I'd read them all out to him tomorrow. It would do him good to know so many people were thinking of him. Maybe it would give him extra strength to fight this thing. There was a parcel at the bottom of the pile and I opened it carefully. It contained an almost full bottle of aftershave, a card and a letter on crumpled paper torn out of an exercise book. It was from Craig's best friend Lee.

To Craig,

Hope you get better soon, because we have been haveing a good time at school and we have been haveing good football matches. Me and Jay's dad have billt a tree-house down the park and I havent got any one to argue with on the way to school. I no them hospittal beds are uncuftuble becos I have been in won myself. I hope you get better soon from Lee.

P.S. Your probably the goodest boy in the world even when your mum cant see you . . . This aftershave might make you smell a bit better Ha! Ha!"

I stuck the letter on the side of Craig's locker so it would be the first thing he saw when he woke up.

Early in the evening Dr. Hayward's registrar came into the ward and made straight for Craig's bed. "So far so good," he said cheerfully. "Craig's operation went well. We're pleased with him." I jumped up. "Oh, thank you, doctor." I think he was afraid I was going to throw my arms around him because he smiled and said quickly, "I should go and eat something if I were you. We don't want you two cracking up on us. Craig still has a long way to go . . ."

Craig was still sleeping peacefully so obediently we went to the canteen and ordered fish and chips. I had every intention of eating but at the last moment my stomach heaved, and I pushed my plate away—"It's the hospital smell," I said to Ernie. "I can't face it." Ernie could though and he put away first his plate and then mine. It was good to see the old Ernie back. He's a big man with an appetite to match but in the past two days he'd only nibbled at a couple of sandwiches. I had a lump in my throat as I watched him. I loved Ernie so much. He'd always been a wonderful father and husband. And he'd been a real support to me these last two days. I wanted him to know how much I appreciated that. I squeezed his hand. "Nothing's going to part us whatever happens, is it, Ern? 'Cos I do need you, you know." He shook his head and gave me a little choked smile. "We need each other, Mal. United we stand divided we fall. Right?" It had always been our song.

That night someone else needed the reclining chairs in the waiting-room and Ernie had to sleep on the chair next to Craig's bed while I tried to doze on a seat in the playroom. The next morning when I went into the ward I found poor Ernie fast asleep with his head on Craig's bed. He was as stiff as a board when he woke up. I went out to the kitchen to make us a cup of tea and when I came back Craig had woken up.

"Look at all my cards, Mum," he gave me a sleepy smile as I handed Ernie his tea. He looked better this morning, I thought. Not quite so swollen.

While Ernie slipped out for a wash I read Craig his messages, first the letter from Lee, then all the cards I'd stuck up the day before.

The orderlies arrived to take him downstairs for more CT scans and I went too. When we arrived back in the ward there was another huge bundle of cards on his bed-side locker. Nurse Jo settled Craig back into bed and helped me count them. Forty-two cards this time. "We'll have to get a special postman just for you at this rate, Craig," she teased. A big smile spread over Craig's face.

"Do you want Mummy to open them for you, Craig?" I asked.

"No. I want to do it myself." His voice was still slow, but at least the sign language had stopped.

It took Craig nearly two hours but he did it. The only help he let us give was in reading who they were from. His face was a picture. It was the first time he'd shown a real interest in anything since he'd come into hospital. Yesterday at least half the cards had been from people I knew through work and today it was the same story. Some cards were from people we hadn't seen for ages. I'd never been so grateful for being a waitress. Through my work I'd met hundreds of people over the years and now the bush telegraph was working.

Ernie held up a card with an elephant on. "This one's from Betty. She must have known your mum thought elephants were lucky." I was puzzled. "I don't remember telling Betty that." I pointed to the green furry elephant on the shelf above Craig's head. "I still don't know who that belongs to either. D'you know, Ernie, I think my mum's watching over us."

Sandra, one of my friends had covered her card with packets of *Sun* football stickers. Craig had been collecting them for months and he was thrilled. It was while Ernie was helping to stick them in his album that my eyes wandered around the ward, and I realized that none of the other kids had as many get-well cards as Craig did.

"Craig," I said gently when Ernie had put the last sticker in, "I don't think I'll put today's cards on the wall. I think it might look a bit greedy to the other kids, is that all right?"

"I don't mind." Craig's head slipped back on his pillows and he closed his eyes. But the smile stayed on his face.

That Tuesday was a wonderful day. Ernie and I knew the real test, the big op, was still to come. But for now we just enjoyed the fact that he'd gotten over this first hurdle so well.

Our visitors shared our relief. Steven was working as a building laborer just down the road at Shell House and he popped in during his lunch-hour to bring Craig some fruit. It was Craig's fifth lot of fruit that day. His bed looked like a Covent Garden stall—and there were dozens of packets of sweets and chocolates. Craig couldn't eat them—he was still on a drip and he hadn't eaten anything since that first vomiting attack—but Ernie tucked in. I tried to eat a bit myself but I still felt sick, and we shared most of the goodies out among the kids on the ward.

Craig couldn't move his head much but he was able to see the other children in the ward properly for the first time that day. When they saw the sweets being dished out those that could walk about came shyly up to his bed and introduced themselves. There was little Danny who screamed whenever he saw a doctor, Caroline who looked normal but all day kept singing like a stuck record, "Don't Worry Be Happy," and Simon who I'd met the first day and was almost ready to go home. Not all of the kids were able to get out of bed. In the cot next to Craig's bed the poor little baby whose head was covered with rows of stitches and clips still sat and cried for most of the day. I'd spoken to his mother in the "fag-room" and she'd told me that her son had been born with the bones of his skull already fused, so he had no soft spot like most babies have. The doctors had separated the bones to let his brain grow. He was going to be all right now, she said, but he did look awful. I caught Craig staring at him that afternoon. I thought he was worrying that he might look like that too. But no. He looked away from the baby and up at me. "Isn't it sad, Mum," he said. "He can't tell his mum how he feels."

On Wednesday morning my dear friend Jan, who had looked after Craig whenever I was working, came into the ward carrying two huge carrier bags full of cards. "From the kids at Craig's school!" she said. "They've made them all themselves." I picked one up. *"Get well tough guy. You can do it."* "We'll find a space on the wall for that one," I said and I stuck it under the Kylie Minogue poster.

Jan put a small red parcel on Craig's bed. "The parents

and Teachers Committee gave me five pounds for you, Craig, so I bought a Kylie Minogue tape at the shop."

"Oh great," said Craig. "I'll play it when my earache's gone."

I looked at Ernie. Craig hadn't told us his earache had come back. Though we'd both thought he didn't seem quite so well this morning. He looked pale again and he seemed a bit listless. He livened up at eleven o'clock, though, when another big bundle of cards arrived in the post. Opening them seemed to take even longer than the day before but he still insisted on doing it himself.

Early in the afternoon Dr. Hayward came into the ward. Craig was asleep and he didn't disturb him. His face was concerned. "I've just seen the latest scan," he said. "It shows that the tumor is growing very fast which means we must operate as soon as possible. It will take too long to get an operating room ready here, so, if you agree, we'd like to do the operation in the National Hospital on Monday. The anaesthetist will be over to talk to you later today."

I felt my heart jump. I reached out for Dr. Hayward's hands and this time he held them out to me as though he knew what I was doing. I held them tightly, willing all my strength into them. It was as he was leaving that Dr. Hayward first noticed the huge pile of cards on Craig's locker and gave me strict instructions to put them up at once so that Craig would have what he called "spiritual upliftment." The nurses thought it was a great idea and we spent the rest of the afternoon stringing them across the ward. But keeping busy didn't stop me noticing that Craig was getting worse. He had turned yellow again and his face and body were swelling back up. His tummy bulged out, and when I put my hand on it, it felt as tight as a balloon.

A play therapist, Janet, was on the ward that day. When she saw all Craig's cards she decided to get every kid on the ward to make him a get-well card as well. I was so relieved that the other kids weren't jealous. Instead Janet was turning it into a project everyone could take part in. The aim now was to completely cover the walls of the ward with Craig's get-well cards.

But the kids' excitement was lost on Craig. Janet had made a badge for him and she brought it over but he showed no interest. The noise was really getting to him. Some workmen in the road outside were using pneumatic drills. And if that wasn't enough, Caroline, the little girl in the cot opposite, was bawling "Don't worry, be happy" over and over. "Please, Mum. Stop her," Craig whispered. "She's driving me mad." I felt my blood rising. They knew Craig had earache. What had they been thinking of to put him in this noisy ward? "Ernie, I think you should call a nurse," I said.

He went out and after a few minutes returned with a young nurse in tow. "What's the problem?" she asked.

"Can you give him something for the pain?" I begged. "Please. I can't stand to watch him."

She shook her head. "I'm sorry. I have to have written permission before I can do that. I'll make a request—and I'll give him something as soon as I get the go ahead." An hour passed but she didn't return. By now Craig had stopped trying to talk and was whimpering like a hurt puppy. I cornered the nurse in the office. "You wouldn't see an animal suffer like this," I said. "Give him something, for God's sake. I'll take the blame."

"I'm sorry," she shrugged. "I really am. But I just can't do it without authority."

I stormed back into the ward. "Right," I said. "Fetch me a glass of water, Ernie." I rummaged around until I found the paracetamols I kept in my bag and when Ernie came back I gave Craig two tablets. "I'm not sure you ought to, Mal," Ernie said. I wasn't sure either but I couldn't watch my son suffer another moment knowing those little white tablets were lying in my handbag.

They did seem to ease the pain a little which was just as well because it was two more hours before the nurse came back to say permission had been granted. I confessed about the paracetamols and she wasn't too pleased but she went ahead and gave him some codeine-based tablets anyway. The combination seemed to knock him out and he dozed off within minutes.

It was quite late when a young lady anaesthetist from the National Hospital came to see us. She asked all the usual questions about childhood illnesses and allergies. She didn't wake Craig up but as she looked down at him

I could see from her face that she was really worried. She looked up and our eyes met.

"I'm so sorry," she said and the pity in her voice sent shivers down me.

Craig stayed asleep or unconscious—I couldn't always be sure which—for the rest of that day. Visitors came and went. My dad, Steven, Carol, Sandra . . . They helped me put cold flannels on his head. He was running a temperature now and the nurses brought a fan to cool him down but he kept shivering and pulling the comforter up and saying he was cold. Soon he became delirious. Doctors came and did more tests. "I don't think he's rejecting the shunt," one of them said. "I think it's an infection that's causing the problem." But I could tell they didn't know.

I was so frightened. Nurse Jo came over to the bedside and cuddled me again. "Don't be afraid," she said. "Sometimes they have to get worse before they get better."

I tried to draw comfort from her words. But I was on the edge of hysterics. I was getting that urge again—the one I'd had the first night—to wrap Craig up in a blanket and run away with him. I wanted to rescue him from this madhouse of radios and televisions and workmen's drills. If only I could get him home. Maybe the nightmare would stop then. Maybe I would wake up.

He only regained consciousness once more that day and when he did he looked straight at me and whispered something. I bent my head closer to hear.

"Mum?"

"Yes, darling, what is it?"

"I'm glad it's me who's ill and not you."

There was a lump in my throat. "Why, Craig?"

He stared up at me with great big eyes. "I love you too much, Mum. You couldn't have stood the pain."

All my resolutions flew out of the window and I hugged him to me and sobbed.

Chapter 6

—⁓—

IT WAS nearly three o'clock before the nurse managed to persuade us to leave Craig's bedside. Ernie and I hardly spoke to each other as we made up our "beds" in the waiting-room. I felt sure Ernie was thinking the same as me. Today was Thursday, and Dr. Hayward had told us that if we hadn't brought him in when we did, Craig would have been dead by Thursday . . .

We were back in the ward by six. The day nurse walked over to us as we sat down by Craig's bed. "He's had a restless night, I'm afraid," she said.

My blood boiled. "Why didn't you fetch us then?"

She shrugged. "I tried to," she said. "I couldn't find you."

"I don't believe her," I told Ernie as she walked off down the ward. "She doesn't care about Craig. I don't think any of the nurses really care. It's just a job to them." It wasn't fair. I knew I was over-reacting, and I knew why too. Yesterday I'd overheard one of the agency nurses complain that there was no swimming-pool or tennis court in the hospital. She said she only put up with it because the money was good. I'd been brooding about it ever since.

"Come on, Mal," Ernie patted my arm. "They're not all like that. Don't get yourself upset." But I was furious at not being called. I needed someone to blame and the nurses were easy targets. I forgot about Jo who'd cuddled me and comforted me. I forgot about Sal patiently explaining the shunt. Now I saw the nurses as enemies—they wouldn't let you stay in the ward all night, but you couldn't trust them to fetch you if your child needed you. I scowled at the duty nurse until she went off duty, seething every time she smiled. It wasn't like me—I've always got on well with people. At the back of my mind I knew the strain and lack of sleep were telling on me.

Craig was listless and far away that morning but at least he was awake and his temperature had gone down. The painkillers seemed to be working better too. The post came early—another couple of dozen cards for Craig. He was in no state to open them so I did it for him and stuck them up along with the ones which the kids on the ward had made the day before.

As the morning wore on he did seem to be taking more of an interest in things. Maybe it was the effect of the cards, I thought. Maybe Dr. Hayward had been right and they had given him some sort of boost.

Alison, a new friend I'd met three months ago in Benidorm, turned up at eleven. She hugged me without saying anything and sat down next to me while Ernie went out to take a break. It was a difficult visit. Alison's first husband had died of a brain tumor and it was hard for both of us to find the right things to say. I was quite relieved when Dr. Hayward came into the ward and headed toward Craig's bed. I was even more relieved when he commented on Craig's cards and made a joke about getting into the *Guinness Book of Records,* because it lightened the atmosphere.

I might have guessed Alison would jump at the idea. She was a born organizer and this sort of thing was right up her street. She was also PA to one of the directors of Gilbey's Gin so she had lots of business contacts. By the time she was ready to go she had a plan of action all drawn up.

"I'll circulate the idea to all the firms we deal with," she promised. "I'll get them to ask all their employees to send a card. We should get hundreds that way—maybe even thousands."

After Alison left I didn't give the *Guinness Book of Records* another thought. That day I had more important things to worry about than record-breaking. Craig was getting steadily worse. If the problem was an infection as the doctors thought, then it wasn't responding to antibiotics. I sat by his bed talking to him, trying to keep him alert. I didn't feel any longer that sleep was healing. Now to me it was the enemy. If Craig was asleep I felt his tumor could take control. I felt certain that to fight it he had to stay alert.

All afternoon I sat by his bed holding his hand through the bars of his cot and talking to him. Telling him how much we loved him, reading him stories, singing to him. Whenever he shut his eyes, I'd bend close and say sternly, "Listen to Mummy." I talked about anything that came into my head. Holiday memories. Being made Prince of the Week at the Golden Sands holiday camp when he was three. Shooting a bull's-eye on the rifle range in Benidorm only last November.

I told him stories of when I was a kid, about playing on the bomb-sites and chasing rats the size of cats round the back of the local factory. I told him how my dad would bring home big slabs of ice from the brewery in summer and put them in the sink in the laundry so everyone could chop pieces off to keep their milk cold. I told him about my rich Uncle George and the day that Kevin and I let the handbrake off his posh car so it rolled into a cobble-stone pillar and brought all the family running out of the pub yelling blue murder. Craig loved that. He liked the idea of me getting into the same sort of scrapes as him.

I opened some of his presents. One of them was a soft toy, a rabbit, which reminded me of a birthday present I'd got from my Aunty Nell when I was seven. I told Craig how I'd torn the parcel open expecting a doll and had screamed the house down when I lifted out a dead white rabbit with a hair-slide clipped to each ear. "The hair-slides were for me but the rabbit was for your nan to make a pie with . . ." I explained. "That's why I've never eaten rabbit since!"

Craig tried to smile but his heart wasn't in it anymore. The effort of keeping awake was draining him. I unwrapped the last few presents. There were about a dozen furry toys at the bottom of his bed now. I arranged them so they were all sitting up, paying attention, and when I looked again Craig was asleep. I went out to the waiting-room, asked Ernie to take over the vigil and set off across the dark damp courtyard toward the chapel. In the past week it had become my second home.

Today, for the first time, I had company. Two shadowy figures were sitting in one of the pews. I felt cross. This was "my" chapel. I wanted a good chat with God. How could I do it with other people here? While I waited for them to go I wandered over to look at the messages in the visitors' book. Tonight there was a fresh one. *"Please God help little Craig Shergold on Punch and Judy Ward to get well and please help his mum and dad. From a nurse who cares."*

Tears rolled down my cheeks. How could I have been so ratty with that nurse this morning? How could I have told Ernie that nurses were heartless? The couple in the far pew stood up and left, smiling at me as they passed. I knelt down in the candlelight and prayed to God to forgive me.

When I got back to the ward Craig was awake. He grinned. "Hello, Mum. I've been to the toilet! I feel a lot better."

Then he frowned. "You haven't been crying, have you?"

"No," I fibbed. "It's just the rain on my face."

Ernie told me they'd given Craig an enema. I was relieved. Craig hadn't had his bowels open since he'd been taken ill and I'd been nagging them to do something for days. But an hour later I was regretting saying anything. He was seized with an attack of diarrhea and vomiting and soon afterward the hot and cold sweats started again. I held his hand, fighting back the tears. Why did my poor baby have to suffer so much? The nurses were wonderful. They were changing his sheets every half-hour but they never complained. I felt completely useless. I've never been much good at what I call the "toilet" side of illness. I can't stomach it. Every time Craig retched I was retching in sympathy. Nurse Jo made a little joke of it but she must have thanked heaven for Ernie who ran backward and forward to the sluice with the soiled sheets without turning a hair. If there was ever a competition for best dad in the world, I thought, Ernie would win it hands down.

By the time it was over and Craig lay once more in a deep sleep I was completely drained. We went out and told everyone waiting patiently outside that visiting wouldn't be possible this evening. All our regulars were there. Steven and Sharon, John and Sandra, and of course Carol. A few of Ernie's workmates had come in too, tipped off by John, who also worked at the LEB. John told us he'd applied for compassionate leave for Ernie, something which hadn't crossed our minds in the confusion of the last few days. I was so grateful we had such wonderful friends.

After they'd gone we started to get ready for "bed." I dreaded the nights now. Tonight especially, with him being so ill, it felt as if we were deserting Craig. "Ernie," I said, "ask the nurses if we can sleep on a chair by his bed just this once. I'd be much happier." Up until now the nurses had always made us leave the ward during the night shift so I wasn't hopeful. But to my surprise they agreed to Ernie staying. Perhaps they thought his efforts in the sluice-room deserved a reward.

That night I tossed and turned on my reclining chair. I missed being able to reach out and touch Ernie for comfort and I couldn't stop worrying. Every night had seen a change in Craig's condition—sometimes for the better but more often for the worse. I dreaded what Friday might bring.

Ernie woke me at six to report that it had been a "wicked" night. "That Caroline was singing and crying," he said. "She kept Craig awake all night. He's only just got off to sleep."

"Right," I said. "That does it." I tackled the sister in her office. "Why do you have to put a child like Caroline next to Craig when he's so ill," I demanded.

She shook her head helplessly. "It's because of the building work," she said. "The other ward on this floor is closed for renovations—that's why this one is so crowded.

At the moment there's nowhere else to put children like Caroline. It'll be better when the other ward reopens."

"That'll be no good to my Craig, will it?" I asked. "What about him? It's like bedlam in there. How is Craig supposed to get better? You'd think he only had the flu the way you expect him to put up with all that din."

She lifted her hands in despair. "I'm sorry, Mrs. Shergold. I do realize you're upset about your son. But we're all doing the best we can under difficult circumstances."

All my anger disappeared. What was the matter with me? I thought. It wasn't her fault. She only worked here. It was just Craig's bad luck to be taken ill while they were rebuilding the hospital. Getting all steamed up about it wasn't going to help. Feeling really depressed I trudged back to the ward.

Last night's change had been for the worse. I didn't need a doctor to tell me that. Dr. Hayward came into the ward early and made straight for Craig's bed. He examined him, studied his charts, then looked at me. "Could I see you and your husband outside for a moment?" he asked.

In the corridor Dr. Hayward turned around to face us. "I'm afraid the poor little chap's in a bad way," he said. "Unless he recovers very quickly we're not going to be able to operate on Monday. It will be a long operation and the condition he's in now he just wouldn't survive it."

I felt numb. Common sense told me he was right and Craig was too ill for a major operation. But the tumor was growing all the time. It *had* to come out. We couldn't afford a delay. "I'm sorry," Dr. Hayward repeated and gave me a sympathetic smile. "Come on, Mother. We'll all do our best, won't we? I'll be back to see him tomorrow."

I couldn't face going back to the ward with Ernie and letting Craig see me upset. I walked downstairs and out of the hospital. Outside I wandered around in circles—into the chapel and out again, round and round the courtyard—feeling as if I was on another planet. I sat down on the wooden bench, and stared up at his window, shivering with cold. People walked past me smiling and I watched them miserably, jealous of their happiness. Then the tears started rolling and I hung my head. After a while I sensed someone come and sit down beside me and I looked up. A little boy, about ten years old, was looking at me with wide eyes.

"Have you got a child here who's very ill?" he asked.

I choked as I tried to answer him.

The boy gave me an inquisitive stare. "Is he dying?"

I was flabbergasted. "I hope not," I said shakily. "But he is very ill."

At that the little boy leaned over and his lips brushed my cheek. "He won't die," he said. "The doctors here will save him. They saved me."

For a moment I couldn't speak. Then I threw my arms around him and hugged him. I hardly noticed the lady sitting down on my other side, putting her arm around my shoulders. When my tears slowed down she introduced herself as the little boy's mother. She told me that her son had received a lung transplant at Great Ormond Street. A few months ago he'd been dying like Craig. Now he was almost ready to leave hospital. "Keep your faith," she said. "Your son will get well."

I flew up the stairs, bursting to tell Ernie about this brave little boy and his mother, feeling full of hope again. I thought of Joan's words, "God will carry you," and realized with astonishment that they were true. Every time I'd felt I just couldn't carry this burden any longer, something had given me the strength to keep going. The sense of peace when I'd first seen Dr. Hayward's photograph, the nurse's message in the visitors' book, and now this wonderful little boy. As I passed Dr. Hayward's photograph in the corridor I stopped and tapped the frame. "Craig's going to be all right," I told him.

The operation was postponed for a week. Dr. Hayward took the decision the next day. But now I didn't feel the same despair I'd felt when he'd first suggested delaying it. I knew God was looking after us. I think Ernie was beginning to share my faith. Once or twice in the next few days he slipped quietly out to the chapel on his own.

As if in answer to our prayers the ward quieted down. The building work stopped for the weekend and to everyone's relief Caroline was discharged. It might have been coincidence but hours after she left, Craig started to eat—only a mouthful of porridge and a sip of tea—but it was his first solid food for a week. Things were looking up. It took Carol to add the final touch. She pointed out that the operation was now scheduled for February 6, and that six was my lucky number!

Craig really seemed to have turned a corner. A few days later his temperature was back to normal, his response to the co-ordination tests seemed better, and, best of all, his sense of fun had come back. It was wonderful to see him smiling and laughing again. One day Alison brought her husband Norman to visit and they gave Craig a huge pair of slippers shaped like bear paws with long nails. Craig loved them, and though he couldn't get out of bed we lifted the sheets and put them on his feet. He gave me a wicked look then suddenly yelled out, "Nurse! Nurse! Look what the medicine's done to my feet. My toenails are growing." One of the nurses came rushing over, then saw the slippers and collapsed in giggles.

Steve had great news that week. He came in very late one evening, long after the other visitors had gone, looking very excited and gently woke Craig up. "Guess what, Craig? They've accepted me into the fire brigade. I've passed the interview and the test." Craig gave him a huge smile. "I'm proud of you, Ugly. I knew you could do it." He closed his eyes. "Now please go. Let me sleep. I'm happy." Steve grinned at us and crept out. Seeing the love between my two sons gave me a warm glow.

The next day when Steven came in again he and Craig seemed to be plotting something. They sent Ernie and me to the canteen saying they had something private to talk about. When we came back Craig grinned. "You'd better listen to Radio GOSH at five to four, Mum," he said. "It's a surprise."

We had to go into the ward kitchen to listen to the radio because there was so much noise in the ward. A nurse helped us tune into the hospital radio station and friends and nurses crowded into the kitchen to listen. At five to four Craig's voice came out of the radio loud and clear. "Mum, I love you, and you too, Dad. I'm sorry I'm ill, but

I'll get better I promise. Don't worry. I'm going to be at my brother's wedding. This song is for you. It's 'I Just Called to Say I Love You.' "

As we listened to Stevie Wonder singing that lovely song there wasn't a dry eye in the kitchen. Afterward, back in the ward, Craig tutted at my tear-stained face. "Cor, I knew you'd cry, Mum. But I do love you and I will get well. Me and Ugly arranged that while you and Dad were having tea. Clever, weren't we?"

Alison had been busy spreading the word about Craig's cards and that week we saw the first results of her hard work. Every day Craig got cards postmarked in Scotland and Wales from people we'd never head of. The nurses had been telling everyone that Craig wanted to break the world record and soon all the kids in Great Ormond Street were involved. Cards were arriving from every ward in the hospital and the other mothers helped me stick them up. The cards had become a project for the Punch and Judy Ward as much as for Craig. Every day when the post arrived there'd be screams of delight and the new cards would be passed round for everyone to have a look at before they were put up. Soon there was hardly a bare inch of wall anywhere and the ceiling was criss-crossed with dozens of lengths of wool and string hung with Craig's cards.

Now that Craig had got the taste of food again, we couldn't stop him eating. Luckily there was plenty to give him. Our visitors had been bringing a steady stream of fruit and sweets, and Joyce, my darling sister-in-law, had baked a huge basketful of sausage rolls, apple pie and cheese straws. I was thrilled to see the way Craig tucked into them. I thought it was a sign that the pressure in his brain was going down but the ward sister said it was a side effect of the steroids. I was a bit taken aback by that. I hadn't even known he was getting steroids but I'd only got myself to blame. I hardly ever asked the doctors or nurses questions. I was too afraid I wouldn't like the answers.

Apparently the reason they were giving Craig steroids was to shrink the tissues around the tumor before they removed it. The sister said it was the steroids that were making him so bloated. "Once he comes off them he'll start to look better," she promised.

I wondered what it would take to make us look better. Ernie and I hadn't been home since the morning we arrived at the hospital, and for the past week we'd lived like tramps, with no bed to sleep in and nowhere to wash except a plastic bowl in the waiting-room. Neither of us was eating proper meals—we were getting by on chocolate biscuits and cups of tea from the vending machine in the corridor. I worried about Ernie. I felt as if I'd got new strength now, but Ernie was exhausted and kept falling asleep. Usually we took it in turns to sit by Craig's bed in the evening but once or twice Ernie had dropped off in the waiting-room and missed his turn. When he was asleep he looked so sad I hadn't the heart to wake him.

Then one day Sister Lindy said, "There's a vacancy in Rainbow House. How would you like to stay there for a couple of weeks?" Rainbow House was a guest-house for the parents of very sick children, just round the corner from Great Ormond Street. We went to see it. The contrast with our seedy waiting-room was dramatic. It was beautifully fitted out with luxury carpets and curtains and there were proper bedrooms with twin beds, wardrobe and dressing table. Down the hall there was a communal bathroom and a kitchen. The thought of sleeping in a proper bed again, taking a shower, and just getting away from the smell of hospital was wonderful.

Craig was quite happy about it. "Go on, Mum—you need a bath," he teased. "You have a rest." It felt as though we'd had a life-line thrown to us. It was only when my head hit the pillow that first night that I realized just how tired I was.

The next morning I noticed a plaque in the living room of Rainbow House saying that the actor Michael Crawford had helped raise money to build it and that Marks & Spencer had donated all the furnishings. I made a vow there and then never to complain about Marks & Spencer prices again.

As the week drew to a close I started to dread the operation. I didn't see it anymore as Craig's big chance. Instead it loomed over me like a big black cloud. I almost started to pray for another postponement. I had a feeling the nurses were nervous about it too. While Craig had been waiting for the shunt operation they'd been reassuring, but now there were no cheerful words. They knew, like us, that this time Craig might die. The thought started to keep us awake at night.

On the morning of Monday February 6 I woke up with one thought running round my head—I had to buy Craig an elephant for luck. The urge was really strong. I was sure it was my mum sending me a message.

Craig was quite drowsy when we got to the ward and didn't want to talk much. I sat by his bedside with Ernie until ten-thirty when I knew the Wishing Well Appeal shop at the hospital entrance opened, then I ran downstairs. "My little boy's having an operation today and I've just got to have an elephant," I told the woman behind the counter.

"I haven't got any elephants I'm afraid," she said. "Would an owl do?"

I felt devastated. I'd been so sure there'd be an elephant here waiting for me. Had Mum let me down? Then I remembered that Craig's godmother Sandra collected owls—maybe that was the lucky sign I was looking for. I couldn't afford to ignore any chance of bringing Craig luck today. I fumbled in my purse but the shop assistant held up her hand. "No. Give him this from me." She pointed to the sign above the shop and smiled. "Tell him I am wishing him *well.*"

Gratefully I took the owl from her and set off back for the ward but as I reached the hospital steps I felt the chapel calling me. They'd be coming for Craig soon and I had to be there, but I knew I had to go and have one last talk with God first. I ran up to the altar with the furry owl tucked under my arm and knelt down. "Don't take him, God," I prayed. I kissed the altar cloth. "Don't take him. I'll die if you take him. Please, please, let Dr. Hayward do it right." I looked up at the arch and read its message again, "Suffer the little children to come unto me," and I felt my heart breaking—it seemed so unfair. "Why should he suffer, God?" I asked. "Let me suffer instead."

Someone opened the door, saw me, and went out again. I looked at my watch. It was nearly eleven o'clock. They were coming for him at eleven-thirty. I got up off my knees and turned to go. As I walked past the visitors' book I picked up the pen—it had become a ritual now. I intended to write, "Please don't take him." But as I read all the sad prayers other parents had written for their sick and dying children something happened to me. I didn't feel sad any longer. I felt angry. I scrawled across the page in great big capitals, "You're not having him!!!" Then I underlined it twice and hurried back to the ward.

The clock in the reception area showed a quarter past eleven—my watch must have been slow—and I ran in panic up the stairs to the ward, terrified they might have taken Craig already. But to my relief he was lying on a gurney in the ward talking to Ernie and clutching the teddy bear that his cousin Kerry had given him. I put the owl on his gurney. It was better than nothing, but I was still upset I hadn't managed to get Craig an elephant. I felt it was a bad omen. If God was going to save Craig's life surely he would have given me a sign and made sure there was an elephant in the shop . . .

I was explaining to Craig how the kind Wishing Well lady had given him the owl when a group of mums came across from the other side of the ward to wish Craig luck. "We wanted Craig to have this," one of them said and she handed me a gray furry elephant. I was speechless. Who had told them? Almost before I could say thank you the orderlies started to wheel Craig out of the ward. As we reached the door Janet the playleader called, "Marion—don't forget Craig's present." She was holding out the green elephant that had been on the shelf above Craig's bed ever since we'd arrived here.

"That's not Craig's," I told her. "It belongs to the hospital." Janet shook her head. "No. This was Craig's admission present. All the kids get a toy when they come in. Didn't anyone tell you?"

I was over the moon. Who could doubt now that my mum was watching over us? Hugging the elephants to me I started to walk after the gurney. Then I stopped. I had a sudden urge to take something of Craig's with me—

something to hold while he was having the operation. I
hurried back to Craig's bed and rummaged through his
locker, grabbing the first thing I put my hands on—a pair
of underpants that he wore when the nurses washed him.
Stuffing them down my jumper I ran back out into the corridor where Ernie was waiting for me. He took my hand
and we followed the gurney carrying Craig and his big
pile of furry toys into the elevator.

I'd thought we'd be traveling by ambulance but I was
wrong. "We're going to walk to the National," the orderly
told me as we came out of the elevator. "It'll give him a
smoother journey." As he pushed Craig's gurney toward
the old part of the hospital where the chapel was, he explained that all the hospitals in this area—Great Ormond
Street, the National, and the University Hospital—were
connected by underground tunnels built during the war.
These tunnels were still used to transfer very sick patients
between hospitals.

As we waited at the tunnel entrance I cuddled Craig's
head. Suddenly the sheet over him slipped and I saw that
his body was surrounded by sachets of blood. It gave me
quite a jolt. It hadn't occurred to me that Craig would need
blood during the operation. It brought the reality of what
was about to happen home to me. Quickly I pulled the
sheet back over the sachets and placed the green elephant
on top. Then the nurses arrived and put blankets over the
gurney to keep him warm and we all walked through some
wide rubber doors into the tunnel.

It felt very cold and a bit eerie—like I imagined an underground station would feel after the trains stop running.
Our footsteps and the sound of the gurney wheels echoed
around us. The walls were white-washed brick with little
dim lights set into them, and every so often we passed
green doors leading into side passages and metal staircases
vanishing up into the darkness. The orderly pushing the
gurney was a big fit man and we had a job to keep up with
him. I grabbed hold of the bar at the side of the gurney
and ran alongside, keeping my eyes fixed on Craig's face.
At last the floor started to slope upward and we emerged
into daylight to find ourselves facing the main entrance of
the National Hospital.

Compared with Great Ormond Street it looked very modern. The orderly pushed Craig through the shining swing-doors of the entrance and into a swish streamlined elevator. We came out on the operating floor and there was Richard Hayward waiting for us. "Hello, Mother. Hello, Dad," he held out his hands to me. I took hold of them and looked into his eyes. "You're going to do it," I told him. "God will bless your hands."

He let me hold his hands for several seconds and then he nodded. "I hope so," he said.

The surgical team came out to meet us, all dressed in their greens and my stomach turned over. How must Craig feel seeing them? I wished he could be asleep already but the anaesthetist had explained that for brain operations they didn't give a pre-med and the anesthetic was given in the operating room itself. Craig stared up at me looking worried.

"You're going to be with me, Mum, aren't you?" he said in a frightened voice. I knew I wouldn't be allowed in the operating room. I thought quickly. "I'm not going to leave you, darling. I'll be right outside this door," I promised.

"Oh no, you'll have to go," a surgical assistant piped up and Craig's eyes went wide with fright.

I glared at her, daring her to open her mouth again. "I don't *ever* leave my son," I said, and I squeezed Craig's hand tight. She looked to Dr. Hayward to support her but he shook his head and she didn't say any more.

"Come on, Craig," a big fat guy came up to the gurney. "Let's label the teddies, shall we?" He put a name tag on each of the two elephants and one on the teddy and the owl, and then, last of all, he put one on Craig's wrist.

Ernie held one of Craig's hands and I held the other as we waited for him to finish. When Craig was growing up he and I had always sung songs together and now it seemed the natural thing to do. After Craig's radio request for me there was only one song I could choose and I sang it gently to him, "I just called to say I love you. I just called to say how much I care . . ." Struggling for each word, Craig sang the next two lines back to me, "I just called to say I love you. And I mean it from the bottom of my heart . . ."

"We're ready for him, Mrs. Shergold," one of the nurses called. Ernie and I stood back and the gurney started to move slowly away from us into the operating room. Craig's eyes, wide and scared, stayed fixed on me.

"Don't forget, Craig," I called after him, "I love you so much . . . And I'm here. I will not leave you. I'm here." I remembered something. "I've got your underpants. Look." I took them out from under my jumper and waved them at him. He pulled a face at me. "Oh Mu-u-u-m!" he said all embarrassed. And then the doors closed behind him and he was gone.

Ernie and I put our arms around each other and sat down on the stairs near the elevator. After a few minutes a sister came up to us. "You must go out now," she said. "Go and have a drink."

"I don't want a drink," I said. "I promised Craig I'd stay here."

"I'm sorry but really you can't." She looked at her watch. "It's twelve o'clock now. He'll be in surgery for several hours. Why don't you go back to Rainbow House and I'll make sure they ring you there as soon as he's out. Then you can be with him when he comes round. He won't know that you haven't been here, and you'll be better off getting some rest. You'll be wide awake then when he really needs you."

I knew what she said made sense and though it still felt as if I was betraying Craig's trust I allowed Ernie to take me back round the corner to Rainbow House. "I'll be sitting by the phone," I promised as we left. When we got to Rainbow House I left Ernie with our visitors in the sitting-room, took a chair to the phone in the kitchen and sat there waiting, rocking to and fro, and hugging Craig's underpants to me.

A support party of family and friends had turned up to sit with us—dear Carol, my dad, John and Sandra, Craig's cousin Sue, Kevin, Steven and Sharon, my sister Kate and her husband Jimmy. All of them took it in turns to sit with me in the kitchen. We hardly spoke. What could anyone say? At seven, knowing it could still be hours yet, all the men except Ernie went off to the pub and Ernie brought a chair into the kitchen and sat with me.

It was ten when the phone rang. I snatched the receiver off the hook. It was Sister Lindy. "Craig's just come out of surgery," she said. "He's very cold and we're wrapping him in silver foil to warm him up but you should be able to see him soon."

"When?"

"About half-past ten. He's on a ventilator and various machines so don't panic when you see him."

I put the phone down. Ernie looked at me anxiously. Behind him another dozen faces waited for news. "He's out," I said. "Come on—we're going to the chapel."

Twenty minutes later Ernie and I led the way up the steps to the Punch and Judy Ward. Craig had been brought to the small intensive-care unit next to the sister's office. We walked in nervously, and Kate and Steve followed, leaving the others in the corridor. Three nurses were grouped around Craig's bed—I recognized one of them as Jo. I tiptoed toward the bed holding Ernie's hand. They'd warned me not to be scared by all the machinery but I didn't even see it—all I could see was Craig. He was wrapped in a shiny case of silver foil and a thick white bandage covered his head. His lips were swollen and held open by the mouthpiece of a ventilator which was pumping air in and out of his chest. His eyes were closed, the long dark eyelashes brushing his cheeks. It was as if I'd stepped back in time. He looked like my baby. Jo put her hand around my waist. "You can talk to him if you want to," she said.

I leaned over and started to sing softly, my face close to his. "I just called to say I love you . . ." I sang the whole song through. He didn't move. His eyes stayed shut. The only sound was the pumping of the ventilator. I was sure he couldn't hear me. Dr. Hayward's words came back to me. "He may be a vegetable . . . He may never speak again . . . He may never regain consciousness . . ." I could feel Ernie's hand clenched tightly around mine. I took a deep breath and started to sing the song again. "I just called to say I love you . . ." I really belted it out, giving it my all, as though Craig's life depended on it. "And I mean it from the bottom of my heart." Every time I reached the end I kissed his face and started again. And

suddenly, as my lips touched his cheek I felt his eyelids
flutter. I drew back and his arm lifted shakily toward me.
His lips moved around the plastic tube. "I . . . love . . .
you," he whispered.

Behind me I heard a soft sighing sound and when I
looked round I saw that everybody in the room was crying. I was crying too, completely overcome. I kissed Ernie.
I kissed Steve. I kissed the nurses. I was looking around
for someone else to kiss when through the glass I saw
Richard Hayward standing outside in the passage with his
registrar. I went out and he held his hands out to me. I
took hold of them. "I told you God would bless you,
didn't I?" I said.

He smiled and nodded. "You did." He looked exhausted. No wonder. He'd been operating for ten hours.
"You must be absolutely knackered," I said. "God bless.
Thank you from the bottom of my heart." And I gave him
a quick cuddle—I couldn't help myself.

He smiled. "I'll talk to you both in my office in the
morning," he said. "Don't forget there's still a long way to
go. These first twenty-four hours are critical. We're not
out of the woods yet."

A faint warning bell was ringing in my head. But I
wasn't going to listen to it. Craig was alive—he could see,
he could speak. At that moment, nothing else in the world
mattered.

Chapter 7

—◆—

It was nearly lunch-time the next day when Dr. Hayward called us into the sister's office. Craig had been asleep the whole morning. The Indian nurse looking after him said it was because he'd been given morphine for the pain. "Sleep is important for him right now," she said. "He doesn't have to talk to you. He knows you're here. That's what matters."

Dr. Hayward didn't look so tired this morning. Ernie and I sat down opposite him. There was a big colored poster of the brain on the wall in the sister's office. I didn't want to look. It made me feel squeamish, but my eyes kept being drawn back to it. Dr. Hayward said he wanted to explain what he had done during the operation. He didn't seem as cheerful as I'd expected, considering he'd just saved Craig's life.

"We managed to cut out almost three-quarters of the tumor," he said. "As you know it was growing right at the center of Craig's brain, very close to the brain stem. That's the area which controls breathing, heart rate and blood pressure. It meant we had to tread very carefully, and we were forced to leave some of the tumor behind. If we'd cut any deeper we might have lost him."

I felt uneasy. When I'd pictured the operation I'd imagined them removing the whole tumor. "Won't it grow back?" I asked.

"Not necessarily," Dr. Hayward said. "I hope not. But we'll have a better idea when we get the results back from the Path Lab. They'll do an analysis on the part of the tumor we've removed and let us know whether it's malignant or not."

Ernie caught hold of my hand. "How long will that take?"

"About a week."

A whole week more of hoping and praying ... "Don't you have any idea just from looking at it?" I asked.

"From its appearance we're fairly certain that it's a teratoma," Dr. Hayward said carefully. "It's the first time I've ever seen this kind of tumor in the brain. Usually we find it growing in the abdomen. It's a congenital tumor, which means it's there at birth but it usually doesn't start causing trouble until puberty. Then it can grow very rapidly. When these tumors develop in the ovaries or testicles they can get very big indeed."

My stomach was turning over. "How big?"

"Up to fifteen pounds in weight. But, of course, it wouldn't reach that size in the brain. It's a very unusual tumor—it's actually a living thing. It has hair, it has nails, sometimes it even has teeth."

I stared at him in horror. What was he telling me? That some sort of monster was living in Craig's brain? It was outrageous. How *dare* that dirty thing be in my beautiful son's head? I couldn't speak. I was afraid I was going to be sick. Dr. Hayward looked understanding. "I'm sorry," he said. "I can't tell you any more at the moment. All we can do until the pathology report comes back is to wait and hope."

For most of the afternoon Craig slept peacefully. His nurse stayed the whole time at his bedside watching over him. "Try and talk to him," she said when we came back into the unit. She passed me a swab. "Here, clean his little mouth for him." I obeyed, talking away to Craig about all sorts of nonsense as I swabbed the dried blood away from the cracks on his lips. He was still on the respirator and was lying on his back, propped up on pillows. From time to time he opened his eyes but he didn't try to speak.

I'd felt really down in the dumps when I came out of

Dr. Hayward's office but my depression didn't last. That day I lived for the moment, enjoying the fact that he was alive, and not paralyzed or blind, not letting myself think any further ahead. Neither Ernie nor I mentioned the teratoma. The very idea of it filled me with such horror that I blotted it out.

As the day drew to a close I let myself start to get hopeful. Craig had come through the first critical twenty-four hours without any dramas. "We must be over the worst now," I told Ernie. "Why don't you go back in to work tomorrow for a couple of hours? You'll be getting the sack if you're not careful."

I was tempting fate. The next morning while Ernie was away, the pain started. It was terrible. I'd thought Craig was in pain before, but it was nothing compared with what he went through that day. Every sound was torture for him. I crept around his bed in bare feet. I even had to stop opening his cards—just the sound of the envelopes tearing made him moan. Worst of all, he hated the sound of my voice. I've always had a loud voice, and since my dad went deaf it has got louder. Now Craig begged me not to speak. Every time I said anything he screwed his face up in agony. Even when I tried to whisper he shushed me to be quiet.

By Wednesday, although he was still on a drip he didn't need the respirator any longer and he was moved out of intensive care into a cubicle. But he didn't show any other improvement. In fact, he was getting worse. Ernie didn't dare go in to work again. By Wednesday evening the pain was so bad they had to increase the dose of morphine and at last, at ten o'clock, Craig fell asleep. I refused point-blank to leave him on his own while he was so ill and the nurses found a Z-bed for me to sleep on which we crammed in the cubicle beside Craig's bed at night.

All the following day Ernie and I kept up our vigil. Visitors were only allowed to look at Craig through the passage window and we took it in turns to go to the canteen with them. To keep myself busy I fetched his things from the main ward and hung his Chelsea scarf and hat on the wall behind his head to make the cubicle look more homely. Then I went back to the main ward and opened all the get-well cards which had been piling up since Monday, brought them back to the cubicle and stuck them up—there were about a hundred. His nurse was amazed—she was doing relief duty from another ward and hadn't heard about the *Guinness Book of Records* project.

No one told us what was wrong with him. Every morning since the operation an orderly had lifted Craig on to a gurney and wheeled him away down the corridor for scans and tests but we never found out what the results were. I asked to see Dr. Hayward but I was told he was away from the hospital. It may have been unfair to the medical team, but I felt we were being deliberately kept in the dark, and on Thursday morning when Craig started moaning worse than ever, I flipped and demanded to see a doctor. One of the nurses disappeared and came back with a young doctor. I could tell from his expression as I followed him out into the passageway that he thought he had better things to do than talk to me.

"Thank you for seeing me," I began. "I just want to know what's wrong with Craig. Why is he in so much pain?" The doctor studied the floor and said in a bored voice, "He's got blood clots." His attitude was the final straw.

"*Look* at me when you talk to me," I exploded. He glanced up startled. I glared at him. "I'm only a mum," I said. "I'm only a waitress. I don't understand. What do you *mean* he's got blood clots?"

He hesitated, then shrugged. "Well, you can have a look at the scans if you want." He went into the sister's office and came back a few moments later carrying a scan which he held up to the light. "Look," he pointed. "Each of those dark areas is a blood clot." I stared at the scan, not believing what I saw. Craig's whole brain was a mass of blood clots. Why hadn't anyone told us about this?

"What's going to happen? What are you going to *do?*" I was shouting now. But he wouldn't meet my eyes. "We're hoping they'll self-disperse," he said. He sounded so indifferent I could have hit him.

I stumbled back into the cubicle and started to tell Ernie about the blood clots. I was still trembling with shock and anger when the door opened and Bobby Campbell, the manager of the Chelsea football team, walked in. What timing! He'd brought a football and a team photograph, signed by all the players. I knew Bobby Campbell quite well. The last time we'd met I'd been serving him dinner at a Christmas function in the executive club at Stamford Bridge. He was a big strong man, always in control of himself, but now he took one look at Craig and his face just crumpled. "Oh Marion," he said. "I'm so sorry. I'd no idea he was so ill."

I nodded. I could hardly speak.

"What's wrong? I'd heard he was getting better."

I explained to him about the blood clots and he looked more and more upset. Perhaps it was because he'd just had a new baby grandson but I sensed he was about to break down. He made an excuse and went outside for a few minutes. When he came back he looked more composed. He pushed a note into my hand. "Read this. We're all praying for you." A photographer from our local paper appeared wanting a quick picture and Bobby put his arm around the top of Craig's Chelsea pillow and forced a smile. Craig just stared blankly at the camera.

After he left I opened Bobby's note. "Listen to Capital Radio at five to six tonight," it said. "Keep your chin up." At ten to six a nurse found the station for us on my little portable radio and turned the volume down till it was quiet enough for Craig to bear it. They played a couple of requests then we heard the DJ's voice say, "Hi out there. This is a very special message for a great Chelsea supporter—Craig Shergold, who is nine years old." Craig's eyes had been shut but when he heard that they opened wide. "He's in Great Ormond Street Hospital with a tumor on the brain," the DJ continued, "so hi there, Craig. Are you listening? This is from all your friends, the players at the Chelsea Football Club. We know you're a very sick little boy at the moment but we also know that you're going to get well. We miss you at the Bridge." Then the first notes of the Chelsea team song, "Blue is the Color, Football is the Game," rang out and Craig beamed from ear to ear. When the record finished the DJ said, "When your bus is late tonight and you're moaning away, remember this little boy, count your blessings and say a prayer for him."

Craig was so happy. Good old Bobby. This was just what he'd needed.

Bobby Campbell had commented on all the cards around Craig's bed and he must have told the team about the record attempt because the next day a get-well card was delivered with personal messages from every single player. "Get well soon, Craig." "Hurry up and get back down the Bridge. We all love you and miss you." The way Craig reacted you'd have thought the card was a check for a million pounds.

But the improvement didn't last. On Friday evening the pain got worse. And by Saturday it was so bad that at times it took three of us—Ernie, me and a nurse—to hold Craig down on the bed. It was terrible to see him suffering. I telephoned Carol to ask her to stop our visitors coming that day. I knew it would upset them too much to stand outside and see him throwing himself around with pain.

All day I stayed by his bedside, rubbing his hands to try to get them warm—his hands and feet had been icy cold ever since the operation—and talking to him non-stop. "Come on, Craig. You can do it. Fight it. Come on, you can win." I only left him once, when Ernie took my place so I could go downstairs to the chapel and desperately beg God to intervene.

At last, late on Saturday evening, Craig fell into a little sleep. Until then he'd been so restless with the pain that you couldn't say he'd slept at all—he'd laid still for a few seconds between spasms, but that was all. But now he slept quietly on his side for a whole hour, his face calm, his breathing deep and regular. I hardly dared to move in case I broke the spell. Then at nine o'clock he stirred. His eyes fluttered open and he stared at me with a puzzled look on his face. "Hello, Mum," he said. "Have I got any visitors?" The pain had completely gone. It was as though he'd come back from another world.

The next day as I sat by his bed, watching him lying peacefully at last, and thanking God that the torture was over, Craig turned his head toward me. "Mum," he said slowly, "I've had a very funny experience."

"Have you, darling? What's that?" I asked.

"You was there, Mum. Nanny was there." He stopped.
"Yes?"

"And someone else was there. I don't know who this other person was though." He frowned, trying to remember. "It's as if I was two person—" he hesitated, "two personalities," he said at last, struggling with the long word.
"Yes?"

He moved his hands around, anxious for me to understand.

"It was so clear," he said. "I was lying on the bed, but I could see myself lying on the bed. And Nanny was there . . . But you kept calling me, Mum. You kept calling me. You wouldn't let me go."

I was at a loss for words. "Was it nice there?" I asked at last.

"It was very bright." He smiled. "It was really quite— you know—pretty." He closed his eyes and slept.

Later on, when Ernie came in, I went upstairs to the smoking-room. Sitting in one of the chairs was a lovely old lady I'd met a few times that week. Her granddaughter had leukemia and she'd come into GOSH to give her daughter a break from looking after her. One afternoon over a cup of coffee she'd told me that she used to be very religious but after her son had died and her granddaughter had fallen ill, she'd lost her faith in God.

Now, after I'd sat down and lit a cigarette, I told her what Craig had just said. She gave me a piercing look. "You do understand what happened to Craig, don't you?"

"I think so. I'm not sure. I know he's had some sort of spiritual experience."

"He passed over," she said. Then as if she thought I might not have understood she leaned forward and said slowly, "He died."

"Yes," I said slowly. "I did think that might be what had happened."

"And you had the power to call him back . . ." She stared at me. "Did you talk to him while he was unconscious?"

I thought back. I had been talking to him, calling his name, all day long.

"That was it then," she said simply. "It was you calling him that did it."

Craig's nurse had been nearby when he'd spoken to me and she'd told the young doctor what he'd said. To my surprise he was very interested too and he came in to discuss it with me. "I'd like to get a psychoanalyst in to talk to Craig if it's all right with you," he said.

It certainly wasn't all right with me. I didn't want anyone telling me my son was crackers or investigating this phenomenon. "No thank you," I smiled sweetly at him. "I know what I think happened, and I don't think he needs a psychiatrist . . ."

The rest of Sunday was wonderful. Visitors were allowed again and they crowded in with presents and cards. Craig's dear cousin Sue brought in the most enormous teddy bear I'd ever seen—she must have spent well over a week's wages on it. The pain had completely gone now but Craig was still having trouble seeing clearly. Late in the afternoon the door opened and a very attractive man walked in. I did a double take as I realized who it was—Georgie Best, Ernie's football idol. Ernie was sitting on Craig's bed and nearly fell on the floor.

Georgie grinned. "Hello," he said. "My good friend Bobby Campbell asked me to come in and see you." Craig squinted up at him looking puzzled. "Who *are* you?" he asked.

I thought Ernie would die of embarrassment but I just cracked up. "I bet that's the first time anyone's said that to you, isn't it?" I said.

He grinned. "I think it's been a while."

Ernie was so excited. He was like a silly boy, as my old mum used to say. He hardly knew what he was doing. He even managed to squeeze himself between the bed and the partition so he could face Georgie and get a good look at him. "Craig," he gulped, "this man was my favorite. He was the best."

Georgie laughed. He stayed a long time with Craig, talking football—teams, players, famous goals—men's talk. He was really good with him. He signed the football Bobby Campbell had brought in, admired all his cards and examined his pictures. "Chelsea don't need any other supporters with you around, Craig, do they!" he teased. They had a good laugh together.

After Georgie's visit Craig really bucked up. He was still weak and he couldn't sit up on his own, so he had to be propped up on five or six pillows. But he looked miles better and he started to read his cards and to chat to his visitors. He even started to eat again and he certainly made up for lost time. He was ravenous. Ernie went to work every day that week—the LEB were letting him work short days on compassionate grounds—and as soon as he'd finished he'd dash to Sainsbury's for a special Premium pie, or to Woolworth Road near the Elephant and Castle for pie, mash and liquor, Craig's favorite cockney dish. None of the nurses on Punch and Judy Ward had ever tried it before but Ernie soon had them all guzzling it down. He waited till they'd finished before he told them the "liquor" sauce they all thought was so delicious was made from the juice of stewed eels ... Their faces were a picture. I couldn't stop laughing. In the past two weeks I'd almost forgotten *how* to laugh but now the slightest thing set me off.

One night Ernie's sister-in-law Joyce came in and told us she'd had a dirty phone call, asking what color her knickers were. Joyce said she'd laughed and put the phone down. But when it rang again Ernie's brother Fred had answered and the man had asked Fred what color *his* pants were. Now if that had happened to Ernie he'd have laughed his head off but Fred isn't like Ernie, he's quite abrupt, and he'd given this nutter a real ticking off. "You've got a serious problem ..." he'd told him. "You need treatment, you do." I don't know why, but that story really tickled me. I just collapsed. I had tears rolling down my face. The nurse in the kitchen next door was all doubled up too at the sight of me. We were all laughing and crying. "That's the best tonic I've had," I told Joyce. I hadn't laughed for so long.

On February 13, the day before Valentine's Day, there was great excitement on the ward. Janet the playleader was helping everyone make Valentine cards in the playroom. Craig had fallen asleep and I'd left Ernie with him and gone to the playroom to give the kids a hand with cutting and gluing. Suddenly a voice said, "Mrs. Shergold—where's your husband?" I looked up. Sister Lindy was peering round the playroom door.

"He's sitting with Craig," I said.

"Would you fetch him and come in to the office please."

I stood up slowly, my stomach turning over. I knew what her summons meant—the results had come back from the path lab ...

Sister Lindy gave me a kindly smile as Ernie and I walked into her office. "Would you like tea?" she asked. I knew then I was right. This was it. The day we'd all been dreading.

It was Richard Hayward's registrar who stood behind Sister Lindy's desk. "Please sit down," he said. I could feel myself trembling and I gripped the arms of the chair. Oh God, I prayed. Let it be benign. Please make it benign. But I knew. Even before he spoke I knew. His face gave him away. He couldn't look at Ernie or me. He was looking down at the desk. Into the corner of the room. At the sister. Anywhere but at us. "I'm very sorry to have to tell you this," he cleared his throat then continued, "I'm afraid it is cancer, and it's very aggressive. It's already showing in Craig's water. We need to start treatment straight away."

I felt Ernie go rigid beside me. "What sort of treatment?" he asked.

"Initially radiotherapy—then chemotherapy."

"Oh no! Not again!" I felt the tears rolling down my face.

"We can't do the treatment here I'm afraid," the registrar continued. "There are two options. One is the Royal Marsden which has the advantage of being quite near your home."

"No!" I shook my head.

"Mrs. Shergold," he said kindly, "we do know about your mother. We're aware that she was in the Royal Marsden last year so it's quite understandable if you don't want Craig to have his treatment there. If you prefer he could receive it at the University College Hospital."

Both Ernie and I were in tears now. I could feel him sobbing quietly beside me. I appealed to Sister Lindy, sitting in the corner. "Is it really that bad?" She nodded sadly.

"I'm afraid it is," she said. Sister Lindy had been on this ward for twenty years and she must have seen it all before, but her eyes were brimming.

"Do you believe the treatment will work?" I asked her. "Please tell me the truth, Sister Lindy. Because if it was me, I wouldn't want the treatment. I watched my mum. If it's not going to work I don't want him to suffer the way she did."

"You've *got* to give him a chance, haven't you?" she said softly.

My mind was in such a muddle. My thoughts went back twelve months. I remembered visiting Mum in the Marsden. Finding her distorted with pain after the last short sharp shock of chemotherapy. I remembered her consultant telling her, "Katie, we're going to give you some more chemo." And I remembered the way she'd smiled at him. "Darling," she said, "you save that for the youngsters. I'd rather fly."

"Fly?" he'd asked stupidly. "What do you mean?"

She'd chuckled, "Up there," she'd looked up. "With the angels. I've had my life. You save that chemo for the little kids."

Was it possible she'd known what was going to happen to Craig when she said that? Had she somehow seen into the future? Were her words that day really meant for me, telling me what I ought to do now? I shook my head. Don't be daft, Marion, I told myself.

"We'll leave you both for a little while," Sister Lindy said. "I'll get you a drink of tea." She disappeared and we sat in her little office lost for words. It's not fair, I kept thinking. It's just not *fair!* I dabbed at my eyes with my soaking-wet hanky but the more I dabbed the faster the tears came. I wanted to be brave but I just couldn't. Poor Ernie—he was hurting as much as I was, but still he tried to comfort me.

By the time Sister Lindy came back with a pot of tea on a tray I was in a terrible state.

"I could get you something stronger if you like ... ?"

she offered. But I shook my head. She poured me a cup of tea and I drank it but the pain was still there.

"Do you want to go back to his room?" she asked gently.

"I can't go to him," I said. "I can't go to him like this." I could hear the rain beating a tattoo on the office window. "Every time something happens it's bloody well raining," I sobbed.

"Take her to the pub," Sister Lindy said to Ernie. "Craig's asleep. You two go out and have a drink."

"Come on," said Ernie. "Come on, love. Do as Sister says. Let's get a breath of fresh air." I let him lead me outside down the stairs and out into the street, but I wouldn't go into the pub. To me drink was for good times, for parties. The idea of drinking to drown my sorrows didn't hold any appeal. I'd have to drink myself unconscious to drown my sorrows today.

We wandered aimlessly down Emerald Street, and along Theobalds Road, the rain mixing with our tears. "Where *do* you want to go?" Ernie asked patiently, when we reached Gray's Inn Gardens. He was soaked. *I* was soaked. "Let's look for a card shop," I said suddenly. "I'm going to buy him the biggest Valentine card there is." We found a shop in Leather Lane market. It was packed with people in steaming raincoats, all with the same idea as us and there weren't many cards left, but suddenly I saw the one I wanted. It was on the very top shelf. About two feet high. Covered in hearts and flowers. I knew Craig would think it was dead soppy but he was going to get it anyway. As I was paying for it, I saw a white teddy with "I love you" written on it. "I'll have that as well," I told the assistant. I tried to tell her about Craig. But I was gabbling, not making any sense. I was in such a state I dropped my purse and the coins went everywhere. "Come on, Mal," Ernie guided me to the door. "Let's get you out of here."

"Right," he said as we came out of the shop. "Now I *am* going to get you a drink. You look terrible." But I wouldn't. I had to get back to Craig. It was still bucketing down, and we looked like drowned rats by the time we got back to his little room. "Stop crying," I ordered myself. "Don't let him see you're upset."

As we went through the door dripping water all over the polished floor, I saw he was wide awake. I sneezed, pretending I had a cold. "We've just been to the shops," I said. "Oh, achoo—I can't stop my eyes watering."

He peered at me puzzled. It was the only time I'd been glad of his blurred vision. "Here," he handed me a piece of Great Ormond Street notepaper folded in half. "I've made this for you." I opened it. Inside, in wobbly green felt-tip writing, it said, *To Mum, Happy Valentine. Love you lots. Love Craig.* Then there was a green heart and a long row of shaky kisses. "Oh," I stammered. "I can hardly see. I think I've still got rain in my eyes."

"Well you'd better hurry up and dry them." He was bubbling with excitement. " 'Cos two of the Chelsea footballers are coming up to see me!" Sure enough, a few moments later, Gordon Drury and Clive Wilson walked in and I didn't have to make any more excuses about my cold. For the rest of the afternoon all Craig's thoughts centered on football.

The two players sat with him for well over an hour telling him all the Chelsea news, promising he could be team mascot, and joking about how terrible the breakfasts were now his mum had stopped working there. Then a press photographer appeared and took pictures of them cuddling him. Craig was on cloud nine. I'd never be able to thank those boys enough. Thanks to them he had no idea his mum and dad had just been breaking their hearts over him out in the rain.

After the players left Craig fell asleep and Ernie and I sat watching him quietly. I felt numb now. I had no more tears left to cry. Ernie put his arm around me.

"Come on, Mal," he said. "We can't give in. Look how Craig enjoyed himself with those lads. He hasn't given in, has he? He's fighting every inch of the way. He's got to be over the worst. They've taken most of that tumor away. If we let him have the chemotherapy we'll get rid of the rest of it. We've *got* to let him have it. He's come this far— we've got to keep going now."

It wasn't the first time I'd thanked God for Ernie. He might be quiet and shy, but when I needed him he was always there, solid as a rock. If Ernie hadn't supported me through the past four weeks I'd have cracked up. No wonder my mum had always thought the world of him. I hugged him, knowing he was right about the chemotherapy. Think positive, I told myself. Craig had cheated death once—why shouldn't he do it again?

Chapter 8

———ᴍ———

WE DECIDED to let Craig have his cancer treatment at the Royal Marsden Hospital in Sutton after all. Cynthia, a lovely staff nurse at GOSH, talked me into it. She was doing an oncology course and had just spent a week on the children's ward in the Marsden. "Craig will love it there," she promised us. Although I was still scared of the memories it would bring back I let myself be persuaded. From a practical point of view it made sense because the Royal Marsden was only a twenty-minute journey from our home.

Dr. Hayward was anxious for treatment to start as soon as possible and it was arranged that Craig would be transferred on Friday February 17. But as luck would have it there was an ambulance strike and we had to transfer him between hospitals in our own car. Cynthia helped me make a little nest of pillows and blankets on the back seat and Ernie and I lifted him gently in, trying anxiously not to touch his head. Two days before they'd taken his clips out and the ugly eight-inch scar ran all the way from the top of his head to the nape of his neck.

The journey was only about eighteen miles but because Ernie drove so carefully it took us two and a half hours. I sat in the back seat with Craig plucking up courage to explain about the biopsy results. I'd put it off for three days but time was running out.

"Craig," I said, "the hospital where we're going is special. There are lots of children there who are very ill and they'll ask you what's wrong. They'll probably tell you they have cancer [the word nearly choked me] and—"

He interrupted me. "Oh blimey, Mum, I hope it's not catching. I've got enough to put up with, with this brain tumor."

My eyes filled up. "Oh Craig," I said, "you are funny. Tumors are called cancer as well. But I don't want you to worry—they have some very good treatments here."

He seemed to accept it and fell asleep, but he wasn't at all well. His forehead felt very hot and he was moaning as he slept. The day before he'd had a painful enema and he really hadn't recovered from that. Being driven over bumpy South London streets in our little Fiat wasn't helping him at all.

By the time we turned into the driveway of the Royal Marsden he was in a dreadful state. He opened his eyes as we parked the car and gazed up at the building. "My nan was here, wasn't she?" he said suddenly.

I stared at him open-mouthed. I'd never told him Mum had cancer. The whole time she was ill I'd been really careful not to mention the name Marsden in front of him in case it frightened him. How did he know?

A specialist had been waiting all afternoon for Craig to arrive but as soon as she saw him Diana Tait shook her head. He was far too ill for treatment, she said, he needed to recuperate first. "I think the best plan is to send him back to Queen Mary's for a week," she told us. Ten minutes later Craig was put into one of the Marsden's own ambulances and transferred back down the road to the hospital where his tumor had first been diagnosed.

So far, the day had been one long nightmare but the moment we arrived at Queen Mary's everything changed. The staff were so welcoming—they came out to meet us and the nurse who had taken Craig to Great Ormond Street planted a big kiss on Craig's cheek and then hugged me. "We've been ringing up every week to check how he was doing," she said. "He'll be fine now. We'll look after him." He was put in a cubicle at a quiet end of ward B2 and we gave him some of the tablets they'd sent with us from GOSH and held hot compresses to his head and after an hour or so he started to look a lot better. "It was probably just the long journey that upset him," a nurse reassured me.

We stayed in Queen Mary's for ten days. At first I felt frustrated by the delay but by the time we left I was grateful for it. A breathing space was what we'd all needed. It did Ernie and me good, while Craig just blossomed. On the day we arrived, the nurses made a chart for him with targets they wanted him to achieve during his stay— bathing himself, walking a few steps, cleaning his own teeth, and so on. They'd expected him to take a week to do all the tasks, but the very first morning Craig woke up bright as a button and asked if he could give himself a bath. The surprises weren't over. As I helped him out of the bath he said, "Mum, do you think I could go to Janet's wedding?" I couldn't believe my ears. Janet was the daughter of our next-door neighbor, Theresa. We'd been invited to her wedding months ago but when Craig got ill I'd put it out of my head. But Craig was absolutely determined to go. "It's Steve's birthday," he said as if that explained everything. And for me it did. Going to the wedding was to be Craig's birthday present to Steve—it was his way of telling the brother he loved so much, "Stop worrying yourself silly about me. I'm going to be all right. Look how much better I am."

After a conference the staff gave their blessing and found him a wheelchair. While Ernie dashed home to fetch my best green trouser suit, I dressed Craig in his Chelsea Football track-suit.

We only stayed an hour at Janet's wedding reception but it was a very special hour. Craig even got up from his wheelchair and swayed a few shaky steps with me in the disco while Steve watched us, his eyes shining. I was so proud. What guts my little boy had. My friend Penny had baked a special cake for him with "Get well" in blue icing on the top, and back in the ward that night we shared it with our visitors.

The get-well cards had been flooding in for nearly a month now. They'd really boosted him while we'd been in GOSH and I knew that the cards would play an important part in keeping his spirits up when we got to the Marsden too. But I didn't know that one of the most important get-well cards of all was already on its way from the other side of the world.

It arrived on Monday morning. Ernie had the day off work and I'd left him in Queen Mary's minding Craig while I nipped home to pick up my bank book. I was nearly broke by now. Money just seemed to disappear in hospital, what with phone calls, stamps, cups of coffee, biscuits and so on. Last week Carol's dear mum, Thelma, had sent in £50 to tide us over—she'd organized a raffle for us at the OAPs' Bingo Club—but that had nearly gone. Ernie's wages for January had only been flat rate with no overtime and most of it had gone to pay the mortgage and on petrol. There was only one thing for it. I was going to have to break into my savings.

It felt strange turning the key in the lock again—I hadn't been through our front door for a whole month. The door wouldn't open all the way—I had a real squeeze to get through the gap—and as soon as I got into the hall I saw the reason. There was a great pile of envelopes on the floor and the door had just jammed on top of them. Most of them were addressed to Craig. I gathered them up and carried them into the living room where I found another huge pile of get-well cards that Steve or Ernie must have picked up.

I started to sort them into bundles to take in to Craig but then the same old worry started to nag at me. Would the other kids be jealous? No one at Queen Mary's knew that we were trying for a record. Maybe I'd better open them here and stick them up at home. But then the whole point of having the cards was to cheer Craig up. I dithered. In the end I put them all in a suitcase. I thought if I took the case in to the hospital I could stash it under Craig's bed so he could look at the cards when he wanted but the other kids wouldn't have to stare at them all day.

I'd just put the kettle on for a cup of tea when the doorbell rang. It was our postman John. He grinned at me. "What's going on in this house? It's worse than the Christmas deliveries! Here you are." He handed me a big brown paper package. "This was too big to go through the letterbox." The package was addressed to Master Craig Shergold and was covered with Australian stamps. "I think I know what this might be, John," I told him. With butterflies in my tummy I went into the kitchen and held the package over the kettle so I could peel the sealed end open. I didn't want Craig to get excited for nothing if I was wrong.

But I wasn't wrong. Oh bless you, Alison, I thought. Sealing the flap back down, I grabbed my portable cassette player from under the telly, jumped in the car and tore back to the hospital. In my excitement I forgot all about my bank book and the suitcase of cards. This was going to be the best medicine Craig had been given so far.

I ran into the ward, winked at Ernie and put the package on Craig's bed.

"A present for you, darling," I said, trying to look casual. I held my breath as he opened it, and emptied it on to the bed. Out tumbled a photograph, a record and a tape. "Oh yeh!" he yelled. "Yeh!"

One at a time he picked them up, his eyes popping. The photograph was a head-and-shoulders portrait of his idol Kylie Minogue with a handwritten message. *To Craig, Get well. All my love, Kylie.*

"Put it up where I can see it, Mum," Craig said. He picked up the record. "Her latest single!" he exclaimed. " 'Especially For You.' That's the one she made with Jason Donovan, and it ain't even been released yet!" I thought he was going to fall out of bed he was so excited. Then he saw the tape cassette. He frowned, "I dunno what's on this though."

I passed him my cassette player. "Here, you'd better find out."

We all listened as Kylie's voice said, "Hi, Craig—Sorry to hear you're not well. Hang on in there. You'll be better before you know it. Keep smiling and I hope to see you some time. All my love, Kylie Minogue."

Craig went potty. He didn't come down to earth all day. The news spread around the ward and all the kids and their visitors came over to his bed to have a look and a listen. Next day, Andy Coulston, a reporter from the *Sun* newspaper, rang up—I never discovered how he found out about it—and he wrote a story about Craig for the show biz page. "KYLIE SENDS MESSAGE OF HOPE TO CANCER KID," said the headline. I bought a scrap-book and stuck the *Sun* story in it next to the two articles from our local paper about Bobby Campbell and the Chelsea players visiting GOSH.

"Watch it, Craig—you'll be famous if you carry on like this," I teased him.

There were lots of other cards that week. Somehow Alison was stirring people into action from one end of the country to the other. Since we'd left GOSH she'd been giving people our home address so Ernie or I collected the post each day from Selby Road—usually there were at least thirty cards—and brought them in. My suitcase idea worked. Every day I sorted through the new cards with Craig and picked a few out. Then I'd exchange them with some cards on the wall and shove the old ones in the suitcase under his bed. By the end of the week the case was bulging at the seams. Usually it was funny ones I put up—I was so anxious to keep Craig laughing.

I didn't count the cards. Breaking the world record was still only a hazy idea in the back of my mind. For me their importance lay in the way they cheered Craig up. When my mum had been dying I'd read lots of articles about cancer which said how important positive thinking was. What could be better than the cards for getting him to think positive?

But they weren't the only weapon I used. That week I thought up one idea after another to keep Craig's spirits up. I quoted Steven's kung fu at him. "I am the master. I am going to win! Come on," I ordered, "say it after me. I am going to *WIN!*"

When Steve had first started martial arts and had come out with all this stuff, I'd teased him something rotten, but Steve had educated me about self-control, and mind over matter. And seeing the effect it had on him had convinced me. Steve had blossomed after he'd taken up kung fu. He'd started applying himself at school, and bringing books home to read. And very quickly he'd moved from the bottom stream up to the top stream. When he was sixteen he'd become National Junior Kung Fu Champion. How could I scoff at kung fu after that?

Anyone who heard me that week in Queen Mary's would have thought I was a martial arts instructor myself. "I am in charge of my body. Bad guys get *OUT*," I'd growl. Craig laughed at me. You're nuts, Mum." But he did say it, to please me.

Some people had sent pins or badges with their get-well cards, and I decided a badge collection would give him something else to take an interest in. I stuck them all on a pillow at the bottom of his bed and added one or two new ones each day.

His clothes were another area where I took control. He was allowed pajamas now instead of the awful white hospital gowns but I felt wearing pajamas all day would make him carry on feeling like an invalid so I brought in the brightest, most colorful clothes I could find—bright pink Bermuda shorts and emerald green T-shirts. It made him look a lot better.

But it wasn't enough. I wanted to see again the look that had been on his face when Kylie's tape had arrived. Before we left Great Ormond Street Dr. Hayward had given Ernie and me a pep talk. He'd been keen on positive thinking too. "Every kid needs a dream," he'd told us. "Do you have a dream you could share with him?"

I'd told him that Ernie and I had always joked about taking Craig to Disneyworld when Ernie was fifty.

"Do it," Dr. Hayward urged. "Give him something to look forward to. Hold up a light at the end of the tunnel for him."

At first I'd dismissed the idea. A trip to Disney would cost thousands and here were we, worrying where the next mortgage payment was coming from. But now I decided to go for it. To hell with the mortgage, I thought. Carol egged me on. "We'll get people in Carshalton to fund-raise for him," she said. "Mum'll help organize it. Tell him you'll take him there for Christmas." She helped me draw a progress chart like a Monopoly board. "Go" was England, the finish was Disneyworld and every property in between was a country on the way. £5 got us to Wales. £10 got us to Ireland and so on. Our geography was all to pot. Our chart had him going to Florida via Russia, Greenland and Japan but Craig thought it was brilliant. Everyone who came in that week put a pound or two in his Disney tin and by the weekend we'd got to Belgium! We still had a long way to go but I was determined we'd make it.

Our time in Queen Mary's went quickly and Craig really did buck up a lot. With every day that passed he seemed to get stronger. He was sitting up in bed now rather than slumping and he could even walk a few steps unsupported. After a week Craig was given an MR scan. Up to now he had just had CT scans. The MR scanner worked by using magnetism and radio waves rather than X-rays like the CT scanners. Although I could see the point of not giving him too many X-rays I really hated the whole procedure. Craig was strapped on a hard narrow bed which then slid head first into a tight tunnel in the scanner. It must have felt like being buried alive, I could see why its nickname was the magnetic tomb. It made me feel claustrophobic just to watch.

When they switched the scanner on there was a hard metallic knocking like a dentist's drill and Craig started to panic. The radiographers talked to him through a little two-way microphone in the scanner until he calmed down. But the whole thing was a nightmare. "Never again," I said to Ernie afterward. "You can go with him for magnetic scans from now on." I kept to that. I never did watch another one.

At last on February 25 the doctors judged that Craig was well enough to be transferred to the Royal Marsden. I didn't find going back as upsetting as I'd feared. Craig was admitted to the Princess Chula Ward, the children's cancer ward. Compared with the cramped Punch and Judy Ward it seemed huge, but Craig was in a side ward with just four beds which was nice and cozy.

Craig's consultant at the Marsden, Diana Tait, called us in to see her on the first day. She was young and very attractive and as she sat casually on her office desk, her white coat unbuttoned, Craig fell instantly in love with her. "Hello, Craig," she said.

He gazed at her spellbound. "Hello, Dr. Tait."

She smiled. "Would you like to know a little bit about what's going to happen while you're here with us?"

Craig nodded, open-mouthed.

"Well," Diana Tait said, "today you'll be going down to the operating room for what we call a lumbar puncture. That'll help us learn something about the way your body is fighting the tumor. Then in a couple of days' time we'll start your chemotherapy." The doctors at Great Ormond Street had told us Craig would have radiotherapy first. I didn't ask why she'd changed the plan though. I doubted I'd understand. Half the time now the technical terms being used were going straight over my head.

Diana Tait told us a little bit about chemotherapy and how the drugs would weaken the cells in the tumor. She warned him that he might feel sick afterward and his mouth might get sore. "You'll probably lose your hair too I'm afraid." She smiled. "What's left of it." (Craig still only had a downy covering on his scalp after the operation.)

"Oh well," Craig grinned, patting his head. "It'll save me having a haircut."

There was one thing about chemotherapy I didn't know. I learned it later that day from the hospital registrar, and it came as a terrible shock.

Craig and Ernie had gone down to surgery for the lumbar puncture and the registrar was describing the different types of chemicals they'd be giving Craig, when he said casually, "You do realize that Craig will never be able to have children after his treatment here, don't you?"

I felt as though I'd been kicked in the ribs. I hadn't realized any such thing. I fled outside to the car and drove to Carol's house and when she answered the door I collapsed in tears. Carol sat me down at her kitchen table and made me a mug of tea. "Now stop crying and tell me what's the matter," she ordered.

"He'll never be able to have kids, Carol," I sobbed. "Oh, it's not fair. Craig loves kids."

Carol banged her fist on the table. "Marion, stop crying."

I sat up startled.

"Don't you realize what this means?"

"No. What?"

"If they're saying he can't have kids then they're talking *long-term!*"

"Oh!" I gasped. "Oh yes. So they are!"

If they were talking long-term they must think Craig was going to live! I drove back to the hospital with my heart singing.

They'd warned me that Craig would have a terrible headache after the lumbar puncture and might be sick, so when I got to the ward entrance I wiped the relieved smile off my face and tried to look sympathetic. I needn't have bothered.

Craig was sitting up in bed surrounded by visitors— Dad, Uncle John, Aunt Mary and "little" Joyce. He was eating a big sticky doughnut, and there was a huge smile on his face. "Hello, Mum" he said. "Look what Joyce brought me. My favorites!"

The following day Craig had to go back to Queen Mary's to have something called a Hickman line inserted. Neither Ernie nor I felt happy about him having another general anesthetic but when we heard the benefits we felt we had to agree to it. Dr. Tait carefully explained that a Hickman line was a fine piece of tubing which was inserted directly into a vein and left there permanently. Once it was in place they would be able to feed the chemotherapy drugs and others straight into Craig's body without having to give him a fresh injection each time. They'd be able to take blood samples any time they wanted as well. I could see that made sense. His arm was getting black and blue from all the needles and they were having more and more trouble finding a vein.

The operation went well and two days later Craig started his chemotherapy. He received it in his bed in the ward, a bit like a blood transfusion. A plastic bag of chemical was hung on a stand behind the bed and connected to his Hickman line and then it was a matter of waiting. Each bag took hours and hours to go in, but Craig's reaction to it didn't take nearly so long. Before the treatment started we'd agreed to him taking part in a trial of new anti-sickness drug. They said that hopefully it might reduce the severity of the vomiting. Two hours after the chemotherapy started I wondered why we'd bothered. He couldn't possibly have been any sicker than he was. Then the diarrhea started. It went on for hours, but through it all Craig didn't once complain. He knew he had to have it and that was that.

His stomach contents were colored by the chemicals—yellow, green, or orange. I found it hard to cope with but over the next few days Craig became quite philosophical about it. "What color was it that time, Mum?" he'd ask curiously when he'd finished being sick. Not surprisingly he went off his food again. Ernie would go home after work and cook things to try and tempt his appetite—roast lamb with mint sauce, meat pie, a nice piece of fish. He'd turn up at the hospital carrying the day's delivery of get-well cards in one hand and a foil-wrapped plate in the other. But Craig hardly ever finished Ernie's dinners. He couldn't cope with more than a few mouthfuls at a time. "Sorry, Dad," he'd say pushing it away, "I just ain't hungry." But Ernie wouldn't give up. Next day there'd be something different to try. He finally struck success with home-made trifle. Craig had a real craze on that for a while and even had it for breakfast.

If Craig had been put in a ward on his own the sickness and diarrhea would have been much harder to bear. The fact that the other kids on the ward were also receiving chemotherapy kept him and us from feeling too sorry for ourselves. There were three other children in Craig's little room on the Princess Chula Ward. Two girls, Emma and Samantha, who were being treated for leukemia, and a little boy, Kelvin, who had a tumor on his leg. Craig was soon good friends with all of them, but it was pretty little Emma that he took under his wing. She was nine, the same age as Craig and very frightened of the treatment—she used to scream in terror whenever they came to give her a blood transfusion. I think Craig felt he had to set her a good example by being brave and he never let her see that his chemotherapy bothered him—straight after he'd been sick he'd always crack a joke about it to Emma.

There was a wonderful atmosphere on the ward. All the parents supported one another and took an interest in each other's kids, and someone would always look after kids

who didn't have visitors and make sure they didn't feel
left out. Ernie was good like that—he'd spend hours playing cards with Kelvin, whose parents ran a pub and
couldn't always come in during opening hours. Other kids
would wander in from the main ward and join in. I was
amazed at how these kids could still laugh. In the next
room to ours there were kids who were too poorly to get
out of bed and sometimes I'd go in and play the fool with
them, doing head over heels and cartwheels. "Bet your
mum can't do this," I'd say and even though they were so
ill they'd have hysterics, "Oh do it again! Do it again,
Marion!" they'd scream. Sometimes Craig would hear the
row from next door and he'd hobble in, put his hands on
his hips and say, "What's *she* been doing now?"

Often Azou, a little five-year-old boy from Jordan,
would peep in to Craig's side ward. He was full of energy—when we'd first seen him tearing up and down the
corridor on a bike we'd thought he must be visiting, because he looked so well—but he had leukemia too. I used
to bump into his father as we sneaked down the corridor
to the Juno Room for a quick cigarette. He told me that
the King of Jordan was paying for Azou's treatment and
for a private nurse. The king had done the same thing for
a lot of Jordanian children, he said.

Azou wasn't the only child from abroad. There was a
little boy from Gibraltar called Philip. His mother was
a schoolteacher, well educated and with quite a different
background to me, but we soon became the best of friends.
Philip was responding very badly to chemotherapy and
was often terribly sick, and I used to take over from Margaret and rub his back for him. I was getting to be an old
hand at coping with sickness and anyway I had Ernie to
help me. Poor Margaret had no one. We became like a big
family. You felt close to these other parents because you
shared this terrible experience with them and understood
what they were going through.

Ernie slept in the hospital most nights, though that
hadn't been the way we'd planned it. It was supposed to
be me who did the night duty. I'd decided on our first day
on Princess Chula Ward that there was no way I was going
to leave Craig on his own at night—not after I'd read the

booklet we'd been handed when he was admitted. It was an awful depressing publication called *Childhood Cancers*—I hadn't let Ernie read it. One of the things it said was that children with brain tumors usually die suddenly in their sleep. After reading that I'd asked for one of the hospital Z-beds and set it up on the floor next to Craig's bed.

But Craig soon got fed up with the arrangement. "Cor blimey, does Daddy have to put up with this?" he asked on the third night. "Do you keep asking him if he's all right and if he's warm enough and keeping him awake?"

I tried to stop myself fussing but I couldn't, it was just my nature.

"Go home, Mum," he said two evenings later. "Please. Just try it for tonight. Both of you go home. I don't need you to sleep with me." He grinned. "I'm a big boy now." I didn't want to but I knew I wasn't helping him by keeping him awake. As we left he handed me a note.

Dear Mum and Dad, thank you for looking after me. I love you very much—you're the best Mum and Dad in the world. Love Craig.

But I couldn't sleep a wink that night so we compromised and after that Ernie slept on the Z-bed instead while I went home so they could sleep in peace (if you could call it peace with a nurse shining a flashlight in his eyes and taking his blood pressure every hour).

I couldn't just walk out and leave him though. I started to write a little note to him each night and leave it on his pillow so that he would have a love-letter to wake up to.

Dear Craig, I love you more than the world. You are gorgeous. Love you today and always, love Mum xxx

I didn't like leaving him but I was glad of a break from the hospital atmosphere. The ward was so hot I often found it difficult to breathe—it felt as if I had a fur coat in my throat. But I hated sleeping in the house on my own. The only time I'd slept away from Ernie was when I'd gone into hospital to have our babies. Now I often woke up in the early hours and couldn't get back to sleep. To pass the time I'd get out of bed and put cards up on the wall. After a few of these night shifts there wasn't space to put a pin in the living room wall.

Ernie and I became like ships that passed in the night. As soon as I arrived at the hospital in the morning he'd be off to work and in the evening when he came in I'd be nearly ready for bed again. I'd always been a night owl—but now I had trouble keeping my eyes open after nine o'clock. I felt exhausted the whole time, even though I spent most of the day sitting down next to Craig's bed. And I was putting on weight. Before my mum was ill I'd never had a weight problem but now when I stood on the bathroom scales I was horrified to find I'd put on nearly two stone. [A stone equals 14 pounds.] It wasn't surprising really, with all the sitting around in hospital and eating junk food—most nights I used to stop on the way home and buy fish and chips for supper. My wedding rings had got so tight I had to take them off and I put my mum's rings on instead. I knew she wouldn't have minded, and wearing them helped me feel close to her.

They were running a test called myelography on the fluid they'd taken from Craig's spine during his lumbar punctures and the results were due any day. I wasn't especially anxious. Craig seemed so much better. I really believed that with the help of the cards and all this positive thinking his body was fighting the cancer 100 percent now. So when Diana Tait told me the results were ready and called me into her office to discuss them I felt quite optimistic.

Ernie wasn't there. He'd fallen off the back of a lorry while delivering a fridge and was up in St. Helier Hospital having his foot X-rayed.

"Our family's keeping the hospitals round here in business!" I joked to Diana Tait but she didn't smile.

"Marion," she said, "sit down."

My heart stood still. "Why? What's wrong?"

She gave a little sigh. "I'm afraid I've got bad news. The myelography shows that the cancer has traveled to Craig's spine. There's one definite tumor and three probable tumors low down in the lumbar region."

I was stunned—it had never once occurred to me that there might be more tumors. I gaped at her. "Where have they come from?"

"The spinal cord and the brain are all connected—it's

very easy for cancer cells to travel between them. They're what we call droplets—they're not very big, and we're going to try and treat them, but I have to be honest with you—it doesn't look good."

"You're kidding." I wouldn't believe it. "It can't have traveled. He's getting better. He's better than he's ever been. Go and look at him."

Diana Tait shook her head. "Marion, I'm sorry, but the tests tell a different story."

"He's *not* going to die," I yelled. I was bursting with anger. I stood up and pushed my chair away. "I"m not going to bloody let him die. You can think what you like. But you haven't finished the treatment yet. He is *not* going to die!"

I stormed out of the office. The doctors didn't know my Craig the way I did. I thought about going to the chapel to pray but I didn't. The chapel here was modern and light and quite nice—I'd been there once or twice—but somehow now sitting in a chapel didn't do anything for me. I went to have a cigarette instead.

Samantha's mother was having a cup of coffee in the Juno Room. She was a big black lady who'd had a lot of troubles—she'd lost her husband very young and now her daughter had leukemia. She took one look at my face and said, "Do you want to talk?" and came over and sat down next to me. I told her what had happened and she took my hand.

"Don't ever lose your faith, Marion," she said. I stared at her. She smiled. "There are two powers in life. There is the power of evil and the power of good. You've got to pray to God *every* day to take the power of evil out of your life."

I wasn't convinced. "How can God let children get cancer?" I asked her. "And what about earthquakes and hurricanes and famines—how can God let them happen?"

She smiled again. "They happen *because* there are two powers and unless we all pray to God and let Him know that we believe in *His* power and think of *His* power then the power of evil can take over. The more people that pray, the more God will answer their prayers. It says so in the Bible."

Samantha's mum put me back on the right road. Because she was right, I had lost it. I hadn't realized it until now but my faith had been really shaken by the suffering Craig had been going through. But after that day I started to pray again. Not in the Marsden chapel, where somehow I never felt at home, but wherever I happened to be. In the ward, in the Juno Room, in my car. And it did help, just as she'd said.

I didn't tell Craig about the new tumors. I was more sure than ever now that the important thing was to keep Craig cheerful. "As long as he's laughing he won't give in to the cancer," I told Ernie. "It's up to us."

Craig had always been a cheerful little boy anyway and that hadn't changed. He still hooted with laughter at his favorite television program, *Only Fools and Horses,* and he had a huge collection of jokes that he would reel off to anyone who'd listen. Often his visitors weren't half as cheerful as him—they were too upset by the way he looked. His appearance was pretty awful now, I had to admit. He was bloated from steroid treatment, his lips were covered in sores and ulcers and his hair was falling out. Even his lovely dark eyelashes had gone. "Never mind, I'll buy you some false ones," I kidded him.

Some people were able to hide their feelings when they saw him but others would sit by his bed with tears running down their faces. My dad especially took it really badly.

Craig would joke to lighten the atmosphere. It was as if he felt it was up to him to put people at ease. "Knock knock," he'd say.

"Who's there?" would come the tearful reply.

"Adair."

"Adair who?"

"Ad air once but I'm bald now!" And he'd chortle at their startled expressions.

There was one side-effect Craig hadn't told me about. I learned about it one morning when Professor Mack was doing his rounds. He was a great big lovely man—Craig wasn't one of his patients but he usually stopped and had a word with us. This morning Craig took the opportunity to have a man-to-man talk with him. Perhaps he'd felt too embarrassed to discuss it with Diana Tait. "Hey, Prof Mack," he said, "I've got these terrible pains in my willy."

"Right, young man. Let's have a look," Professor Mack said. He peered under the bedclothes. I hadn't realized how burnt and sore he'd got down there. The professor frowned. "Well, I don't know what to do, Craig. I really don't," he said. "Perhaps if you could get up and go for a little walk it might help."

Craig looked at him in despair. "Well, you're a lot of good, ain't you!" he said. Prof Mack put his head back and roared with laughter. Then he said, "I'm sorry, Craig. I'm sorry," and walked out chuckling and shaking his head.

The other kids helped Craig keep cheerful. Most of them had great attitudes to their illnesses too. There was a new boy on Craig's ward now, Jason, and he and Philip would whistle around the ward using their chemotherapy stands like skateboards. There was always more laughter in that ward than tears.

In addition to all the targets I had set for Craig he had set one of his own—he wanted to be a pageboy at Steven's and Sharon's wedding. I didn't encourage the idea. He had gone to Janet's wedding, but that was before the chemotherapy started. He'd been stronger then. He hadn't been weakened by all this vomiting and diarrhea. I didn't want him to be disappointed if the doctors wouldn't let him go. But Craig had made his mind up, and when they realized that, the doctors didn't argue. Kevin's sister-in-law measured him up for a pageboy suit (blue for Chelsea—what else?) and on March 18, just six weeks after his brain operation, Craig walked down the aisle behind Sharon. He had trouble keeping his balance and as soon as Sharon took her place at the altar steps, he walked over to Ernie and me in the front pew and collapsed back into his wheelchair, but he did it. I was so proud of him. There wasn't a dry eye in the church. After the ceremony Brian Branche, the vicar, came over and put his hands on Craig's little bald head and blessed him. Craig looked up at him and he didn't make a sound but suddenly tears just flooded down his cheeks. He looked up at me and smiled through them. "I'll be all right now, Mum," he said.

He wasn't all right of course. He still had a long, long way to go. But he did start to get better. The sickness from the chemotherapy disguised it. But underneath I was sure I could see an improvement. Every week he was walking better and his headaches were getting further apart. Most noticeably of all his eyesight was improving. He could recognize people much more quickly now, he could read his cards for himself, and he could watch television and videos with the other kids on his ward.

Each of Craig's chemotherapy treatments was given over a period of about ten days. Then he'd be given a couple of weeks to recover before the next treatment started. On the day Craig was due to start his third course of chemotherapy I was at home getting ready to leave for the hospital when there was a knock at the door. A man stood on the step holding a big bouquet of flowers. "From the *Sun* newspaper," he said. A few minutes later the phone rang. It was Andy Coulston, the reporter from the *Sun* who'd written about Craig back in February. "Kylie Minogue is appearing in the Children's Variety Performance tonight," he said. "How would Craig like to go and see the rehearsal?" I didn't have to ask Craig to know the answer to that one! After checking him over the hospital agreed to put off his chemotherapy till later in the week. They also agreed that Emma could go with us—Andy had said he could take a friend and Craig was determined it should be Emma. They'd become inseparable.

We traveled with Emma and her mum up to the Dominion Theater by taxi and were put at the front of the stalls. We were the only people there for the rehearsal and the cast played straight to us. It was like having a private command performance. All Craig's favorite stars were there. Jon Pertwee, the pop-group Brother Beyond, Philip Schofield, Sue Pollard and of course Kylie . . .

After the rehearsal Kylie came down off-stage and talked to Craig and Emma and posed for photographs. I'd taken three beautiful yellow roses out of the *Sun*'s bouquet for Craig to give to her and she gave him a huge hug of thanks. I thought Craig and Emma would burst with excitement, especially when the other stars came down and chatted to them too.

There was only one cloud over the afternoon. Jason Donovan was appearing in the show but he hadn't been able to get to the rehearsal. When they saw how disappointed Craig and Emma were the organizers invited us to stay on for the evening performance, but the hospital was expecting us back and Emma's mum didn't think we should accept. Emma's eyes were shining. "Please, please, Mum," she begged.

"It's the chance of a lifetime," I said to Heather. "Don't take it away from her. I'll be responsible. I promise." And she agreed.

It was wonderful. They gave us seats in the second row of the stalls, and after Jason and Kylie had stopped the show with the duet, "Especially for you," Jason stepped forward. "We've got two very special kids here tonight," he said, and he came right down off the stage, introduced Craig and Emma to the audience and gave them a big cuddle.

It was after midnight when we finally took a taxi back to the hospital. Emma put her little head on her mum's lap and closed her eyes. Even in her sleep she was still smiling. Craig leaned against my shoulder and snuggled up. "How do you feel, Craig?" I asked.

"Great," he murmured.

"Who is the master?"

He grinned up at me. "I am the master," he said.

Chapter 9

CRAIG'S MOUTH ulcers were causing real problems—they'd spread outside his mouth and up to his nose. He was also getting a lot of nosebleeds because of the chemotherapy, which irritated the ulcers and made them worse, so that the area all around his mouth was inflamed and sore. The nurses gave me a little sponge on a stick which I had to dip into a jar of brown liquid and dab all around the inside and outside of his mouth. Craig hated the taste of the liquid and always tried to spit it out. One day early in April we were going through this routine when a voice behind me said, "Hello, Craig," and I turned around to see Diana Tait.

Craig pursed his lips and tried to wolf-whistle. It had become a bit of a joke between them—Diana Tait often wore shorts under her white coat because of the heat on the ward and Craig always whistled if it was a shorts day. But this time his lips were too cracked and he couldn't quite make it. Dr. Tait grinned at him, then turned to me. "Marion, I'd like to see you for a minute." My heart sank. Surely not, I thought, as I followed her out of the ward. Not again . . .

But this time the news was good. Out in the corridor Dr. Tait smiled. "Marion, I don't see why you can't take Craig home for a day or two." I stared at her. "When?"

"Today if you like," she said. "Take him home overnight. See how it goes. It'll do him good. Being with other sick children all day isn't helping him to get well. What he needs now is a bit of home life."

I could have kissed her. Craig had been getting really low recently. He was beginning to feel like a bird in a cage. All his mates had gone or were going. Kelvin had finished treatment and gone home and Emma seemed to be a lot better and was also due to be discharged soon. Sadly Philip had got really ill and been moved to Great Ormond Street. Even little Azou no longer came whizzing into the ward on his bicycle (I didn't dare tell Craig that poor Azou had died a few days ago).

I dashed to telephone Ernie—he had the day off work and was at home doing a bit of cleaning—and screamed the news down the phone at him. "We can come home!"

Craig was so excited. He couldn't wait to see how I'd papered the living room with his cards. Twenty minutes later Ernie arrived and Craig and I got into the back of the car. It was a lovely warm day. All the cherry blossom was out in Carshalton Beeches—the posh part of Carshalton where I always joked we'd live one day—and Craig and I started singing "I'll Be with You in Apple Blossom Time," full of the joys of spring. On the way home we stopped at the video shop and Ernie got *Crocodile Dundee* out for Craig to watch that night. When we pulled up outside the house I ran around to open Craig's car door, but he'd hardly swung his legs out before he started to retch. Luckily I'd brought a sick bowl and I put it in the gutter between Craig's legs. It was no big drama. Throwing up was an everyday thing now. When he'd finished he stood up and carefully we made our way up the garden path. Craig's walking was still unsteady and he held my arm to keep his balance.

The last time Craig had seen Selby Road there'd been snowdrops peeping out in the front gardens. Today there were pink buds on the roses in front of the house. He stopped, his hand on my arm and looked around him. "It's good to be home, Mum." He sounded like a soldier coming back from the wars. My eyes filled up and I put my key quickly in the lock. For some reason it wouldn't turn. "Here let me do it." Ernie took it from me. But he had no more luck than me. While he was trying I glanced through the front-room window and saw that the brass box where I kept my video tapes and magazines was in the middle of the room. I wondered why Ernie had left it there.

"It's no good," Ernie said. "The latch must be down inside. I'll have to climb over and get in the back door." He heaved himself on to the garden fence and down the other side and then I heard him shout. "Oh no!"

"What's the matter, Ern?" I called.

"We've been burgled," he yelled. "They've cleaned us out."

I waited, clutching Craig's hand until Ernie came round from the back and opened the front door. Then nervously we walked inside and looked around. The cards were still all over the walls as I'd left them, but they were the only things that hadn't been touched. The whole place had been ransacked. All the drawers were open. The telly had gone, the video . . .

I sat Craig down on the settee and left him with Ernie while I ran upstairs to our bedroom. Our bed was upside-down on the floor and my dressing table was smashed to pieces. I remembered that my jewelry case had been on the dressing table with my wedding and engagement rings in it. I scoured the room and finally found the case open under the bed. I picked it up. It was empty.

In a daze I wandered into Craig's room. He'd had his own little fourteen-inch telly and video in there and a computer. I wasn't surprised to find them missing. What I hadn't expected was to see the Chelsea wallpaper hanging off the walls in shreds, or the ripped-up Chelsea posters, or the muddy footprints all over Craig's Chelsea bedspread. Even his bookshelves were smashed. I stared around in horror, feeling absolutely numb. My mind just refused to accept it. Craig mustn't see this, I thought. Craig mustn't know what these bastards have done. It was the only thought in my head.

Downstairs Ernie was sitting on the settee with his arm around Craig, who was still looking sick. "I've rung the police, Mal," Ernie said. "They're sending someone round. They said we're not to touch anything."

I sat on the other side of Craig cuddling him until the police arrived. Ernie showed them into the front room and the two great big coppers looked round, taking it all in—the upside-down drawers and shelves, the scattered magazines. Their faces were deadpan. I guessed they must be used to scenes like this.

"Well, they've done a proper job here, haven't they?" The one who'd spoken turned toward me and his face changed as he saw Craig's bald head and the big scar down the back of his head. He glanced down at the sick bowl on the floor. "My God," he said. He went upstairs to see the bedrooms and when he came down again he looked as though he'd seen a ghost. He stared at the layers of get-well cards on the wall. "Are these all his?"

I nodded.

He looked at his mate and shook his head. "I've met some villains in my time," he said, "but I don't think any one of them would have done this. The hardest criminal would have come in here and said, no—this is the wrong house."

That did it. The floodgates opened and I just howled. I hadn't cried in front of Craig since we'd left Great Ormond Street. But I couldn't help it—I couldn't take any more.

"What else can happen to us, Ernie?" I sobbed. "What else can possibly happen?"

Craig looked concerned. He put his arm around me. "Never mind, Mum," he said. He reached to the table for his bottle of tablets and held it up with a grin. "Look, they never nicked me medicine, did they?"

They never did find out who did it, though the state of Craig's bedroom and the way his Chelsea gear had been smashed made the police think it was most likely local teenagers who supported a rival football team. Whoever they were, they can't have guessed the publicity the break-in would bring. We were overwhelmed by the reaction. The *Sutton Guardian* ran a story on the burglary and the next day dozens of letters arrived sympathizing and offering prayers for Craig. The evening after the robbery, when Craig was safely back in hospital, I was getting ready for bed when there was a knock at the door and I opened it to find two of our neighbors, Chris and Carol Pilbeam, holding a television set. Chris was the manager of Sutton Athletic Football Club and he told me the club had organized a whip-round to buy a new TV for Craig. Soon afterward a local builder, Len Carpenter, came round with a replacement video for Craig's room.

Both events were written up in the local paper and in the course of one article the reporter mentioned Craig's Disney fund. The idea caught people's imagination. Within days Peter Pink, the owner of Pink's gym in Carshalton, had organized a body-building display for Craig's benefit which raised more money toward the Disney trip and as an extra thrill Peter arranged for Mr. Universe, Lance Dreher, to present the check to Craig. Thelma, Carol's mum, had already been running small raffles to help get Craig to Disney. Now she decided to take advantage of all the publicity to organize some serious fund-raising. She did her job well. Over the next few weeks a pub in South Croydon raised £1,000, a postman from Battersea volunteered to run in the London Marathon to raise money for Craig's trip, and the firemen from Croydon fire station also started collecting for him.

Ironically, thanks to our burglars, this trip to Disneyworld was beginning to look like a real possibility. The climax to the story of the break-in came early one morning when I had a phone call from the fiancée of a notorious South-London gangster who was serving a life sentence for murder. "Hello, Mrs. Shergold? My feller's heard about the robbery at your house, and he's very upset about it. He told me to let you know that if he'd been on the manor it wouldn't have bleedin' happened. I mean, ten to one everyone's going to be burgled sometime but you don't burgle a kid dying of cancer, do you?" She didn't wait for an answer. "Anyway he wants you to come up to Broadmoor and meet him."

"Ooh! oh!" I stammered. "I don't think I could get all the way up there . . ." How could I tell her that the idea of a day-trip to a top-security mental hospital scared the pants off me? "Oh, don't you worry about that," she said. "I've got a nice gold Roller. I'll pick you up."

I wriggled out of it by saying I didn't have the time because of looking after Craig—it was true anyway. Her fiancé can't have taken offense because a few days later a letter arrived in a brown envelope with "Her Majesty's

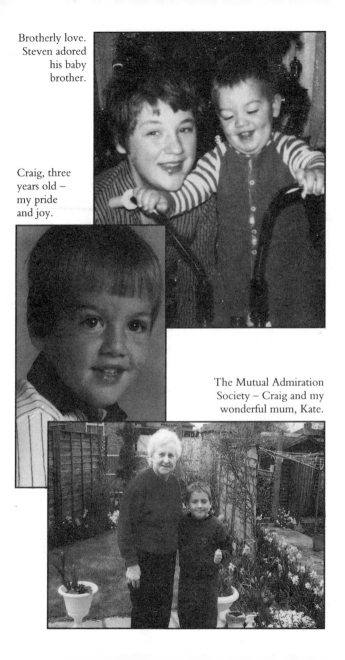

Brotherly love. Steven adored his baby brother.

Craig, three years old – my pride and joy.

The Mutual Admiration Society – Craig and my wonderful mum, Kate.

December 1987. Despite feeling really unwell, Craig didn't want to let anyone down and was determined to appear as King Herod in his school nativity play.

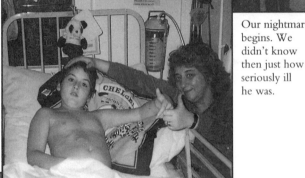

Our nightmare begins. We didn't know then just how seriously ill he was.

The start of "the cards." Under doctor's orders, we strung them up all over the ward.

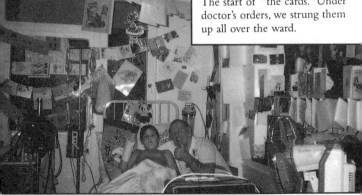

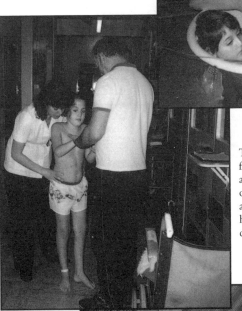

Craig's first major operation had to be postponed because he was too weak to undergo surgery.

The first faltering steps after his operation. He always tried so hard and never complained.

A great supporter of Chelsea Football Club, Craig was thrilled to meet the team manager, Bobby Campbell.

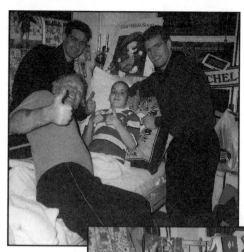

Ernie getting in on the act when Chelsea players, Steve Clarke and Gordon Durie, dropped by to see Craig.

Putting on a brave face for St. Valentine's Day 1989. Only the day before, the doctors confirmed that Craig had cancer.

GET WELL SOON CRAIG

It was my good friend, Alison Ingram, who took up Dr Hayward's suggestion of trying for the Guinness World Record.

News of our record attempt was reaching far and wide. Here's Craig with his precious card and message from Kylie Minogue.

"Bad guys get OUT!" Craig demontstrating his kung fu techniques for my dad.

Craig at The Royal Marsden Hospital, with the Hickman line in place, just before the start of his chemotherapy treatment.

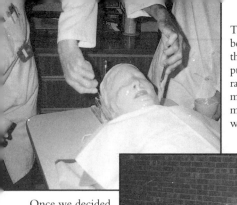

The chemotherapy hadn't been a success, but we thought long and hard before putting Craig through radiotherapy. This is the mould being prepared for the mask that he would need to wear during radiation.

Once we decided to make Craig's world record attempt official, tons of get-well cards began to arrive – as many as 70,000 a day, in fact!

Steven fighting back the tears on his wedding day. He knew that Craig had made an enormous effort to be with him on this special day.

Now an out-patient, Craig had a terrific day at the *Sun* newspaper. Here he is with Peter Cox, assistant editor. (The *Sun*)

Just a tiny selection of the autographed celebrity photographs that arrived. (The *Sun*)

After the initial rejection, Guinness eventually recognized Craig's world record and he received his certificate. (The *Sun*)

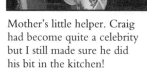

Mother's little helper. Craig had become quite a celebrity but I still made sure he did his bit in the kitchen!

Up, up and away! Actor Brian Blessed made a special request to meet Craig and they had a great day out.

St Peter's Square in Rome just before we had to make a hasty exit.

This young man flew over from Berlin just to meet Craig.

I was optimistic about Craig's condition, so, with the help of many people, we headed off to Disneyworld. It was a dream come true for Craig.

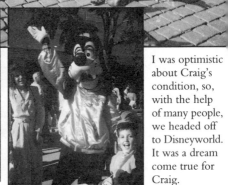

Another memorable day out. Craig desperately wanted to visit the set of *The Darling Buds of May* and meet one of his favorite actors, David Jason.

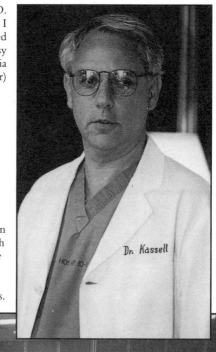

Dr Neal F. Kassell, M.D. After reading his letter I knew God had answered my prayers. (Courtesy of University of Virginia Medical Center)

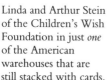

Linda and Arthur Stein of the Children's Wish Foundation in just *one* of the American warehouses that are still stacked with cards.

A wish granted. Craig gets to meet two of his idols, wrestlers Sting and Lex Lugher.

Wonderful friends, Ward and Sandy Griner, and Sandy's mother, Mimi, welcoming us to Florida. They carefully scheduled rest periods for Craig to enable him to enjoy his holiday as much as possible.

Craig and Ernie at Gatorland. Despite the smiles and the suntan, we couldn't deceive ourselves – Craig was still desperately ill.

The University of Virginia Medical Center, Charlottesville.

Home again and back to the cards. The card counters kept us going through those dark and depressing days. (John Pennington)

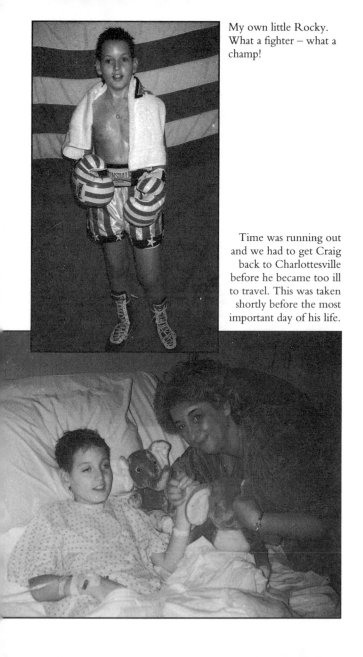

My own little Rocky. What a fighter – what a champ!

Time was running out and we had to get Craig back to Charlottesville before he became too ill to travel. This was taken shortly before the most important day of his life.

Craig made a remarkable recovery after his operation. Here he is, tired but happy!

A moment of peace after all the celebrations.

Joan, Craig's occupational therapist, helping Craig to regain his balance.

Craig finally meets his guardian angel, Mr John Kluge. This was a very moving, very special moment. (Matt Gentry)

Mr. Kluge told us that he was going to send Craig a card, "But then it was as if God touched me on the shoulder and told me I had to do something more." (Matt Gentry)

Tears of joy as Steven and Craig are reunited at Heathrow Airport.

What a welcome home! Here's our celebrity conducting yet another interview.

Wonderful Bill Wyman, always a great mate and a true friend. Of all the thousands of photos taken of Craig, the portrait Bill is holding here is my favorite. To me it is a moving tribute to a child who has suffered and survived. (Richard Young/ Rex Features)

We could have danced all night ...

Back to school and enjoying (almost) every minute of it. It's been a long, hard road, but he made it! (The *Sun*)

Prison" stamped on it. I opened it nervously. Inside was a check for £500 made out to Master Craig Shergold and a letter. *Dear Craig, I was a boxer and I'm tough but you're really tough. You're the bravest . . .*

We paid the check into the Disney fund account we'd opened for Craig.

The word must have spread amongst his friends on the outside because soon afterward some of them got together to organize a Derby Eve ball for Craig. I had a phone call asking me to meet them at a pub in South London. I was quite nervous—I hadn't had any contact with this type of person before and I wasn't sure I wanted any now but Kate said she'd come with me so I went along. The men were just as I'd imagined them—all wearing crombies with velvet collars while the women were all very glamorous and dressed to kill. They pressed offers of help on me. "When you get to Miami you'll be looked after, don't worry. We'll arrange for you to be picked up," one man with gold rings on every finger promised. "Crikey," I whispered to Kate. "I don't want people like that picking me up—I'd be terrified!" But the Derby Eve ball went ahead. Some big television stars came along and at the end there was a collection. Days later I got another check in the post for Craig's fund.

When the Press found out they took an even bigger interest in the story. TV-am wanted Craig to go to the studio to tell viewers what he thought about convicts and their friends taking such an interest in him, but although he'd been allowed out of hospital for a couple more days he wasn't well enough to travel up to London. But he was well enough to give interviews and while he was home the *Sun* newspaper sent a pretty young girl reporter called Ruki Sayid to talk to him. Ruki was very bright. I could see her looking at the gap where our video had been, and the broken furniture that Ernie had patched together. When she heard I'd had to give up work and Ernie could only work part time she asked very tactfully if I'd like the *Sun* to launch an appeal for Craig. "It would help you look after him," she said. "Not just now—in the future too." But I had to turn her down. I knew a national appeal would raise a lot more money than our little local events for the

Disney fund, but I knew too I wouldn't be able to face
the neighbors if I said yes. "Every time I walked down the
street in a new jumper, I'd be worrying in case people
thought I'd paid for it with Craig's money," I told Ruki.
She accepted my decision and wrote the story instead as a
simple tribute to Craig. *Our Kid Courage*, the *Sun* headline said.

I didn't tell Ruki about the card record. It just didn't occur to me, which sounds silly, because obviously a newspaper is the ideal way to ask people to send you cards. But
to my mind the main point of the get-well cards was to
keep Craig's spirits up, and I thought thirty or forty cards
a day was quite enough to cope with. It took Craig a couple of hours to open them each morning and finding room
for them was getting to be a problem. We just had no more
wallspace at home. I'd had to stack several hundred old
cards in a sack in the garage. At a rough guess we must
have opened about two thousand cards now. Once or twice
I'd thought of asking Alison to find out how many more
we needed to beat the world record but somehow, whenever I saw her, it slipped my mind.

Most of the cards were coming from workers in companies that Alison had sent letters to like Ladbrokes, British
Aerospace and British Oxygen. But occasionally there'd
be a surprise and we'd find one from a celebrity. As well
as Kylie, Craig now had cards from Frank Bruno, Michael
Barrymore and Bill Owen. There were cards from footballers too. In addition to all the Chelsea cards, every Arsenal
player had sent one and there were team cards from several other first-division clubs. I put those above his bed
along with the funny ones. The new kids in Craig's ward,
Jay, Sarah, and John, didn't take any notice of them. I was
still strict about the number I allowed on display and most
kids had just as many cards as Craig stuck up behind their
beds.

Craig continued to come home for a few days at a time
between treatments, and getting away from the hospital atmosphere did seem to help. He was a lot brighter these
days. We still hadn't told him about the spinal tumors. Ernie and I felt he didn't need to know. He understood that
he was fighting cancer—that was enough for him to cope

with. That summer we tried to keep all bad news from him, for fear it would drain his will to live. It was why I hadn't told him when little Azou died. And I didn't tell him either when I heard that Philip had died suddenly in Great Ormond Street Hospital. That really upset me—Margaret and I had been so close—and it was hard to keep it from Craig, but I had to. I didn't want Craig to think that dying was even a possibility for him. Chemo—and radiotherapy might help him fight cancer but in my heart I still believed it was Craig's own will-power that was going to pull him through. And I guarded that will-power like gold-dust. Every single night I still repeated:

"I am the master. What do you say, Craig?"

And he would stand by his bed, fold his arms in front of him and answer, "Bad guys get out!"

In June, Craig completed his final chemotherapy treatment and the following week he had more tests to assess how well the treatment had worked. While we waited for the results we took Craig home again. This was to be a longer break than usual. The doctors wanted to give him a couple of weeks to recover before they started radiotherapy. He'd lost a lot of weight and was very weak now—he'd been having some very heavy nosebleeds and he needed transfusions of special blood cells called platelets, which helped with clotting, to try and control them. They seemed to give him a short burst of energy. One night after going up to the hospital for a platelet transfusion we couldn't get him to sleep until four in the morning—he was absolutely bubbling and wouldn't stop talking. "Whoever they took these platelets off must have had ten pints of beer inside him," I joked to Ernie.

Before he was allowed home I'd been warned not to take Craig into shops or public places where he might pick up an infection. The doctors were especially concerned about chickenpox which they said was very dangerous to children receiving chemotherapy. I wrote a big notice in red felt tip pen and put it on the front door at home.

PLEASE DO NOT ENTER THIS HOUSE IF YOU OR YOUR CHILD HAVE CHICKENPOX OR ANY INFECTIOUS DISEASES. CRAIG

**HAS NO IMMUNE SYSTEM AND I'M SURE
YOU'LL AGREE HE HAS BEEN THROUGH
QUITE ENOUGH!!!**

He got tired quickly and had to spend most of the time in
his bedroom but he enjoyed that break at home. Lots of his
schoolfriends came in to visit him and cheer him up. Lee,
who had sent him the aftershave, came daily—he was a
gem—and Maxine, who'd sent Craig a card or a letter
nearly every day since he'd been ill, also visited regularly.
On June 24 he was ten years old and we had a little birthday party for him. Afterward we took a birthday cake in
to the Princess Chula Ward to share with the children still
there. To Craig's joy we discovered Emma in the isolation
room. She'd been brought back for a bone marrow transplant. The two of them sat for an hour chatting and nib-
bling birthday cake.

On June 29, just before the radiotherapy was due to
start, Sharon's and Steve's baby girl was born and they
kept their promise to Craig by calling her Kylie. Craig was
able to visit them in hospital which gave him a big lift.
The same week I drove him up to the Marsden because
Diana Tait wanted him to have a CT scan before starting
radiotherapy. While we waited for her to assess the scans
Ernie and I took Craig back to Great Ormond Street to see
Dr. Hayward. He was absolutely delighted with the progress Craig had made since February. He could stand on
one leg now and count to nearly fifty. We came away feeling very optimistic.

We were completely unprepared for the bombshell
waiting for us. The following Tuesday we had a routine
appointment with Diana Tait and Craig was very bright
and breezy as he did his usual tests. After ten minutes Dr.
Tait said, "Craig, I want you to go with the nurse to be
measured. Your mum and dad can stay here." The nurse
took Craig away, and she waved us toward two chairs.
"Marion, Ernie, sit down a minute." We obeyed. "I'm
sorry," she said. "The chemotherapy hasn't been very successful. There's some change in the spine, but it doesn't
seem to have touched the brain tumor at all," she sighed.
"We could give Craig radiotherapy but it's not very

pleasant—it would have to be very deep radiotherapy and the chances are the end result would be the same."

I went crazy. After all he'd been through. All the pain. All the vomiting. And for what? For what?

"I'm sorry." Diana Tait looked upset.

"Is he dying?"

She shrugged helplessly. "He could be. Look, it's up to you. If you want to try radiotherapy we can. Why don't you go away and think about it."

Poor Ernie looked shell-shocked and I was completely distraught as we came out of the office. Jane and Shirley, two of the nurses, came over and offered their support. "Come on now," Jane said. "You haven't given up before. Don't do it now."

"I don't believe it," I said. "You just have to look at him. Don't you think he looks well?"

"Yes," Jane nodded. "Yes he does."

"Why Craig?" I asked. "He's so cheeky, so full of fun. Everyone loves him. It's not fair."

"It's never fair," Jane said.

Shirley put her arm around me. "Marion, whatever happens, the quality of life you've given him, what you've done for him, will have been worth it . . ."

I glared at her. "Sod the quality of life . . ." I said. "I want him to live. I don't want a box of memories—I want him to *live!*"

Ernie went to find Craig while Maureen, one of the hospital's social workers, walked with me up the corridor to the Juno Room. There was a terrible smell of sweetcorn everywhere—you smelt it whenever they did a bone marrow transplant. I wanted to escape. Everything about this place made me feel sick. I couldn't take it. I just couldn't take it.

I fell sobbing on to a chair in the Juno Room.

"Oh Marion, please stop," Maureen said.

"I can't," I gasped. "I can't."

I asked her to leave me on my own for a minute and she went but seconds later one of the mothers walked in. "Oh Marion, we're so sorry. We're so sorry." Behind her stood Emma, looking worried. "Are you all right, Marion?" she asked. Then Sarah, a little Mongol girl, came in and held her arms out to me. "Marion. Marion. Marion . . ." she said. I hugged her to me.

Hours seemed to pass. Someone gave me a couple of cigarettes and brought me a cup of tea and poor old Ernie came up the stairs about three times before I felt ready to face Diana Tait again. There was no argument. Ernie and I were agreed on what had to be done.

"We want you to do the radiotherapy," I told her.

She spread her hands. "All right. If that's what you want. But I'm not promising anything—you must remember that."

The radiotherapy was scheduled to start the following week. As she'd warned, it was to be very deep radiotherapy—one of the Marsden doctors told me they'd never gone so deep before with a child, which meant the side effects would be quite severe. But having made the commitment I tried to think positively. Bill, one of the parents on the ward, had assured me that radiotherapy was the only thing that would touch brain tumors. I didn't ask him how he knew, but I clung to that belief. I told myself it was too soon yet to judge the success of the treatment.

Craig could receive radiotherapy as a day-patient which meant that I would take him to and from the Marsden by car each day. The treatment would be given every day for nine weeks on his head and on his back.

The chemotherapy had been given while Craig lay in his ordinary hospital bed, but the radiotherapy took place in a windowless thick-walled room in the basement of the hospital. Before it started he had a mold taken of his head so that a perspex mask could be made to immobilize his head during radiation. Marks could then be made on the mask to allow the radiotherapists to target the tumor sites exactly. Marks were also tattooed on his head and on his spine. Ernie and I weren't allowed in during the treatment but we could stay with him while he was prepared. By the time they'd finished getting him ready for his first treatment he looked like something out of a horror film—his head was completely encased in perspex except for a small hole for his nostrils, but Craig didn't seem at all bothered by it. He wasn't worried either by the yellow radiation signs or the red warning light outside the room. He wouldn't even be sedated. "I don't need that," he said, and he waved the needle away.

We'd been warned that Craig would be just as sick after the radiotherapy as he'd been after the chemo. That turned out to be true. But at least the diarrhea and the terrible nosebleeds stopped. He was put back on steroids and his weight, which had been falling, started to creep back up. He was still weak though, and he was getting weaker. There was no let-up in the treatment now—no rest-and-recovery period like there'd been with the chemo. And the journey to and from the hospital each day was one more stress. Every morning I had to load the wheelchair, half-carry Craig out to the car, strap him in and drive for twenty-five minutes through the rush-hour traffic to the Royal Marsden. The radiotherapy itself only took a few minutes but there was always a long queue for treatment and it was usually after midday when we got home. It was exhausting for me so it must have been even more so for Craig. By the end of August, after eight weeks of treatment, he looked listless and bloated and his speech had got very slow. His coordination was bad too. His hand had a bad tremor, which made eating hard work and since he didn't have much appetite anyway he often didn't bother. The only good sign was that his eyesight didn't seem too bad now.

I was sure the radiotherapy treatment was causing most of his symptoms. It was due to finish at the beginning of September and I really expected a magic improvement then. But I was disappointed. The only improvement in the first few days was that he stopped being sick. He was still lethargic and depressed. When I took him in for his weekly check-up on Princess Chula Ward he wasn't cheeky and full of fun any longer. It was as though a light had gone out. At home he spent most of his time lying on the bed. Sometimes, looking at him, I had a terrible suspicion that he had given up. The thought terrified me. I'd just heard that Gary, one of the teenagers in Craig's side ward in the summer, had died. I tried not to brood about it. It couldn't happen to Craig, I told myself. It just couldn't.

The news that Craig had been chosen to present a bou-

quet of flowers to Princess Diana couldn't have come at a
better time. The Princess was opening a Malcolm Sargent
holiday home for the families of children with cancer at
Jaywick Sands near Clacton. After the ceremony Craig
would stay at the home for a week's seaside holiday to
celebrate the end of his radiotherapy.

I was thrilled. I didn't know why Craig had been picked.
Maybe it was because for the short time after we were
robbed he'd been quite famous. Or perhaps they just knew
they could rely on Craig not to get stage-fright or forget to
bow to the Princess. I didn't really care why. I was just
happy they'd chosen him. No matter how ill he was feeling
Craig always sparkled when he was in the limelight. Gary,
the *Sun* photographer, had noticed it back in April. "He's a
natural," he'd told us then. Perhaps an afternoon of stardom
was just what he needed.

But he was too ill. The morning of the opening he
didn't get out of bed when I called him. "Don't you want
to go, Craig?" I asked. He didn't answer. He seemed to be
far away. I put away his freshly ironed blue pageboy outfit
and rang up Maureen O'Sullivan, the Marsden-based organizer for the Malcolm Sargent Fund, to call the whole
thing off.

Maureen consoled me. "Never mind, Marion," she said.
"There's a royal film premiere in aid of the fund at the
Odeon, Leicester Square, in ten days' time. I'm sure he'll
be feeling better by then. I'll see if I can get Craig an invitation to that so he can meet Princess Diana then instead.
Prince Charles will be there too." A few days later she
rang to tell me it was all fixed. Craig and two little girls
from the Marsden would meet the royal couple at the premiere of *When the Whales Came*.

Maureen was right, Craig did start to look better that
week. It looked as if we'd make it this time. When I realized that I started to panic. Craig could wear his pageboy
suit but I hadn't a thing suitable to wear to a royal film
premiere. When I tried on my best wedding outfit I nearly
passed out. The skirt wouldn't meet around my waist let
alone do up. For the first time in months I forced myself
to stand on the bathroom scales. My clothes hadn't shrunk.
I'd put on nearly three stone. Fortunately my friend Alison

is a "larger lady" too and she lent me her best suit, the one she'd worn for her wedding to Norman the previous year—a silver-gray silk number with a dark stripe. Very posh. On the day itself I really threw myself into the occasion. A nice hair-do in the morning. Plenty of warpaint . . .

Craig looked lovely in his pageboy suit. He did seem quite a lot better—the only thing that worried me was that he was having problems with his Hickman line. The skin around it was inflamed and sore. It was the weekly outpatients' clinic at the Marsden the next day. I made a mental note to have it checked then.

The performance was due to start at seven-thirty. Ernie drove us up to town to arrive at Leicester Square in good time. I don't think Craig was as excited as me—he would rather have seen *Batman* which was also showing in the West End. He certainly wasn't as excited as the two little girls. They'd arrived before us and were over the moon at the idea of meeting Princess Di, both giggling and sick with nerves. Their hair was just starting to grow again in little wisps after their chemotherapy and they did look lovely—their mums had bought them long dresses specially for the occasion.

At seven o'clock we were all told to get into line and the little girls took their places next to Craig in his wheelchair. By seven twenty it was clear there was a panic on—the royals were late. Officials rushed around speaking into walkie-talkies, then without any explanation a man in a dinner jacket ushered us down some stairs. We found ourselves squashed into a room with three other sick children and their parents. I recognized one of them, a little boy called Oliver who'd been in GOSH, and we spent a few minutes chatting to him and his mum and dad.

Suddenly there was a buzz of excitement outside and we all surged to the door to see what was going on. But the man in the dinner jacket was blocking the door and the cinema staff were standing in front of him and although we saw the flashbulbs going off we didn't even catch a glimpse of the royal couple. Charles and Di were ushered straight into the cinema—we never even saw the back of her dress.

I couldn't believe it. Both the little girls were sobbing their hearts out and their mothers looked pretty choked. I sat through the film absolutely seething. Not for Craig, he wasn't bothered—Kylie Minogue had meant more to him than Princess Di—but for those little girls, still sick from chemotherapy, in their pretty long dresses. All that effort to make them look nice. All that excitement.

Next day when I took Craig into Out-patients at the Marsden I was still seeing red. I stood beside the examination bed while a doctor checked his Hickman line. As I'd suspected it was infected and the doctor decided to re-admit him for a week's antibiotic treatment. That news didn't help my frame of mind.

The two little girls had come in for their weekly check-up too and their mothers came over to Craig's bed. We were grumbling away to each other about the fiasco of the night before when Brian Sadler, the Appeals Director for the Royal Marsden, walked into the treatment-room and headed toward us. The other mothers scurried away but I stood my ground. I knew Brian quite well and anyway I was in the mood to stir up trouble.

"What do you want, Brian? Have you come about last night?" I asked. "I think it's disgusting. The papers ought to know."

He shook his head. "I've heard about that. It was unfortunate. But it's not worth getting upset about. It won't get you anywhere." He smiled. "I want to talk about something much more important. What's all this about the *Guinness Book of Records?*"

All the wind was taken out of my sails. I don't often color up but I could feel the blood rising in my cheeks. "How did you know about that?" I asked.

He gave me a teasing look. "You can't keep secrets here." Then he relented. "I've had a phone call from ICI in Cheshire asking about Craig. They said someone called Alison Ingram had written asking them to send get-well cards to Craig because he was trying for a world record—is it true?"

I had to admit it was.

"How many have you got now?"

I shrugged, "I don't know really. Maybe about three thousand."

Brian Sadler stared at me thoughtfully. "How would you feel about going for it properly?" he said. "Making it an official world record attempt. With the Marsden behind you." Before I had time to say anything he added, "You'll never break the record if you do it on the quiet, you know. Have you any idea what the world record is?

I shook my head. "We were going to ask Guinness."

"I've asked them." Brian gave a little smile. "It's over one million cards."

My jaw dropped. "We'll never do that."

"Oh, I'm sure you could. You just need to publicize it better. The Marsden could help you with that. We could let the papers know, the TV people, all the radio stations, we could turn it into something really big."

I frowned. "What for?"

"Because the publicity wouldn't just help Craig—it would help the Marsden."

I didn't understand. "How?"

"Well, you know we have a big fund-raising appeal going. We need to keep the Marsden in the public eye. Anything that brings the Marsden's name to people's attention helps."

"So you think Craig's cards could help raise money for the Marsden?"

"I would imagine so," he said. "But it's entirely up to you. It'll be a lot of work for you. I don't want to force your hand."

I thought about it. Now Craig was back at home permanently—apart from these hiccoughs with his Hickman line—I didn't have to worry about the feelings of other kids on the ward. There didn't really seem any good reason to keep the appeal quiet anymore. I'm not really sure what it was that finally decided me. Perhaps it was because Craig had just missed meeting Princess Di, perhaps it was because I knew it would take our minds off his cancer. Whatever the reason I suddenly found myself grinning at Brian Sadler.

"Right. You'd better tell us what to do," I said.

Chapter 10

—⁓—

EVERYTHING STARTED to happen very quickly then. The Marsden Appeals Office didn't hang about. The next afternoon Craig was playing with Kelvin, Jay and Hannah in his side ward, when a reporter and photographer from the *Daily Mirror* turned up. I'd taken the morning post in for Craig to open and at Brian Sadler's suggestion I'd also brought in his card suitcase and covered the wall behind his bed with cards. The photographer's eyes lit up. "Magic," he said. He moved the bed to one side then posed Craig in front of the wall and got me to tip the rest of the suitcase out on to a table in front of him so it looked as though he was swimming in a sea of cards.

Later that day several reporters from local papers also turned up wanting interviews. A day or two later Ruki Sayid and Gary Stone, the *Sun* photographer, staged yet another photo session. That morning two huge cardboard boxes full of cards had arrived from ICI in Cheshire, and we tipped them out to add to the pile for the photos. Ruki pretended to be cross with me. "Why didn't you tell me about the cards, Marion?" Then she smiled. "Never mind—we'll make up for lost time now. Maybe we will launch an appeal for Craig, after all. We'll just make it an appeal for get-well cards."

The story broke in the *Daily Mirror* on Monday September 25. *You're a Card Craig!* the headline said. There was a big picture and an article telling of his wish to get into the *Guinness Book of Records*. Two days later the *Sun* launched an appeal under the heading, *Help Brave Craig Beat "Get Well Soon" Record*. They printed a coupon with space for a message and our home address in Carshalton at the bottom which they asked readers to paste on to a get-well card and send to Craig. The *Sun*'s interest didn't stop there. Ruki rang to say they wanted Craig to come into the *Sun* office at Wapping that Sunday and be their "editor for a day."

The Marsden publicity people had really gone to town. That week Craig's address was given out on BBC's *Good Morning Britain* program, and on ITV's *This Morning* with Richard Madeley and Judy Finnegan. Radio presenters also plugged the appeal—Gary Davies on Radio One, Derek Jameson on Radio Two, and *The Chris Tarrant Show* on Capital Radio.

The public response was dramatic. Craig was due to be discharged on the day after the *Mirror* story was published. At eighty-thirty that morning I was going round the house switching all the heaters on to make the house nice and warm for his return when there was a knock on the door. I opened it to find John, our postman, holding a great pile of cards between his hands and his chin. "I thought Craig had his birthday back in the summer?" he frowned. I took them from him and dumped them on the sofa— there must have been a couple of hundred cards. At midday Ernie had just brought Craig back from the hospital when there was another hammering on the door. This time John was on a moped and I could hardly lift the bag he handed me.

"I think you'd better come in, John," I said. John sat down on the settee and stared at me flabbergasted as I told him about the appeal. "Oh dear," he kept saying. "Oh dear, oh dear.

"Well good luck, mate, I hope you make it," he said to Craig. "I'd better get myself a bigger bike."

At tea-time Carol called in to see Craig and we were all having a cup of tea when a post office van pulled up outside and we watched the driver—a different postman this time—carry four bulging mailsacks up the path to the front door. He and Ernie struggled to carry them in. Craig was still lying on the settee and he laughed so much I thought he was going to make himself sick. "Oh *Mum*, I don't believe it," he said. "I just don't *believe* it."

Then the phone rang. It was Pauline, the receptionist for Princess Chula Ward. She could hardly speak for laughing. "Marion, you should see behind my desk! The mail-sacks are blocking up the foyer. They're everywhere. Do you think Ernie could come up and get them?" Ernie set off in the car and while he was away there was another knock on the door. I was almost afraid to answer it, but this time it was a tall, pleasant-looking man with glasses and a moustache who introduced himself as Charlie King the delivery office manager at Wallington Post Office. I asked him in. Craig was sitting in the chair in the corner looking really very ill, and Charlie seemed quite upset when he saw him. I trusted men who showed their feelings, so I liked Charlie at once.

He sat down on the settee opposite Craig. "I read the story in the *Sun*," he explained. "I just wanted to ask you if you know what you're letting yourself in for. Are you sure you want to go ahead with this? It's going to be a lot of work."

I knew he meant well but I was quite cross. "Of course I'm sure," I said. "It's going to make him better. I want to do it. Don't you worry about us. We'll manage."

He smiled. "I'm not trying to stop you. I only wanted to say that if you do go ahead the Post Office will be right behind you. We'll give you all the help we can. We can even make the Princess Chula Ward one of the Post Office's nominated charities this year. That way, when problems arise, you can always call on me to help."

"What sort of problems?" I couldn't think what he meant.

"Well, one of the difficulties is going to be actually physically counting the cards." He leaned forward. "Where are you going to do it? Who's going to help you do it? You can't count a million cards yourself. It'll take you years . . ."

I shrugged. It really didn't seem that much of a problem to me. "I've got loads of friends, a lovely family," I said.

"They'll help—I'll get the vicar to loan us the church hall."

Charlie nodded. "Good idea, but you'll have to organize the counting very strictly. For an official record you can't have any cheating or mistakes. It'll have to be done like a vote count at an election."

I hadn't really thought about the practical side of this appeal before. Suddenly other difficulties started to occur to me. "What'll we do with the cards after we've counted them, Charlie?"

Charlie looked around him and laughed. "Well you can't put any more up on the walls, can you?"

"I could put them in the garage, I suppose."

Charlie shook his head. "You'll soon fill that. You'd need half a dozen garages to store a million cards. Maybe we can find some paper recyclers to take them."

I wasn't keen on the idea. So much love had gone into the cards, "It doesn't seem right to destroy them," I said.

"No. But paper recyclers pay money and the money could go to help other people with cancer," said Charlie. "No one would mind that, would they? We could raise money from the stamps too. There are firms that'll pay for used stamps—they package them up and sell them to stamp collectors." He was getting quite enthusiastic. "We'd have to make sure people rip them off carefully though. So they don't get torn. I'll see if I can find out who takes them." He looked at his watch. "I must go." He stood up and touched Craig gently on the shoulder. " 'Bye, Craig." He hesitated and you could see his heart going out to him. "Don't worry. I'll help you."

At the door he turned. "This could go on for a long time you know, Marion. These things are difficult to stop once they've started. I hope you won't regret it."

"I won't." I felt so certain about that. This record attempt was going to help Craig more than anything that had happened so far. I knew it. If I'd ever had any doubts, then seeing Craig's face when the van had driven up this afternoon had settled them. I didn't care what problems it created. How much work it meant. We were going ahead.

The response was more than even Brian Sadler had bargained for. He rang the next day to tell us the telephones

at the Marsden were jammed, and they were having to put
in answer-phones to deal with inquiries about Craig. The
cards, he added, were also causing "a bit of an administra-
tive problem." On Friday, when we went into the Marsden
for Craig's weekly check-up, I saw what he meant. Poor
Jean, the Appeals Office secretary, didn't know if she was
on her head or her heels. There were cards everywhere, in
the entrance hall, in the corridors . . . I carried a sack into
the Juno Room to open while I was waiting for Craig. The
other mothers in there thought it was a great idea and
helped me count them. After half an hour there were cards
all over the floor. The babies were rolling in them. The
older kids were building houses with them. My last worries about jealousy disappeared.

Each day the avalanche of cards continued. A week before, Craig had been getting thirty or forty a day. Suddenly
it was more like ten thousand a day. Brian had discovered
that the current card record was held by a little boy from
Leicestershire called Mario Morby who had collected post-
cards. The number we had to beat was 1,000,265 cards. If
I'd known that when Dr. Hayward first mentioned the
Guinness Book of Records I might have abandoned the
whole idea but now, seeing all these sacks of mail flooding
in, I knew it wasn't an impossible dream.

But Charlie had been right. There were far too many for
us to open ourselves. Every night that week Dad, Carol,
Thelma and Fred came round to help but even though we
stayed up till three in the morning, we only managed to
open a few thousand each day. By the end of the first
week we'd counted 22,500 cards, but there was a growing
mountain of unopened sacks in the garage. We had to have
more help.

I went to see Bill, the vicar of All Saints, Hackbridge,
just down the road, who agreed to lend us his church hall
the following Tuesday. The minute I got home I picked up
my address book and started to telephone people asking
them if they'd be willing to spend three hours opening
cards. No one escaped. Friends, neighbors, relatives, all
got an invitation. I rang all my old friends from work. In
the past people used to laugh at me for having so many
irons in the fire but now it paid off. People agreed to come

from every place I'd ever worked in—the Grange Restaurant and the Cavalier Pub in Wallington, Liberty's in Regent Street, the Chelsea Football Club, Turks Launches on the Thames, Eagle Star Insurance, the Fox and Hounds in Carshalton ... I'd even run a slimming club once, and I still had all the clients' names in a file. Because of the state of my figure I felt a bit embarrassed about asking them—but what the heck, let them laugh. Nearly everyone said yes.

The publicity was still going strong. Local radio stations mentioned the card-opening night, and the papers were still very keen to know how we were coping. On Sunday, as Ruki had promised, the *Sun* sent a big limo to pick Craig up and took him to Wapping where he had a wonderful day, meeting all the staff and touring the newsroom and the news library. He even sat in the editor's chair and both Kelvin McKenzie and Peter Cox, the assistant editor, were wonderful with him. Peter Cox even gave us his home telephone number ("In case you ever need help," he said). But it was a long day and at the end Craig started to flag, so, sadly, the party that had been planned for him had to be abandoned. But he was presented with his party cake—an iced sponge with "Get Well" and the *Sun* logo on the top and a framed copy of the *Sun*'s front page with *Craig Edits the Sun* as the lead story.

Tuesday's card-opening session was due to start at seven. Fred and Ernie went early, ferrying sacks to the hall in Fred's big van. By the time Craig and I arrived the church hall was overflowing with people. Outside in the street there were dozens of cards, at least ten post office vans and also, to my surprise, a big ITV van. I put Craig in his wheelchair and went inside. The church hall had been transformed. Charlie had brought his whole team of posties from Wallington and with Ernie's help they had arranged long trestle tables around the hall. Charlie, looking ever so posh in a dark-gray three-piece suit with a pale silk tie, was already getting people seated around the tables and explaining what they had to do. He saw me and came over beaming. "We've sorted out the stamps," he said. "The Leukemia Research Fund are going to take them."

Well over a hundred people had turned up—aged from eight to eighty. There were lots of familiar faces, mostly family, old friends and local people, but there were some surprises—on a table at the far end I found Brian Sadler and a group of Royal Marsden nurses. And Alison Ingram and her husband Norman had come all the way from Harlow on the other side of London. "I couldn't miss this," she laughed. "Not after being in at the start."

The counting continued steadily for three and a half hours. Charlie had organized it like a military operation. The posties brought in the sacks of unopened cards from their vans and tipped them on the tables. The people working as openers had to slit open the envelopes with knives and check every card to see if it had a special message or money inside. Then they collected the cards into bundles of two hundred and put a rubber band around each bundle. The bundles were put into sacks and carried to the end of the hall where John, our own postman, counted them and entered the running total in the official tally book. Other people were given the job of tearing the stamps off the envelopes and putting them in boxes at the middle of the table ready to go to the Leukemia Research Association. The torn envelopes were put into special "waste-paper sacks" under the table.

I was anxious for people to enjoy the night and not get bored and I'd brought my party tapes so we could have a sing-song while we counted. It worked, and the atmosphere was great. Soon everyone had settled into a routine of counting, singing and chatting. Every so often someone would shout "more cards!" and a postman would carry over another full sack of unopened cards and take the sacks of waste paper back to the mail-vans. Charlie had put up a blackboard at one end of the hall and every half-hour or so he wrote up the running total of cards opened so far. By half-past eight it had reached 21,000, nearly as many as we'd managed to count in the whole of the past week.

There was a buzz of excitement when men holding TV cameras walked through the door. It turned out to be ITV's *This Morning* team. Soon afterward crews from a French television company, TF1, and from SKY Television arrived—they'd heard about the card evening from Brian Sadler. Charlie had arranged for Postman Pat and Jess the cat to present Craig with sacks of mail which made great TV pictures and while the pictures were rolling Charlie grabbed the opportunity to make his request. "We hope there is a waste-paper company somewhere out there who will give a donation if we take the paper out to them," he said. The ITV interviewer promised she'd try and get his appeal included in the broadcast the next day.

The cards were no longer just from Britain. That night we opened cards from France, Germany, Switzerland and America. They came in all shapes and sizes. Funny ones, religious ones, home-made ones and huge expensive ones. Most carried just a short message written on the card, but some had long letters tucked inside, which I collected to take home to read later to Craig. Several contained money—prisoners in the carpenters' shop at Wandsworth Prison had sent a check for £50 for the Princess Chula Ward, and there were some smaller checks too, as well as postal orders, fivers and even coins. We put them all into a special box marked "Royal Marsden" for Brian Sadler to collect at the end of the session.

I'd hoped we might get a few cards from famous people and I wasn't disappointed. Early in the evening my friend Jean suddenly waved her arm in the air. "This one's from Des O'Connor!" she yelled. There was a cheer and I rushed over and brought it back to show Craig. The card carried a hand-written message. *Dear Craig, Hope you make the record—I've broken a few records in my time . . .*

I put it carefully away in my handbag. Twenty minutes later someone else put her hand up. "I've got a card from Seve Ballasteros." Ernie ran over for that one—he's always been a nut about golf. Soon afterward one of my ex-slimmers brought a card over. "Look Craig, this one's from Linford Christie." After that we found cards from Tessa Sanderson and Henry Cooper.

Brian Sadler was very interested in the celebrity cards. "These might come in useful one day. Don't lose them," he told us. He gave Craig a secret smile. "We've heard at the Marsden there's one from President Gorbachev on its way. Don't ask me how I know, but keep your eyes open for it."

Ten o'clock, the official finishing time, came and went. No one seemed to want to stop. "It's more exciting than the bingo!" one of Thelma's pensioners' club ladies said to me.

Finally, at ten-thirty, Charlie called it a day. As everyone packed away the last torn envelopes he stood up and announced that since seven o'clock we'd opened 43,000 cards. On top of what we'd already opened that made a grand total of 69,000. Everybody went crazy. Cheering and laughing. "When are we going to do it again, Mal?" someone called.

Clearing up and putting away the tables looked as if it would take at least another hour but Charlie insisted we take Craig home. "He's tired. Get him to bed. I'll sort things out." He promised to drop the opened cards off in my garage the following day—in spite of what he'd said I still felt they were too precious to recycle. Charlie said he would take the waste paper back to the sorting office. "We can store it in the post office canteen for the time being," he offered.

The ITV film of the card opening and the interviews with Charlie and Craig were broadcast the following morning. We'd expected that the TV publicity would help swell the number of cards but it helped us in another way too. That afternoon a man turned up at our house from Securicor in Sutton. He said his boss had been at home ill watching Daytime TV when she'd seen Charlie's appeal about the waste paper, and she wanted to help. It seemed that one of Securicor's subsidiary activities was recycling paper. The man said they would pick up the waste envelopes directly from the Post Office, and pay the Royal Marsden for every ton they recycled. Everything was falling into place.

It was evening before I got a chance to sit down and take out the box of letters I'd saved from the night before. I started to read them to Craig but I was soon in tears. Craig raised his eyes to heaven at my "soppiness" but I couldn't help it. The letters were so moving. Every pupil in the Belfast school had sent a letter and a card. A little boy of five, also called Craig, said he'd spent all his pocket money on his card. There was even a poem and a long letter from a prisoner in Shepton Mallet Prison in Somerset. *I read your case in the* Sun *and we hope and pray that your spirits will pick up again. Go for it son, get in the* Guinness Book of Records. *We might be in prison but we have got hearts as well and we are human.*

"I've got to answer some of these letters," I said to Ernie.

"Love, you haven't got time," Ernie protested. "And we can't afford the postage. There must be a hundred letters there. It'll cost twenty quid to answer all those."

Charlie came to the rescue. He told me to draft a standard letter of thanks. "We'll get someone at the office to type it and duplicate it and the Post Office will supply you with 2,000 pre-paid envelopes," he said. Charlie was proving to be an absolute gem. "Don't be silly," he said when I tried to thank him. "The Post Office is doing good business out of this. The least we can do is to put a bit back."

Dear Charlie put more than a bit back. He got more and more involved, not just in his official role but in his free time too. The day after the first opening session he contacted a firm in Harlow and talked them into lending us two big letter-opening machines. It meant we'd be able to open many more cards in a session. The same day he contacted Sutton United Football Club, where he was a member, and asked them if they'd let us use their ballroom for future card sessions. I was very relieved when they said yes. The first session had been such a success it was obvious we'd have to organize more but Hackbridge church hall really wasn't big enough. We could fit twice as many people into the ballroom. Charlie booked it for Thursday evenings and Sunday mornings. "There's about 200,000 cards in the sorting office now, waiting to be counted," he said. "We're going to need at least two sessions a week to keep on top of them. Maybe even three."

By looking after the bookings Charlie was taking a real weight off my shoulders. I had enough on my plate dealing with the Press. Craig was flavor of the week with the TV and radio. The phone hardly stopped ringing with people wanting to interview him. I never said yes without asking him because I didn't want to overtire him. But when he was asked to go to the ITV studios that Friday to appear on *Good Morning Britain* with Mike Morris and Richard Keys there was no chance of him saying no. He loved being interviewed at any time. To be on television as a celebrity guest was a dream come true.

It went really well. Craig was tired because of the early start—the ITV car had picked us up at six—but he perked up the minute we got there. Richard Keys asked the questions and Craig didn't have any stage-fright at all. He was quite relaxed and with a bit of prompting from me reeled off all the facts and figures—how many cards we'd opened, which famous people had sent cards and so on.

Richard and Mike Morris each gave him a get-well card, then they asked who else he'd like a card from and he said the Queen. But they said they were sorry all they could manage was Timmy Mallett, the children's TV presenter. Up he popped from behind the settee and handed Craig a card and a T-shirt and video and the two of them did a "wacka-wave" for Jay and Jo and Kelvin and all the nurses and doctors. I embarrassed Craig by joining in. "Mum, you did it all *wrong!*" he complained afterward.

After the program we had to go to the Marsden for Craig's weekly check-up. Craig was standing on the scales being weighed when the registrar came and stood in the doorway and gave me a beaming smile. I still had my TV make-up on—I looked like Joan Collins on a very bad day—and I thought he was either smiling at that, or he must have seen us on TV. But he was smiling about something much, much more important. "Good news, Mrs. Shergold," he said. "The latest scans show that the tumors in Craig's spine have completely cleared."

I was so ecstatic I screamed. Since Craig's radiotherapy had finished I'd been completely in the dark about his condition. I hadn't asked the doctors a single question because I was so afraid the answer might be bad. Surgery and chemotherapy had both failed to beat Craig's cancer. I knew that if the radiotherapy had failed too we had nothing left to try.

The registrar smiled back at me—he looked as pleased as Punch. I took his hand. "It's the cards," I said. "It's all those people praying for Craig. Do you know what this is? It's a miracle." I meant it too. I really, really, believed it.

I didn't ask the registrar about the brain tumor. I didn't want to risk spoiling my happiness. Instead I told myself that no news was good news . . .

Hearing that the spinal tumors had gone really gave me a boost, and for the next few days I had more energy than I'd had for months. I wanted to thank every single person who'd written to Craig and tell them the effect their letters and cards were having. I took up Charlie's suggestion and drafted a thank-you letter. He came back the next day with 2,000 copies, each with a great gap at the bottom for me to add a little personal message. It was a mistake. Charlie didn't know me. Instead of just signing my name and adding a brief note, I filled each page up with reams of writing because I thought it would be rude not to. Before long it was taking up nearly all my time. When I wasn't opening cards, I was writing letters.

We held the first meeting at Sutton United Football Club at ten-thirty on the morning of Sunday October 8. Charlie had booked a morning session because of all the children who wanted to help. The Carshalton Brownie and Cub leaders had rung to say their packs wanted to be involved and so did most of Craig's school. Even more people turned up than at the church hall. Once again the posties were very efficient. They'd arranged tables all around the room and put bundles of cards—already opened by machine—on each table before anyone else arrived. I did my bit too by putting "special" boxes out. The boxes were labeled *"money"* (for the Marsden), *"famous"* (for celebrity cards), *"funny"* (for anything people thought might make Craig laugh), *"holy"* (for things like prayers, mass cards and religious medals) and *"presents"* (for any furry toys, badges or charms).

The session was another great success. By the time I packed away my music tapes at two-thirty we'd opened another 59,000 cards. Everyone seemed to have had a really good time and Charlie announced that we'd meet again on Thursday.

The list of stars who'd written to Craig had grown longer. This time the *"famous"* box contained cards from

George Cole and Dennis Waterman. And though we hadn't found Mr. Gorbachev's card yet we had found one from the Duchess of York! She'd enclosed one of her Budgie books and a hand-written note—*Dear Craig, get well soon. I hope this will add to your collection of cards. Good luck, Yours Sarah.* It thrilled Craig. One which thrilled him even more came from Captain Al Haynes, an American airline pilot who, three months before, had saved his passengers from drowning when his plane crashed into a river in Iowa. Captain Haynes didn't just send him a get-well card—he sent him his pilot's wings, the ones he'd been wearing in the crash. *I hope these bring you as much luck as they brought me,* he wrote. Craig put them in pride of place on his bedroom wall.

A mail-van had been delivering about ten sacks a day to the house but because I was storing the opened cards at home as well our garage was getting fuller and fuller. When the garage door finally jammed and refused to open, Charlie decided to stop delivering mail to our house. Instead he said the Post Office would hold it all for us and bring it along by van to the card sessions. Because of the volume of mail Craig now had his own computer at Mount Pleasant sorting office. That was quite something, Charlie said. Normally only counties had their own computers. It was the first time a person had ever been given one. Not even the Queen had a post office computer of her own!

On Tuesday the Carshalton Brownies held a session in their church hall and the count went up to 160,000 cards. But we still weren't keeping up with the flood coming in. The Post Office estimated there were still over 200,000 waiting to be opened. Not all of them were being sent in response to the newspaper publicity. Some were from companies like ICI, Shell, McDougall and Kwikfit, who'd set up collecting points in their factories or workshops. The local bingo halls, supermarkets, churches and police stations had also put in collecting points, and the traders in Croydon market went one better—they not only had a collection bin, but anyone who bought ten pounds of potatoes was being given a free card to send to Craig. The appeal was just snowballing. The local fire brigades had sent faxes to fire stations all over the country asking for cards. Banks were asking their employees to help.

Then on Wednesday Craig picked up an envelope from a sack I'd brought home, opened it and yelled, "Oh no! I don't believe it!" My heart jumped. I could see the envelope contained a letter, not a card and I was frightened it might be from a crank. We'd only had one so far, but that was enough—it had said that Craig had been very wicked in a previous life and that cancer was his punishment. Luckily Craig hadn't opened that one but it had made me nervous—I took the letter from him and read it quickly. It was type-written.

> *Dear Craig,*
>
> *I have just heard that you have been in hospital and wanted to write at once to wish you well. Nobody ever likes being in hospital but you are obviously keeping busy and I hope this get-well message helps you achieve your ambition.*
>
> *With warmest good wishes to you, your family and all those looking after you at the Royal Marsden Hospital. With love and all very best wishes ... Margaret Thatcher.*

I yelled so hard I swear the windows rattled. "You've made it, Craig! You've made it!"

I found a frame for the Prime Minister's card and put it on the hearth in pride of place. Craig was on top of the world for the rest of the morning. And because he was laughing, so was I. At dinner-time the phone rang and I skipped to answer it.

"Marion? It's Brian Sadler here. Have you heard from Donald McFarlane?"

"Who the heck is Donald McFarlane?" I asked.

"He's the editor of the *Guinness Book of Records.*" He hesitated. "You haven't heard then?"

"No. What?"

"Donald McFarlane has announced this morning that Craig won't be allowed an entry in the *Guinness Book* even if he does break the record."

"What?" I sat down suddenly on the stairs.

"He made a statement to the press this morning," Brian went on. "I'd better read out what he said, shall I?" He paused. "Long experience of similar situations tells us that such appeals have the potential to get out of control. In the long term they cause more distress than positive value." That's about it. I don't know what to say, Marion. What do you think?"

What I thought was unprintable. I was livid. Absolutely beside myself.

Craig had heard my side of the phone call so I had to tell him. His face fell. "Ain't they mean, Mum?"

"Never mind, darling, don't give up hope," I told him. "I'm not going to lie down and take this."

The phone started straight away. All the papers had heard the news and wanted to know my reaction. "How do you feel about it, Marion? What are you going to do?"

When I said I was going to fight Donald McFarlane's decision most people said they were behind me. But not everyone. Later that day I had a very sympathetic phone call from Esther Rantzen. "Marion, Donald McFarlane only has your best interests at heart," she said. "This could cause you such a lot of problems. The people at Guinness are afraid you'll have a nervous breakdown if you go on with it."

"What do they know about nervous breakdowns?" I snapped. "I have a nervous breakdown once a month. I'm used to them."

She laughed. "Yes, but this is a bit different. You might not be able to handle this."

"I'll handle it," I said. "I'll do anything if it gets him better. It's my problem not Guinness's and I'm not worried."

"Perhaps you should be worried though," she said quietly. "The last couple who tried to do something like this for their son couldn't handle it. It got too much for them. They wished they'd never started it."

But I'd heard that story already. "That family didn't have anybody helping them," I said. "We're asking people to help us and we've got hundreds of people coming along every week. They *want* to do it. Why should Guinness tell them not to do it?"

Soon afterward Ruki telephoned from the *Sun* newsroom. She sounded upset. "What are you going to do, Marion? Are you going to carry on?"

"Of course I'm going to carry on," I said. "It'd be bloody silly not to. It'd be like me going up Mount Everest, getting halfway and saying, 'Sod it. I've had enough of this I'm going down.' I can't stop now. How can I? The garage is exploding. There's sacks everywhere you look. Anyway if I stopped I'd be letting people down."

"Good for you," said Ruki. "Don't forget we're on your side."

Most people seemed to be on our side. All over the country people were up in arms about the decision. I even had phone calls from the police to say they'd put up protest petitions in their stations. At the end of the week Derek Jameson did telephone interviews with Donald McFarlane and me on his radio program and asked for an explanation of the Guinness decision. Donald McFarlane said it was now policy not to accept any more records that depended on media appeals.

"Come on, come on, all the great British public out there are saying they want this little boy to have this record," Derek Jameson told him.

But he wouldn't budge. He said the book would only consider recognizing something that Craig had done himself, rather than something he'd asked other people to do. "So if Craig were to sit on top of a pole in the local pub parking lot for twenty-four hours you'd give him a place in the *Guinness Book of Records*, would you?" Derek Jameson asked. Donald McFarlane agreed they would consider that kind of record.

"What do you say to that, Marion?" Derek Jameson said.

I told him just where Donald McFarlane could put his pole.

After that broadcast the Guinness phone lines were jammed with calls of protest and Brian Sadler told me the Marsden had received angry letters too. Ruki had contacted the *Alternative Book of Records* and she rang to tell me they'd agreed to publish Craig's record but it didn't satisfy me. The aim had always been *Guinness*. I didn't see why they should get away with it. "It's a public book," I told Ruki. "Without the public they wouldn't have a book. They want to start listening to the public. They want to come along and spend three hours at a card session."

Ruki's story in the *Sun* was headlined, *"Guinness Meanies."* But it did no good. Donald McFarlane had made up his mind. He said he had no intention of doing a U-turn. No matter how many cards Craig received he would not win a place in the *Guinness Book of Records,* and that was that. As far as Guinness was concerned the matter was closed.

The hall was booked for the next session. Ernie and I had to decide what to do. Like Craig, Ernie was disappointed but he wasn't as mad as I was and he left the decision to me. It wasn't difficult. These cards were helping my Craig to fight his cancer and that mattered far more to me than the record. I telephoned Charlie.

"Tell everyone that the meeting at Sutton United Club on Sunday is *on,"* I said. "We're going to carry on counting as if nothing has happened.

Chapter 11

As I walked into the Sutton United Club ballroom on Sunday morning everyone was hovering around as if they weren't sure what to do. People looked over expectantly as I came in. I took a deep breath and raised my fist in the air.

"Guinness! Up Yours!" I yelled. "We're going to go for it!'

The hall just exploded. Old Peggy came scooting across to me and gave me a big kiss. "They don't know you, Mal. They don't know Craig's muvver, do they mate? We'll show 'em."

That morning, enclosed with the cards, we found hundreds of letters saying, *Don't give in.* One man had sent a bundle of cards with a note saying, *I hope I'm not cheating by sending fifteen cards but anything to help you get your own back on Guinness.* Every single national newspaper had sent a card to support us. The *Daily Express* had even sent a Rupert Bear outfit for Craig to wear. "That Donald McFarlane should be here today!" Charlie said.

We counted 60,000 cards that day. The following Thursday, two hundred and fifty people turned up, and we counted 70,000. But even that wasn't enough—Charlie reckoned 200,000 cards were arriving each week now—and for the rest of October we decided to hold three card sessions weekly and to appeal for even more volunteers.

Charlie wasn't really happy about it. He felt that if we roped in too many complete strangers some of the presents or money in the envelopes might "walk." Until he said that it hadn't even occurred to me that people might be tempted to steal things. But it just wasn't feasible to question people's motives for volunteering. And there wasn't time to worry about it. I told Charlie that if anyone wanted to be dishonest they would have to live with it on their consciences.

The ballroom had an extra advantage over the church hall, apart from its size—it had a bar. It meant the card sessions could turn into real knees-ups. And they did! Counting cards was still what mattered, but now people would have a beer or a vodka and tonic while they worked and we'd always have my tapes going or somebody's records. One or two people even started to turn up in fancy dress. Smokey the Clown lived nearby and came along most nights in his clown's make-up bringing a box of magic tricks. Sometimes the Joan Collins and Boy George look-alikes would turn up from the Model Agency in Clapham. One family even used to wear full Red Indian costume.

Our family and friends never flagged. Steven and Sharon came whenever they could, though Sharon's mum was very ill and Steven was studying for his fireman's exams so they couldn't always make it. But some people, like my dad, and Tony and Jean, my old friends from work, never missed a night. And there were several other regulars—Sue, Reg, Mick, Eileen, Shirley, Lyn and Vic and their kids, dear Cis and Bev, the Guide and Brownie leaders, and Chris and Carol Pilbeam (who'd given Craig his TV). Ernie's brother John and his wife Pat were two others who came like clockwork. I don't know what we'd have done without them. John owned a big van and anything that needed shifting—cards, waste paper or stamps—he's shift it.

Most nights at about nine o'clock Jan's mum Peggy would start playing the piano and I'd get the singing going with "He's Got the Whole World in His Hands." Then Smokey the Clown would pick up His accordion and play "On Mother Kelly's Doorstep," or "Maybe It's Because

I'm a Londoner," and we'd have a real old cockney sing-song. Now and then someone who'd opened a brilliant card or a big check would stand up and shout, "Yeh, hold it everyone, look at this!" and the singing would be interrupted by a big cheer. Every evening was so exciting. You never knew what would turn up next or what corner of the world it was coming from. Everyone was in a state of elation. It was like having Christmas three times a week.

The list of celebrities who'd written to Craig grew longer and longer. I started to give a small prize—a plant or a box of chocolates—to the person who opened the best "famous" card each session. By the end of the month the celebrity box contained cards from the Rolling Stones, Sean Connery, Roger Moore, Eric Clapton, Neil Kinnock, Ronald Reagan (including a beautiful hand-written letter from Nancy Reagan), Richard Gere, Tom Cruise, Tom Jones (I grabbed that one!) and Arnold Schwarzenegger (*Keep pumping iron*). Craig was thrilled by all the big names but when an interviewer asked him who his favorite card was from he didn't have to think twice about it. "Buster Merryfield . . ." he said.

She looked puzzled. "Who?"

Craig gave her a despairing look. "You know—Uncle Albert off *Only Fools and Horses.*"

Craig really loved card nights and went to as many as he could. Since the radiotherapy had finished he hadn't been able to go out much because the weather had been so cold and windy. It meant he'd been spending a lot of time with grown-ups. His friend Lee popped in each day, but he was really missing his other mates from school. On card nights he could get back together with them and be one of the gang again. We'd usually set up one table just for the kids and they'd chat away to each other all night. Everyone had got used to Craig's bald head now and no one at cards stared at him the way people did when we took him out. When he'd had enough of counting he'd wander round the tables telling jokes. "Why can't Frankenstein have kids?" he'd ask innocently, then chortle, "Cos his nuts are in his neck!" Craig couldn't manage to last through a whole session yet—round about nine his eyelids would start to droop—but even an hour at cards did him good. All the fun and excitement were making him glow.

The sessions at the football club weren't the only card nights being organized. Everyone wanted to join in the fun now. The local Brownies and Scouts were counting cards at Bishop Andrew's Church Hall. Parents and children met at Craig's school. Brian, the vicar who'd married Steve and Sharon, let sessions be held in St. Peter's Church Hall. And it wasn't only people in our local area. One dear friend, Brigitte St. John, had recruited all her friends from John the Baptist Church in Guildford, fifteen miles away. They were collecting up to a hundred sacks a week from the Post Office and returning them days later in neat bundles of two hundred, ten bundles to a sack. Charlie was very strict about that. "You never know. The Guinness people might change their minds," he said. "We don't want them throwing us out for not following the rules."

For some people card-opening became an addiction. Some of our counters at the football club started to take sacks of cards home to count between sessions. One lady, June, who lived in Willesden, used to sit up in bed all night counting cards. The people of Willesden did a lot of counting for us. Brigitte St. John's sister, Mary Hurry, lived there and was always coming up with bright ideas to rope more people in. "How about an all-night session?" she suggested one day. "I could get it publicized on the radio." I agreed and Mary took charge. The marathon card-count was mentioned on the Jameson show and Chris Tarrant, on Capital Radio, also gave it a plug. Even local CB enthusiasts spread the word.

When the night arrived, McVities Social Club at Willesden was packed. The session was due to finish at eight in the morning but by three o'clock most people couldn't see straight and drifted off home. However, a faithful crew carried on counting doggedly and when the groundsman opened the door the next morning he discovered four snoring bodies, two male, two female, lying on top of a pile of sacks! I won't name the ladies concerned for fear of embarrassing them, but Chris and Willy, the two male "bodies" that morning, became enthusiastic regulars. I christened them Slippery Chris and Wandering Willy because they never sat down while they were opening cards but wandered from table to table chatting up all the women!

Chris was a commanding officer of the Thames Valley Rescue Unit Cadets and he roped the cadets in to open cards too. He also had a car trailer and he used to run around everywhere delivering and picking up cards and waste paper for us. He drove a battered old blue Cortina and his trailer was a ramshackle yellow thing which looked as if it belonged in the scrapyard. John, Ernie and Charlie were helping with transport too and the funny thing was that over the next few weeks as they drove round late at night all three of them were stopped by the police. ("What are you doing with those mail-bags, sir? We'd like to search your car.") But Chris was never stopped. It really upset the others. "He's the most suspicious looking of the lot of us," grumbled Ernie.

The sacks of opened cards had overflowed out of my garage now and were piling up in the garden. They were getting to be quite a tourist attraction. People were driving from Mitcham to come and gape over the fence at them. I didn't know what to do with them. Everyone was urging me to recycle them but I still hated the thought of it. Then I had an idea. A lot of handicapped kids had been sending us hand-made cards which they'd made by cutting up old Christmas and birthday cards. I thought maybe schools for the handicapped could use Craig's cards for occupational therapy. It turned out they could. And Charlie and his mate Tony in the Post Office were soon sending sacks of cards to handicapped schools all over the country and even in Ireland. I felt relieved. At least this way someone would get pleasure out of them. People had gone to so much trouble over these cards they deserved to be appreciated.

We weren't just getting run-of-the-mill get-well cards anymore. People were thinking up all kinds of ideas to make their cards a bit different. One card, the size of a football pitch, arrived in separate rolled-up sections. Another one, 40 feet long, had been printed on computer paper. There were miniature ones too. Someone had sent Craig a card the size of a postage stamp with a message you could only read with a magnifying glass. There were cards he could wear, hats and T-shirts with "get-well" printed on them. And there were cards he could eat, get-well pizzas, get well loaves of bread, and get-well giant cookies. One man in Germany had sent a piece of the Berlin Wall with "get-well" carved into it, and someone from Easter Island sent a message written on a whole coconut shell.

Easter Island was the most remote place we'd heard from so far. But the cards were coming from all over the world. In one session we'd often open cards from all five continents. Everyone's geography was getting better. "Where the heck is Swaziland?" someone would say. My sister-in-law Pat and my cousin Kathleen were good at geography and one of them would usually come up with the answer. If they didn't someone would look it up on the map of the world Charlie had stuck up behind the big card-opening machine.

After each card night I'd collect the "special" boxes. The "money" box for the Marsden would be taken up to the appeals office by Charlie or John the next day. Checks were continuing to pour in and the hospital had opened a fund in Craig's name to receive all the money, *The Craig Shergold Appeal for the Royal Marsden*. We didn't count the money at the club but by the end of October I guessed we'd sent in several thousand pounds, between the checks and postal orders and the ten-pence pieces which kids and old-age pensioners used to Sellotape to their cards. Not all the donations were made directly. Several big companies from abroad wrote to say they'd made donations to cancer foundations in their own countries in Craig's name.

I would usually take the other boxes home to sort out later. Sometimes it would take hours to go through them. The *"funny"* box wasn't usually too much of a problem. I'd stick the cards up wherever I could find space. The funniest cards came from Holland and from India—on the front of the Indian cards there would often be beautifully painted portraits of Craig and when you opened the card a frog or a mouse would jump out on a spring.

The contents of the *"present"* box took up most room. Craig's bedroom was filled with furry animals now, so he decided to give the rest to the kids on Princess Chula

Ward. Soft toys weren't the only presents arriving. There were pounds of sweets and dozens of bars of chocolate. There were also books, video tapes and literally hundreds of cassette tapes. The tapes covered all sorts of subjects. There were straightforward music tapes. Tapes of birdsong and sounds of the sea. "Healing" tapes with people reciting positive thoughts about cancer, often in foreign languages. There were even songs that people had written especially for Craig.

Sadly there were far too many to listen to. Craig would have to spend a whole year plugged into a cassette player to hear them all. But I kept them all and I promised myself that one day when we had time, we would play them. I didn't use any sort of system to file them. I've never been too good at that sort of thing. Everything just went into boxes and was crammed into the cupboard under the stairs.

The *"holy"* box usually took me even longer than the *"present"* box to sort out. The reason I'd started a holy box was to collect all the mass cards that were arriving, telling Craig that candles were being lit and masses said for him in Catholic churches all over England. But I hadn't expected to get so many things from other religions. Mormons, Hindus, Buddhists, Muslims—you name it—they all sent something to Craig. We had holy ash from a mountain in India with instructions to make a circle of ash around Craig and dab a bit on his forehead (I did that when he was asleep—he always wondered why his face was dirty in the morning). *"Nam Myoho Renge Kyo,"* that he was supposed to repeat six times a day. Like the cassettes, nothing "holy," however weird, ever got thrown away. If people thought it might help Craig I wasn't going to turn my nose up.

Most of the gifts in the *holy* box still came from Catholics. Usually Italian Catholics. They sent all sorts of things—crosses, rosaries, medallions of the saints (which I put under Craig's pillow) and beautiful madonnas. There was a carved figure of Jesus carrying the cross, and a crib scene, hand-carved in wood from Italian schoolchildren. There was a letter from a woman in Italy who'd been the first person to see a statue of Mary cry, and there were dozens and dozens of Bibles and New Testaments. It was a problem knowing what to do with them. How many Bibles could Craig read? I gave a few to regular card openers who I knew would treasure them and I sent the rest up to Brian to use in St. Peter's Church.

We were also getting gallons of holy water, not just from Lourdes, but from every other holy spring in the world. I stored it all in the bathroom, so I could splash some on Craig each night before he went to sleep.

Sometimes I'd find miracle cures in the *holy* box—lotions and potions with messages urging me to feed them to Craig or rub them on his head. These I was more suspicious of. Someone in Russia had sent Craig a living mushroom in a jar suspended in a yellow liquid with black lumps floating in it, which he was supposed to drink. Then there was the bottle of red syrup from Hungary with the letter saying, *This will cure your son.* It didn't say what we were meant to do with it. Stupidly I tried a mouthful and nearly burned my tongue off. I couldn't eat for two days. There was also a jar of black sticky stuff made out of beetroot extract that Craig was supposed to eat. There were boxes of herbal teas, vitamin supplements, hankies anointed with oil, strange-smelling powder from Poland to mix in his tea, dried seaweed from Alaska and a special diet-sheet from India which suggested that Craig should drink his own wee. I took all the folk medicines up to Marsden thinking that maybe they could use them for research. Perhaps some of the herbal "cures" did contain something useful, but I wasn't going to use Craig as a guinea-pig.

It was the box of letters which took me longest to sort through. After all the Guinness publicity we seemed to get a lot more letters enclosed with the cards. Some were from people I'd never have expected to respond to Craig's story—hard-headed businessmen, doctors, even people who had cancer themselves. We also had more letters from people in prison—including one from a man on Death Row in America (*Craig, I think you have the power to forgive me for the murders I have done . . .*).

One company in Israel wrote to say they had planted trees in Craig's honor, which made me very proud.

Lots of the letters had me in tears, especially the ones from people who'd lost a dear friend or relative to cancer, wanting advice on how to cope. I knew I wasn't qualified to help but I felt I had to try. I'd sit up in bed scribbling away while Ernie snored beside me. I couldn't possibly answer them all so I used to choose the ones with shaky hand-writing that looked as if they were from old people, or sometimes I'd pick one out simply because it painted an interesting picture of a different kind of life, like the one from a woman in Alaska who said that as she wrote she could hear a reindeer eating grass off her roof. I remember replying to one letter which really touched me from a very poor family in Romania inviting Craig to visit them. And then there were the notes from children all around the world, saying they were praying for Craig. I wrote to as many of them as I could. I never found out if my letters reached their destinations. If anyone wrote back then their replies were lost in the mountain of mail.

I didn't ask Craig to help me answer his letters. His hand still trembled so much he had trouble holding a pen and I felt writing would use up too much of his precious energy. But I'd get him to sign his name at the bottom of my letters or sometimes on a photo of himself that I'd tuck in the envelope. Eileen, one of our volunteers, offered to help me answer letters and whenever I got overloaded I'd pass some on to her. Soon Eileen had pen-friends in Poland, Norway, Austria, Australia and Russia.

By the first week in November we'd opened 700,000 cards and Charlie estimated the sacks still waiting at the sorting office contained at least another half million. Despite all our efforts the backlog was growing. The Post Office canteen was full now and they'd started to use the wash-house where the Post Office vans were washed. Unfortunately stray cats were wandering into the wash-house and discovering that the sacks made comfortable beds. Sometimes the smell of cat pee when the posties pulled the sacks into the ballroom was enough to knock you out.

Despite the warnings I didn't feel in the least as if I was going to have a nervous breakdown—we were all having so much fun and it was doing Craig so much good that both Ernie and I were on a real high. How could we feel ill when we were surrounded by all this love and affection? How could we possibly feel alone with all these people sharing our concern for Craig? There was one thing worrying me though. All our household bills were being delayed because everything with our address on it was being put into Craig's sacks. At the Post Office new sacks were often put on top of old ones and some of the sacks would be stored for weeks before we got around to opening them. We were so late paying the electricity bill we were nearly cut off twice and in November our telephone was disconnected. After that I started giving people my friend Jan's address if they wanted something to come direct to me.

The media interest in Craig was as strong as ever. When Guinness said no to Craig it back-fired on them because it gave reporters another angle on the story. Trish Ingram from Thames Television News came to the house to interview him about the record attempt. Craig was getting quite an old pro now. He had all the facts on the tip of his tongue. The number we'd opened so far. The number waiting to be opened. The more recent celebrity cards. I didn't have to step in to help him out.

Trish asked him if he thought Guinness were mean. He shrugged. "Oh yes, they're mean," he said carefully, "but it doesn't matter now. It's taken my mind off being ill. And I feel much better." Then he looked straight at the camera—you'd have thought he'd rehearsed it, but he hadn't. "Thanks, everybody who sent the cards," he said. "And all the children who've been making them. You're all good," and he gave a big beaming smile.

"Craig—you're a smasher," said Trish.

After that item was broadcast, the TV interest snowballed. While most kids got nervous and clammed up on TV Craig seemed to have no nerves at all. He just acted naturally and the cameras loved that. Word spread, and TV companies and reporters from all over the world began to turn up on our doorstep. Sometimes I had to pinch myself to make sure I wasn't dreaming. New Zealand TV filmed Craig at the Marsden for a Christmas Day broadcast. Australian TV visited us at home. Two days after the Berlin Wall came down on November 12 we even had a visit from two East German reporters. Then, at the beginning of November a TV crew from Monaco arrived at the house bringing 100,000 cards with them. Better still as far as Craig was concerned, they brought Glen Hoddle, the former Spurs player, who was now playing for Monaco. Glen gave Craig the shirt he'd worn when he'd played in the World Cup—if he'd given him the World Cup itself Craig couldn't have been more thrilled. While the camera crew were getting ready to film, Glen took me aside and told me that from the moment he'd first seen Craig on TV he'd felt drawn to him. "It's his smile," he said. "There's something about it. I just had to meet this little boy." I laughed and told him that only that morning I'd opened a card addressed, *To the little boy with the biggest smile in the world.*

Craig was really more interested in talking to Glen than in being interviewed, but he answered the reporter's questions cheerfully and even managed to say *"Merci beaucoup"* at the end. That day French TV turned up unexpectedly as well and at one point we had twenty-seven people crammed into our house. After that whenever foreign TV companies rang I learned to warn them that we lived in a "government house." Some of the TV crews must have thought all English people lived in castles, the amount of equipment they brought with them.

Although Craig had improved a lot since the cards started, the infection in his Hickman line kept coming back, and every time it did he had to be readmitted to hospital for a few days to be treated with antibiotics. For a short time afterward he would look very pale and ill. He still had no hair which made him look even worse and I think the TV crews often had second thoughts when they saw him. Somehow, though, he would always perk up when the moment came. It didn't matter how rotten he was feeling, when the camera switched on, he switched on too. His attitude affected the crews. More than one cameraman was in tears by the time he finished filming.

The programs brought a lot of response. We started to get letters from viewers all over the world saying that they'd been inspired by Craig's courage. Perhaps it was his cheerfulness when he had to struggle so hard to get each word out, but something about him seemed to reach out and touch people.

We had so many interviews in October and November that they started to fall into a routine. Usually I'd sit on the settee next to Craig, and Ernie would stay in the background videoing the interview. I knew that all the Press were interested in the cards from famous people and I'd keep the latest ones handy in a box near the settee ready to pull out to show the cameras. Craig had a huge selection of celebrity cards now, including the promised card from President Gorbachev and one from President Bush. There were cards from famous people in every walk of life you could imagine—pop singers, television actors, film stars, politicians, royalty, wrestlers, golfers, jockeys . . . the list went on and on. But the Press weren't only interested in our celebrities. There was one question nearly every reporter asked me—"Why do you think this has taken off in such a big way?" It seemed to puzzle them. "It takes a bit of effort to go to a card shop and buy a get-well card," one young man pointed out. "Why do you think people do it for someone they don't even know? I mean there's nothing in it for them. Why don't they just give a pound to charity instead?"

In the early weeks when we'd been so busy handling the avalanche I hadn't really had time to wonder *why* it was happening. But now it began to sink in just how extraordinary this whole thing was. And I started to puzzle about it too.

A few people explained in their letters why they'd sent a card. Some had lost a loved one to cancer, and had never expressed their feelings so they told Craig instead. Others were dying of cancer themselves, and wanted Craig to know he wasn't alone. Some had beaten cancer and wanted to tell Craig he could do the same.

But those reasons couldn't account for *all* these cards, surely? Then lying in bed one night I remembered the words of Samantha's mum when she'd tried to comfort me a year before. *The more people who pray, the more God will answer their prayers,* and suddenly I knew the answer. Every card being sent to Craig was a prayer—a prayer for the defeat of cancer. For whose lives hadn't been touched by this wicked disease?

And the prayers were working. Craig looked so much better. He still had to go up to the Marsden once or twice a week for assessment. But I was sure in my own mind now that he was on the road to recovery. Diana Tait said how well he looked. The cards had been the best medicine in the world. Of course there were still problems. Walking was quite an effort—he would need his wheelchair for months yet—and the infections had knocked him back a bit, but nothing could disguise the fact that he had a real light in his eyes these days. He'd lost the wilting look he'd had back in September. He'd even started getting cheeky again. Telling rude jokes and teasing me about how fat I'd got.

I did sometimes worry that Craig might be overdoing it. Some weeks there was a photocall or an interview or a presentation every single day. I tried to pace it so it didn't get too much for him. I told the media I would only do what Craig wanted to do. But Craig loved going to TV studios and waving to the kids on the ward and he hardly ever said no. The opportunities coming his way were just too exciting to turn down. "There's a letter here inviting you to meet Frank Bruno, Craig," I'd say. "Do you want to do it?" "Oh yeh, Mum! Yeh!" he'd say. The Craig Shergold Fund was attracting a lot of donations and now when stars made goodwill visits to the Royal Marsden, Craig was invited to meet them. One day, when he was back in the ward for antibiotic treatment, the RAF Black Knights Display Team did a fly past of the hospital in Craig's honor, and later on that day the pilots came into the ward to meet him and present him with a signed photo. That was a big thrill.

On Bonfire Night, Carshalton Athletic Football Club held a charity football match for the Princess Chula Ward with Craig as special guest. He loved every minute of it. My dear friend Margaret from Gibraltar came to the match. It was our first meeting since Philip had died, and we cried and cuddled each other. When she told me tearfully how she had taken Philip back to Gibraltar to be buried it brought home to me again just how lucky I was.

The following week Securicor made the first payment for our waste paper and I took Craig up to the Marsden on Armistice Day to present the check (for £1,000) to the hospital. But Brian Sadler stopped us at the entrance to the Princess Chula Ward and took me aside. "I'm sorry, Marion, you can't go in," he said. "Jamie has just died." The day crashed around my ears. Jamie had been in the ward right at the start when Craig was admitted. His parents were Spanish and didn't speak much English, but we had spent a lot of time in the same room. Now I could hear their grief echoing up the corridor. Craig could hear it too. We made the presentation in the foyer and I whipped Craig away before he started asking questions. Luckily there was plenty to divert him. We were due to go to Charlie's house and then onto the Crown pub at Morden where Craig had been asked to start a marathon Post Office bike ride in aid of the Princess Chula Ward. He never remembered to ask what happened that day in the hospital.

The count was rapidly approaching one million now, and Charlie worked out that we should finally break the world record on Thursday November 16. We set about organizing a gala celebration. The atmosphere that night was electric. By seven, Sutton United's ballroom was jam-packed with people. There were nearly as many reporters as card openers. Television crews from TV-am, Sky TV, France and New Zealand had turned up and everywhere you looked there were camera lights, microphones and cameras. Ray and Neil, two old friends of mine, were running a free disco and they already had their light display flashing "Well Done Craig."

With the cameras filming every move we counted madly for nearly two hours. Craig was on top form. Ray had found a curly blonde wig for him to wear and he entertained the crowd by singing along with a Kylie Minogue record. Then at five to nine Charlie went up to the microphone and called for a bit of hush.

"I forecast we would hit this record tonight by eight-thirty," he said. "Well yes, we've hit it. Not only have we hit it. We have *smashed* it. By a quarter of a million! Our total of counted cards so far is one million, two hundred and fifty thousand, two hundred and sixty-five cards."

There was a wild cheer and everyone started clapping and hugging each other. It was like the finish of a marathon.

Charlie handed Craig a card in a frame. "This is for all the hard work you've caused me and my postmen, mate. And good luck with the next one million." Everyone roared, but Charlie shook his head. "No, I mean it," he said. "We have not stopped, folks. This is not the end. I need your support because we need to count again. And again. And again. We're going to get to two and a half million. We'll show the *Guinness Book of Records* people just what they can *do* with their bloody book!" The whistles and cheers when he said that nearly took the roof off.

Craig took the microphone and said slowly but clearly, "Thanks everyone," which brought another roar. Then it was my turn to thank all the card people from the bottom of my heart. "And thank you, world," I added, almost overcome. "Let's have three cheers for everybody that's sent cards." As the last cheer faded Cliff Richard's voice blasted out from Ray's speakers. "Congratulations . . ."

The celebrations went on until nearly midnight, and a dear friend, Doreen, took Craig home so Ernie and I could stay to the end. I sang until I was hoarse. All the good old happy songs. "We'll Meet Again," "You'll Never Walk Alone," and, of course, "I Just Called to Say I Love You." What a night.

Next day, November 17, was Children in Need Day. It was also out-patients' day at the Marsden and I had to dig Craig out of bed and drive him up to the hospital. After the usual eyes, ears and balance tests we arrived home in the early afternoon. Craig was tired out after all the excitement of the night before and went up to bed for a nap. I was downstairs sorting through the "special" boxes when the phone rang.

"This is Norris McWhirter's secretary," a woman's voice said. "I'm ringing to tell you that Mr. McWhirter has agreed to recognize Craig's record. He will receive an entry in the next *Guinness Book of Records.*"

The scream I let out must have deafened her. She waited a moment then said, "Norris is appearing on the Children in Need program on TV this evening. When he's finished his spot he plans to come straight to your house to present Craig with his certificate."

I screamed again. After I'd put the phone down I rushed upstairs to wake Craig and tell him. "Craig, Craig, they're going to put you in the book! Norris McWhirter's coming to see you!" Craig gave me a sleepy little smile.

"Magic," he said.

In fact, Craig missed being presented with his certificate. Norris McWhirter's TV spot was delayed and his secretary rang to say he would come to see us at the weekend instead. But on Saturday Craig had been invited to see a matinee performance of the show *Starlight Express* and at one o'clock a car arrived to take Ernie, Craig and me up to the West End. We had a wonderful time. The show was great and there was a special surprise. After the performance the cast lined up to meet Craig, and Tom, the show's drummer, presented him with 9,000 *Starlight Express* get-well cards. It turned out that for the past two weeks they'd been getting everyone in the audience to sign a card for Craig!

We arrived home at seven, tired but happy. Soon afterward there was a knock on the door. I answered it to find a neighbor from a few doors down standing on the step, looking all excited. "Here," he said, "I've got something for you. Some geezer knocked on my door and he left this . . ." And he handed me a large piece of card.

This is to certify that Craig Shergold of Selby Road, Carshalton, Surrey, England, became the first person ever to receive more than one million get-well cards.

I took the certificate back into the front-room and waved it at Craig. "Guess what, Craig? What do you think?" He took it from me and screwing up his eyes, read the words slowly out loud. "Wow! I'm in the *Guinness Book of Records!*" He gave me a great beaming smile. "Thanks, Mum, that's because of you."

"Don't be daft," I planted a kiss on his cheek. "It's because of *you!*"

Chapter 12

——❦——

IN JUST two short months Craig had become a celebrity. There was no escaping it. Something about him had caught people's imagination. Everybody wanted to meet this little boy who had fought Guinness and won. He was asked to appear on television, to open fêtes, to start sponsored events, and in the weeks that followed he met dozens of stars—the cast of *EastEnders,* Michael Barrymore, Frank Bruno, Telly Savalas, Tony Bennett, Ernie Wise, Jerry Lee Lewis ... On November 23, while the record was still hot news, Mary Hurry persuaded the Nolan Sisters, Bobby Davro and Hearts of Gold to do a benefit concert for Craig's Disney fund at the Working Men's Club in Willesden. The event was televised by Sky and it was a sell-out. At the end of the concert they got Craig up on stage and he danced with the stars while everyone sang "You'll Never Walk Alone." The audience never stopped putting their hands in their pockets. People were even coming up to Craig and offering to buy his autograph. By the end of the evening we knew for certain that we would be going to Disney. The only question was when.

We knew we'd have to be patient. We couldn't think of going away for more than a few days at a time yet because Craig still needed weekly check-ups at the Marsden. He was having scans every couple of weeks too, and Ernie and I took him for an MR scan a fortnight after breaking the record. We were waiting our turn outside the scanning-room when a bearded man came up and spoke to us. Craig was thrilled when he realized it was Richard Branson, especially when he wrote a "card" on Craig's hand. "All that money and you can't afford a card?" I kidded him and he laughed.

After Craig came out of the scanner we went to look for Emma who was back in the Princess Chula Ward for more treatment because her bone marrow transplant had been unsuccessful. We'd seen her when we came into out-patients the week before and I'd been shaken then by how ill she looked. Emma was such a pretty girl, but you wouldn't have known it that day. She'd lost all her lovely hair and her skin had turned a terrible angry red. But she hadn't lost her spirit. She'd spent our whole visit planning to do things with Craig—she'd been so thrilled by his cards and all the people he'd met. "Do you think you could ask Lenny Henry to come and visit me, Marion?" she'd begged. I promised I'd try but in my heart I knew it would take more than a comedian to make Emma feel better. Today, when we asked after her, we were told she was off the ward having treatment. "Never mind," I said to Craig, "we'll go and see her next week." But the following Friday as we arrived in out-patients one of the mothers took me aside. "Emma's died," she whispered.

I felt as if my legs had been knocked from under me. It shouldn't have been such a shock, after the way she'd looked last time. But it was. I just couldn't believe Emma was gone forever. She'd been so bright, so full of life. Every time a kid died, a knife went through me. But with Emma it was the worst yet. Craig had been so fond of Emma. I had too. We really did love her. She'd been Craig's first real friend in hospital. When they'd been in the same ward that first month, they'd been inseparable.

Somehow I managed to carry on as normal for the next hour. I drove Craig home, took him into the house and left him with Ernie. Then I drove the car up to Mitcham Common, parked in a quiet spot, and howled like a wild animal. I felt absolutely terrified. First Azou, then Philip, Gary, Jamie, and now poor little Emma. My God, who was going to be next? But even in my grief I knew I couldn't let Craig find out. I couldn't risk him giving in. For his sake I had to keep going as if nothing had happened.

Luckily there was plenty to keep my mind occupied. The cards were still flooding in. The flow had actually increased; 70,000 letters a day now, Charlie said. It had taken me by surprise. Once the record was announced I'd expected the cards to die down after a few weeks. But I was beginning to realize that stopping this appeal wasn't going to be quite as easy as that. People told us chain letters were going around the world now, asking people to send Craig cards. We had no option but to carry on counting. Charlie had predicted two and a half million by Christmas. Instead it was three million. Craig's computer at Mount Pleasant sorting office was so overloaded in December that it crashed three times. In Christmas week the Post Office handled eight hundred sacks of mail addressed to him! Charlie had commandeered two warehouses to store the cards until they could be counted and the media were practically camped at Wallington sorting office, photographing and filming Craig's mail mountain. "We haven't had publicity like this since the great train robbery!" Charlie said.

Everyone was working overtime to try and keep up with them. We had to meet three times a week for "cards" even over the holidays, but nobody grumbled. It was as if we were all members of a special club now and I knew we were going to stay friends for the rest of our lives. I would never be able to thank the card people enough but I organized a Christmas party as a token of our gratitude.

I was starting to get worried about Craig's schooling. He'd missed nearly a whole year. It was obvious he couldn't go back to an ordinary school while he was still in a wheelchair and spending most of each day in bed, but he needed something. After a bit of a fight the education authority agreed to pay for a private tutor. Mrs. Dinnage started just before Christmas and taught him on Mondays, Tuesdays and Wednesdays from half-past ten to twelve. Craig loved it. He'd really missed his lessons. I was amazed by what Mrs. Dinnage managed to achieve without a proper classroom to teach in. She even set up science experiments in the kitchen. Craig enjoyed cookery lessons

best and with Mrs. Dinnage's help he cooked a Christmas
cake and toffee apples and his special favorite, ginger pudding.

For a week or two over Christmas, though, schooling
would have to take second place to travel. On December
15 we were due to fly to France. A couple of weeks earlier
Craig had given an interview to French TV thanking all
the French people for their cards and wishing them *"un
joyeux Noel."* Now the same TV crew wanted to interview
Craig again, and to our delight Air Inter had offered to pay
for us to spend five days in Paris and Strasbourg.

None of us had ever been to Paris before and we loved
it. We stayed in a small hotel near the Arc de Triomphe
with shutters on the windows and a wrought-iron balcony.
All the things I'd heard about the French being cold and
unfriendly were proved untrue. The hotel owners treated
us like one of the family. They'd made a nativity scene
specially for Craig and had even put a little Christmas tree
in our room.

That weekend, while we were getting ready for a trip
around the Paris sights, Craig went into the bathroom to
clean his teeth and let out a yell. "Hey Mum, look, my
hair is growing."

I dashed in and sure enough there was a faint dark fuzz
all over his scalp. I was thrilled—the doctors had told us
his hair might never grow again—but Craig pretended not
to be bothered. "I preferred it when I was bald," he said.
Underneath, though, he was tickled pink, I could tell.

After three days we flew to Strasbourg which Craig
loved even more than Paris. There were storks' nests on
housetops and lovely shops. Air Inter spared no expense.
They even took us for lunch in the world-famous
Maxine's. I thought I'd died and gone to heaven. I ordered
salmon en croute and Ernie asked for steak chasseur. But
Craig really let me down. After one look at the menu,
which naturally was in French, he put it down. "Could I
have egg and chips please?" he asked. The waiter didn't
bat an eyelid. Ten minutes later he returned carrying a
plate covered with a big silver cover which he whisked off
to reveal a perfectly fried egg and golden chips garnished
with parsley and watercress. Craig smiled politely and

waited till he went away. Then he went, "Ugh," and pushed all the greenery to the side of his plate before tucking in.

The TV interview went well. An interpreter translated the questions through our earphones and Craig thanked the French people for all their cards and kindness and said how beautiful France was with all the decorations and lights everywhere. The next day we returned home to Carshalton for a quiet family Christmas.

At the start of the New Year, on Twelfth Night, we went traveling again. This time to Italy for five days so Craig could appear on the *Nino de Marti Show,* a big Italian chat show. Again we were spoiled rotten—a lovely hotel, and an escort wherever we went. It was the first time we'd been interviewed in front of a live audience. I'd always heard that the Italians loved kids and after the program we found out how true it was. Just about everyone in the audience wanted to kiss Craig. And how the compliments flowed. One old lady said he had Marlon Brando eyes!

On Sunday we went to St. Peter's Square to hear the Pope's blessing. We couldn't take Craig's wheelchair into St. Peter's basilica because of the steps but I went in and said a prayer. After I'd come back out we were waiting in the crowd for the Pope to appear when suddenly I heard a shout. A woman was pointing at us. Then someone else yelled and everyone started turning and coming toward us. In seconds we were surrounded by people patting Craig on the head and kissing him and taking photos and yelling, "God bless you, Craig." The Pope had appeared and was talking away up on his balcony, but everyone near us was ignoring him. Craig was really quite scared—it's not nice to have people mobbing you when you're stuck in a wheelchair. But George, our driver, called some policemen over to help us out and they got us back into our car and away.

Italian TV did everything they could to make sure we had a good time. They even took us to the circus on Monday evening. I'd told them that elephants brought us luck and as a surprise for Craig they arranged for the elephants to come across the ring and bow to him. The next day they took us to the beach—I hadn't even known Rome was on the coast—which was lovely. But our afternoon turned sour when Craig was taken ill on the way back to the hotel. He turned a dreadful gray color and was sick when we got to our room. I told myself it was something he'd eaten—we'd been quite adventurous in sampling Italian food. It seemed I was right because by the time we left for London the next day he was better.

We arrived home to find another thrill waiting for Craig—an invitation to meet Princess Diana when she visited the Royal Marsden on January 29. It proved to be third time lucky. Craig finally got to shake hands with the princess and was rewarded for his patience with a beaming smile. "Well done, Craig," she said.

Since October our life had revolved around television, radio and magazine interviews. It was just constant, every single day. But at least the media let you know they were coming. Other people dropped in unannounced. The casual callers had started in September. The very first Saturday after the Marsden had launched the appeal we'd had eighty-four visitors, all wanting to meet Craig and see his cards because they'd seen him on telly. That first day they'd been mostly local people, but as the weeks went by visitors had started coming from further afield. Just before Christmas I'd opened the door to find a young German man standing on the doorstep. His shoes had fallen apart and he had great blisters on his feet. He told us he'd flown over to Heathrow from Berlin specially to see Craig. He'd only had enough money for his plane ticket and he'd slept on the Underground all night, then in the morning he'd walked the 9 miles from Morden tube station to the Marsden, only to find Craig wasn't there, so he'd walked another 6 miles from the hospital to our house. We fed him—luckily it was Sunday and I had a roast in the oven—and gave him a pair of Steven's shoes. I tried to lend him some money but he wouldn't take it, so we filled his pockets with chocolate and off he went back to Heathrow.

Visitors only caught me off my guard once. It was a horrible day with the rain sheeting down and Craig and I had decided not to bother getting dressed—I thought no one would come to see us in weather like that. At about ten in the morning we were sitting in our dressing-gowns, eating toast and opening cards in front of the fire, when there was a knock at the door. I peeped through the front-room window to see four foreign-looking people, three men and a woman, all smartly dressed in business clothes, standing outside in the pouring rain. I nearly passed out. "Could you just wait a minute?" I called. I hurled myself upstairs, pinned my hair up, threw some clothes on, came down and opened the door. They said very politely that they were from Malaysia and they'd come to see the cards. I asked them in and to my amazement they took their shoes off before they came into the house. Then they knelt down in their immaculate business suits in the middle of all the cards and rubber bands and bits of toast and started to pray for Craig. I was so embarrassed I could have died.

I always asked people in. If they'd taken the trouble to come and see us then I felt I had to. It never crossed my mind that we were taking a risk asking strangers into our house. We had two Japanese people in once who not only prayed for Craig but wanted Ernie and me to join in. One of them told us to kneel down facing the fireplace and clap our hands while he chanted and prayed over us. The second chap looked as though he'd just come out of jail—he had a shaved head and tattoos everywhere—but we still did as we were told and knelt down. If they'd wanted to they could have murdered us. But if people asked us to pray I always did. It didn't matter what religion they were (and we had every religion under the sun from Catholic nuns to Buddhist monks). We were so desperate we would do anything.

People often told us we should have our heads exam-ined, but after all that had happened to us since Craig had been taken ill, why shouldn't we have faith in human na-ture? We only regretted our trust once. I was upstairs when Ernie opened the door to someone dressed all in black, a real weirdo, who looked like Count Dracula. But Ernie asked him in and left him with Kate and Craig while he went to make a cup of tea. When he came back Kate was beside herself because the bloke was telling Craig he was going to die, as a punishment for being very evil in a pre-vious incarnation. The first I knew about it was when I suddenly heard Ernie yelling at the top of his voice, "Out! Out! I don't want to hear another word!" And he pushed this chap out into the street and slammed the door. Luckily Craig thought it was funny.

I often regret not keeping a visitors' book during that time. We had so many interesting people in our house. Like the rich Texan couple who kept a black cab ticking over outside for one and three-quarter hours . . . "Honey, it doesn't matter at all," the wife told me when I kept reminding her about it. On another day we had the whole of the Mitcham fire brigade in the kitchen (Craig told them a rude joke and they faxed it to every fire station in the country). Quite a few famous people came to the house too. Eddie Kydd the motorcycle stunt-man, all the Chelsea football team and countless TV personalities. Meeting famous people never flustered Craig. He wasn't at all starstruck, thank goodness. I'd been a bit afraid that all this attention might make him big-headed. But he still talked to everyone in the same way. "Hello, mate, how are you?" he'd ask, whether it was a pop star or a neighbor from the estate who'd popped in to see the latest cards.

Mrs. Dinnage was finding teaching more and more difficult. Every time she started on a lesson the doorbell would ring and she'd have to break off. I knew we had to do something about it, but I really didn't want to turn visitors away. After all, it was these caring people who were helping to get Craig better. We decided to buy an old caravan and use it as a school-room. Ernie paved over the garden so we could stand it next to the garage. Once it would have broken my heart to lose our garden. It had been my pride and joy. Over the years I'd filled the borders with cuttings I'd begged off the gardeners at the park near the Grange Restaurant and in the summer I used to spend nearly every evening pottering about in the garden. But it had been looking like a jungle for months now—last year no one had even cut the grass—so paving it over seemed the best solution.

The caravan was a success. Now, if people turned up during lesson time I just made apologies and told them Craig couldn't be disturbed. He was doing quite well in his schoolwork and Mrs. Dinnage was pleased with him.

He still couldn't write very well because his hand was so shaky but she'd got him a typewriter and since then he'd been making good progress. I still wished he could go back to school though. Lee was very good about coming in to see him, but most of his other mates had dropped off—he wasn't part of their lives anymore. As a result Craig was missing his childhood. I didn't see why he couldn't go to school for a few hours now, but the education authorities told me he would have to see the child psychologist first and even if he got the go-ahead he wouldn't be able to go back to his old school because it wasn't suitable for wheelchairs.

The big Christmas rush of cards had died down a bit but they were still coming in at about 70,000 a day. By February the count had risen to six million and I rang Guinness and asked them if they'd change Craig's entry in the *Book of Records*. One million didn't look so impressive now. They agreed but said we had to submit a figure by the middle of May to catch the printing deadline for the 1991 edition.

"That's it then," I said to Charlie. "We'll count like crazy till May and then, somehow, we have to stop it."

Charlie raised his eyebrows. "How?" he asked.

"We'll think of something," I said confidently.

In all the excitement of the cards we'd never forgotten our other aim of getting Craig to Disneyworld, but it was March before Diana Tait finally decided he was well enough for the nine-hour flight to Florida. She seemed really pleased with his progress. She even arranged for him to have his Hickman line taken out so he could go swimming. It had been left in just in case he ever needed more chemotherapy, so I saw taking it out as a further sign that he was out of the woods.

We left Heathrow Airport on March 15, on a Virgin Airline's 747. We hadn't let the Press know about the trip. Ernie and I were tired of sharing Craig with reporters and photographers and we wanted him to ourselves for these three weeks. We were going for three weeks at Diana Tait's suggestion. It would give him time to recover from the flight. "Take it easy," she told us. "Don't try to do everything at once." It was wise advice.

In the end we didn't spend very much time in Disneyworld itself. Although he enjoyed the Magic Kingdom, the crowds and heat were too much for Craig and after a couple of hours he flopped. The one thing he really wanted to see was the Disney parade, and we managed to find a good place for that. Not in the area reserved for the disabled though, because Craig didn't want to feel "different." It turned out to be a wise move. Because Craig's wheelchair was the only one on that bit of street, all the characters came over to him and patted him on the head or shook his hand. He thought it was great. Maybe some ten-year-old boys would have been too grown up for Mickey Mouse and Cinderella but Craig still loved all that make-believe stuff.

I suddenly realized that the Fairy Godmother was heading toward us. She stopped in front of his wheelchair and touched his head gently with her wand. "Hello, little boy," she said. "Now, what do you wish for?" Craig looked up at me. "I've only got one wish, ain't I, Mum? I just want to get better. I want to live." I started to cry, I couldn't help it and the Fairy Godmother stepped back. "I hope it comes true," she said softly. When I looked around all the women around us were crying as well.

People in wheelchairs were taken down the exit ramp to get on the Disney rides. We were heading down the ramp of the Captain Nemo ride when someone in the crowd passing the other way gave a yell, "There's Craig! It's the little boy Craig," and we found ourselves surrounded by excited children and their parents, chattering in foreign accents.

"Craig, can I have your autograph? Can I take your photo?" It turned out they were from Italy and remembered Craig from the *Nino de Marti Show* two months earlier. One of the ride operators came over to find out what all the noise was about. "Hey, have we got a real live celebrity here?" Craig grinned. "Not really," he said.

That was the last day we went to Disney. Craig was just too tired afterward. Now that he didn't have to perk up to do an interview every day he looked a different boy and I realized that I'd been kidding myself in thinking he was almost well again. He still had a long way to go.

Next day he stayed in bed till midday and we decided to take it easy and stay by the hotel pool. There was no point in dragging him around to see everything if it was going to make him ill. Actually Craig enjoyed swimming in the pool as much as anything. He hadn't been swimming since our holiday in Benidorm sixteen months before. It was wonderful to see him doing breast-stroke across the pool. I thought he might have forgotten how, but he hadn't. I did worry that other people in the pool might look at the scars on his head and the mark where his Hickman line had been and think he had AIDS or something, but although one or two kids stared no one took fright and he played quite happily with them. Something else shocked me though—how thin he looked next to the other kids in their swimsuits. I hadn't realized how much weight he'd lost.

Although we didn't go back to Disney we did take Craig to lots of other places. We hired a car and drove to St. Petersburg for four days so he could swim in the ocean. We went to Gatorland. We played Crazy Golf. We fed the dolphins and watched water-ski displays at Sea World. But for the rest of the trip a niggling worry stayed with me— the feeling that perhaps everything was not as well as I'd thought. I didn't say anything to Ernie. As long as I didn't talk about it I could pretend it was all my imagination.

I was still uneasy when we came back. I couldn't get rid of the feeling that he should have been better than this by now. It was nearly eight months since his radiotherapy had finished yet he could still hardly walk. And his speech, if anything, had got slower than it had been last September. I tried not to let my fears run away with me. After all, I told myself, they'd never given such deep radiotherapy to a child before—he couldn't just bounce back. But I was very aware that conventional medicine had nothing left to offer Craig and I began to look around for other help. Just in case.

Chapter 13

---m---

BACK IN December a children's charity had offered to take Craig to Lourdes, but because they wouldn't allow me to go with him, I'd said no. At that time I wouldn't be apart from Craig for more than a few hours. All my instincts told me he needed me. On his own, disconnected from me, I had this picture of him gradually fading away. But now I began to wonder if I'd been ridiculous and should have let him go to Lourdes after all.

I've always been a believer in spiritual things. I know there's a lot more to life than what we can see and hear and touch. When I was a little girl of eleven I started having premonitions—I used to call them my "witchy" feelings. Once, daydreaming in class, I pictured the trestle table which carried our morning bottles of milk collapsing on top of a girl called Margaret Harries. A week later it happened, just as I'd imagined it.

That sort of thing happened a few times over the next twenty years. In fact, I used to pray to God to take the power away from me because it frightened me. The time I remember best was when Steven was a toddler and I was taking him and some other kids to a funfair in Mitcham. I was in the kitchen, checking my make-up in this plastic mirror I had on the wall when I heard it speak to me. It might sound ridiculous, but I actually heard a voice saying, "You're going to have a car-smash tonight. Don't go out." It was so vivid. But the kids were all screaming to go and it had been a couple of years since I'd had any of these premonitions so I told myself not to be stupid and we went. We'd only got as far as the traffic lights at Mitcham when a drunken driver in a refrigerated van jumped the lights and hit us ... the car was a write-off, though, luckily, none of the kids was seriously hurt.

Another moment I'll never forget happened on Cup Final day 1976 when we were living in Tooting. Steven had gone to my mum's for the weekend. Ernie was watching the big match on TV and I went up to bed to read a book and dozed off. When I woke I had an irresistible urge to go to bingo. I'd only ever been once in my life before but I trusted my witchy feelings and I knew I had to obey. I dragged Ernie out with me to the old Streatham Hill Theater. It was in four tiers and I knew exactly where I had to sit—the top row of the top circle. "Blimey, how much higher? What's all this about?" Ernie had puffed.

"It's nearer to heaven up here," I said. "You wait and see."

It happened in the last game—the big Club Flyer, the biggest prize of the night. Suddenly I only wanted two numbers. Number nineteen, which was the number of Mum's and Dad's house, and number six which was my birthday. And I just knew it was coming. Nineteen came out first. Then nine. And then, "On its own Number Six!"

"Eeah! Eeah! Eeah!" I screamed.

I'd won £1,126 and fourpence—a lot of money in those days. It was enough to get us moved out of our awful dump in Tooting back to Carshalton to be near my mum. When we got home that night I read my stars in the paper. "Don't gamble, whatever you do," they said. "You'll never be lucky ..."

After that the power had left me. Nothing like it happened again until the terrible night when I'd dreamed of Craig in his coffin (and, please God, that was nothing more than a nightmare). But because of my psychic experiences I found the idea of faith healing quite reasonable.

We'd had some contact with it already. Brian, our vicar, had introduced us to a faith healer called Tom Caswell who had laid hands on Craig several times. And back in

November Glen Hoddle had put me in touch with a lady faith healer who had visited us twice, but had told me Craig needed someone with a stronger power than hers.

So when I opened the Sunday paper two days after we arrived home from Florida and read an article about a psychic surgeon, my interest was caught at once. This man was supposed to be able to do operations without instruments because power was being sent to him from the spirit world. Two of the paper's reporters said he had diagnosed their illnesses correctly.

"Maybe he could get this thing out of Craig's head," I said to Ernie.

He shrugged. "Up to you, Mal, but you know what I think . . ." Ernie wasn't a great believer in the supernatural.

I might not have taken it any further but the very next day a stranger knocked on the door and asked me, "Did you read a story in the paper yesterday about faith healing?" The man, whose name was Tony Sales, said he'd been reading an article about Craig just before he saw the piece about this psychic surgeon. "I had the feeling it might be the answer for Craig," he said. "Would you let me pay for him to see this man?"

I didn't take much persuading. I said he could go ahead and make an appointment. On Good Friday, April 13 (why didn't that date make me think twice?). Tony Sales picked Craig and me up and drove us 80 miles to the psychic surgeon's house in a beautiful little village. Two women dressed in white coats appeared and one of them showed us into a waiting-room filled with lovely antique furniture.

Craig was quite ill. The long journey had upset him and there was a terrible smell of liniment everywhere which was making him feel sick. I asked for a drink for him and one of the ladies in white coats sighed and fetched him a thimbleful of water in a tiny glass. When I asked if I could use the bathroom she sighed again, then stood outside the door the whole time as if she thought I might steal the toilet paper.

I was already beginning to regret we'd come. But since we were there and Tony was paying I decided we'd better hang on and give it a go. Suddenly a door opened and a great big man came in, all smiles.

"Hello, my love," he said to Craig in a funny cockney accent. "How are you, my darling? Are you all right? Hello there, my boy." He was really gushing and his whole manner hit a wrong note with me.

"Come on then, Craig," he held out his hand. "This way." Craig stumbled into the examination room and I followed and helped him up onto the bed. On the wall there was a picture of a Red Indian. "Who's that?" I asked.

"It's one of my guides," the surgeon said.

The stink of liniment was even stronger in here. Beside the bed was a tray of gleaming metal instruments like you'd find in a real operating room but the surgeon didn't touch them and he didn't ask Craig to undress. Instead he held his hands over Craig's legs and stomach, first touching them, then letting his hands hover over his body. "How are you feeling, Craig? Are you getting hot?" "Well, I am where your hands are," Craig said. His hands moved down over his legs. I hadn't told him what was the matter with Craig, but I was sure he thought, because of the wheelchair and his problems walking, that the trouble lay in Craig's legs. His hair had grown now so you couldn't see the scar on his head anymore.

The surgeon frowned. "Oh this little boy is very ill." Then he looked at me and smiled. "But in ten days he'll be better. Bring him back next week."

"Oh," I said, "Right."

Ten days? Blimey, I thought, what did he think he had? Flu?

Tony was sitting in the waiting-room and he got out his wallet and paid the nurse as we left. I couldn't see how much he gave her. I hoped it wasn't too much. I just couldn't believe this man's "treatment" would help Craig. He hadn't convinced me at all. On the way home Tony told me he'd made another appointment, and I felt trapped. Tony was such a kind man. I just couldn't bring myself to tell him I didn't want to go again.

We paid the surgeon another visit the following week as arranged, though, as I'd expected, Craig had shown no sign of improvement. This time the waiting-room was packed with people, most of whom looked dreadfully ill, and we had to wait quite a while to go in. When at last it was our turn the surgeon bent over Craig and held his hands over his legs again. "You don't know who my little boy is, do you?" I asked him. He frowned at me and I knew he didn't.

"Craig has a tumor on the brain—so why you're doing his legs I don't know," I said. "Your Indian guide has let you down this time."

He looked offended. "I know what I'm doing," he said.

As we drove home, Craig lay on the back-seat of the car, looking absolutely exhausted. "I don't like that man," he said. "Please don't take me back there."

That decided it. We never went again. It had been an interesting experiment and I was grateful to Tony for paying for it, but after two sessions I really didn't believe psychic surgery had anything to offer Craig. But the experience didn't put me off other forms of faith healing. For instance, I still believed strongly in the holy things people were sending to Craig because I knew they'd been sent with love and my faith in the power of love was undimmed. I still kept every single religious thing sent to him. I recited the prayers people had written out for him. I put a piece of carpet that the Pope had walked on under Craig's bed, and I carried on sprinkling the holy water. I didn't necessarily think they would all work. But some of them might and since I had no idea which ones they might be, I tried them all.

Thankfully I didn't have much time to sit worrying about Craig's health the way I had in Florida—we were madly counting cards again now, trying to get as many as we could opened before the Guinness deadline of May 16. A backlog of three million was being stored at the Post Office, waiting to be counted.

Then one day I had a phone call from Keith Wendon, who had taken over Brian Sadler's job in the Marsden Appeals office. (What a coincidence—his wife was Cynthia, the Great Ormond Street nurse who'd persuaded us to take Craig to the Marsden!) "Marion, have you heard of the Children's Wish Foundation?" Keith asked. I had. We'd had whole boxes of cards from America with compliments slips inside saying, *From the Children's Wish Foundation.* But I hadn't a clue what it was.

"Well," he said, "they've got four million cards for you. They want to know when you'd like them."

"Keith, do us a favor," I said. "We can't possibly take them. If we took four million on top of all this lot we're counting now we'd sink."

"What shall I tell them to do with the cards then, Marion?"

"Why don't you ask them to recycle them. Help the kids in their *own* country who've got cancer?" I said.

Keith said he would see to it and I didn't give it any more thought. Card nights had taken over my life again now as the deadline got closer. We were up to fifteen million and people were staying up all night so they could count. At last, on May 16, Charlie let Guinness know that we had a new record—16,250,292 cards. The following day we had a phone call to say Guinness had accepted it.

We were still celebrating when we had a phone call from the Mayor's office in Sutton telling us that two officials from the Children's Wish Foundation were coming over from America at the end of May to meet us. Apparently we had to officially sign over the American cards and parcels to them before they would be allowed to recycle them. The Mayor of Sutton threw a tea party to celebrate the occasion and it was in the Mayor's parlor that we met Linda and Arthur Stein for the first time. Linda was an elegant woman in her early forties who reminded me, both in looks and the way she dressed, of Jackie Kennedy. Her husband Arthur was a real Southern gentleman, a thoughtful, kindly man. He told us that it was Linda who had actually started the Children's Wish Foundation and as we sat sipping tea she told us all about it.

Linda's daughter Susan had died of leukemia at the age of twelve. Afterward Linda had thrown her heart into raising money for the hospital, but she had got disillusioned. "At the end of the day I wanted to see a kid smile," she said. "And I wasn't seeing that." Apparently Susan had set her heart on getting her driving license before she died and it was remembering that which had given Linda the idea

for the Children's Wish Foundation. The fund's purpose
was to grant the last wishes of dying children.

Linda told me how, last year, people had started asking
her if she'd heard of this little English boy and his wish to
get over a million get-well cards. She'd been fascinated
because most of the children she helped wanted to travel
or meet famous people. In contrast, Craig's wish didn't involve spending a lot of money. The Children's Wish Foundation had picked it up in a very big way and had made
its own appeal for him, setting up card-collecting points all
over America. Linda said she had sent me a letter explaining all this but, of course, we hadn't found her letter
yet—it was at the bottom of a sack somewhere.

She'd brought Craig some presents—a Coca-Cola tin
which moved in time to music, which fascinated him, and
loads of bright American T-shirts.

"Did you enjoy Disney, Craig?" she asked.

"Well, yes," he answered, "only I wanted to go to Universal Studios, but it wasn't open."

"Oh really?" Linda looked thoughtful. "And tell me,
Craig, is there any special American you'd like to meet?"

"Yeh, Hulk Hogan and Jake the Snake," Craig said instantly.

Linda looked blank.

"The wrestlers. You know . . ." Craig said. He was really into American wrestling.

"Maybe we can do something about that," Linda smiled.
"Craig, how would you like to go back to America?"

Craig's grin stretched from ear to ear. "Oh *yeh!*" he
said.

Craig would have to improve quite a lot before he could
take up Linda's kind offer. He'd lost even more weight
since we got back and he hardly ever got out of his wheelchair now. But I still remembered Dr. Hayward's words to
me more than a year ago, "Give him a dream." After the
Disney trip Craig really had no dreams left. Now Linda
had given him another one. I was sure it would make a
difference.

I was right, but it didn't happen straight away. One Sunday at the end of May, Craig gave me a terrible fright. Ernie was out, and I was just helping Craig out of his

morning bath when he suddenly gasped, "Mum," and passed out in my arms. I thought he might be having a fit—they'd warned me he might—so I carried him to his bed and laid him down and lay with him, afraid to leave him even to phone. After a few minutes he came round, but he looked vacant and he was very tired. I rang the Marsden and spoke to a male nurse who asked me what had happened. I told him.

"Well, you have to expect this sort of thing I'm afraid," he said. "The tumor's on the move."

I felt myself go cold. I didn't ask him what he meant, but the next day I took Craig to see Diana Tait, who sent him down for a scan. "What did the nurse mean by, 'It's on the move'?" I asked. She frowned. "It is possible it's started to grow again," she said. "But we won't know till we see the scan."

I tried not to over-react. Dr. Tait had only said "possible," and that nurse hadn't even seen Craig, so how on earth could he tell? His bathwater was probably too hot, I told myself, that's all.

Craig didn't have another turn. Instead, over the next few weeks, he seemed to rally. Mrs. Dinnage even said he was doing much better in his lessons. I tried to forget about the incident—I didn't even mention it to Ernie. On June 24 we had a party to celebrate Kylie's christening and Craig's eleventh birthday. He stayed awake almost to the end and I let myself start to feel optimistic again.

Dr. Hayward had written asking to see us and soon after Craig's birthday we went up to Great Ormond Street. "I haven't brought you here for any reason, you know," he said. "I just like to keep an eye on Craig for curiosity's sake." Craig was keen to demonstrate what he could do now. "Watch me, Dr. Hayward," he stood on one leg and counted to seventy-four, then he changed legs and managed ninety-four on the other. He hadn't been able to do that the year before. "Very good. You must have been working hard on that." Richard Hayward looked at me. "Has he been doing his exercises?"

"Only kung fu!" I said. "Show Dr. Hayward, Craig." Craig grinned and folded his arms across his chest. "I am the master! I am in charge of this body!" Dr. Hayward smiled. He didn't say so but I was sure he believed Craig was cured. He looked so pleased with him.

As Charlie predicted, our second try at stopping the mail turned out to be no more successful than the first. We'd sent letters to newspapers all over the world telling them the appeal was over but hundreds of thousands of cards were still arriving every week. By the middle of the summer the Post Office had three warehouses devoted to Craig's mail and we had no option but to keep on opening them. Apart from anything else, some of them contained checks for the Marsden. I'd finally decided to recycle the cards now. I hadn't wanted to but there was nothing else I could do with them. The schools for the handicapped had enough to last for years and didn't want any more. At least this way the cards were raising money to treat cancer.

Everyone seemed quite happy to carry on counting. "Cards" had become more than a duty now—it was a social club. For some of the older people it was their one night out a week. That summer we organized barbecues, karaoke evenings, trips to the seaside and barn dances for the card people. I realized that the predictions had been right. The cards had taken over our lives. But I didn't regret it. Not one single minute. We'd made such wonderful friends through cards, felt such love and unselfishness. We'd really been blessed to have so many people caring for our son. If the clock was put back I knew I'd do it all again.

During Craig's low spell after we came back from Florida I'd turned down most invitations to travel but now I started to accept them again. That summer Craig had another trip to France, this time, to his great excitement, on Concorde, courtesy of a Midlands travel company. Soon afterward Yorkshire Television took us down to the Kent hopfields to see *The Darling Buds of May* being filmed. That was wonderful. David Jason met us as we arrived. "What are you going to be when you grow up then, Craig?" he asked.

"I want to be like you—an actor and a comedian," Craig told him. Later on as we were having lunch in the bus which served as the actors' canteen, David Jason came and sat next to us. Craig was playing with his food as usual. "Come on," David said. "You told me you wanted to be like me when you grow up."

Craig nodded. "I do."

David put on his Delboy voice.

"Well, you've got to bloody eat then, you plonker, Craig. 'Cos if you don't eat you can't be funny." Craig looked at him with great big eyes and wolfed down his whole plate of cottage pie.

"Good boy. Lubbly Jubbly." David rubbed his hands together. Craig loved him.

The same month Penny Thompson, the appeals organizer for the Fulham Marsden, a lovely girl who had become a dear friend, organized the London cabbies to do a collection for the Craig Shergold Royal Marsden Appeal. Craig was guest of honor and before the collection started he was introduced to Fiona Fullerton, the actress, who had started the Save the Humans Appeal. She was a really beautiful and generous lady and after five minutes of chatting to her Craig was head over heels in love.

About twenty taxies drove round the West End in procession while celebrities in fancy dress walked alongside with collecting tins or waved out of the taxi windows. Craig and I sat in the back of the lead taxi and I held a bucket out of the window for people to throw money in. I was in my element. "Come on, darlings. Insurance for the future. Give us your money," I yelled, while Craig sank down on the backseat trying to pretend he wasn't with me. My bucket got so heavy that my arms were banging against the cab window as I tried to hold it up. I was black and blue when I took my top off that night.

The outings carried on. My diary was crammed with engagements that summer. Craig was getting more attention than a pop star and I felt anxious sometimes that he might become spoiled. But I didn't see any sign of it. I know I was biased but I never got the slightest feeling that he was getting cocky. Craig's feet stayed firmly on the ground.

I did worry about his appearance though. Sometimes I half-thought his head was changing shape again. It seemed to stick out at the back more than it used to. But no one else commented on it so maybe it was my imagination. Anyway he was still going to the Marsden for regular scans and no one ever called me in afterward, which gave me confidence. He did still get tired very quickly but I was sure this was due to his weight loss. It was getting more and more difficult to get him to eat. His hand was so shaky that he found it hard to fork food into his mouth and, in any case, he really had no appetite—it was almost as if he'd lost his sense of taste.

By August his weight had gone down to four and a half stone—and he looked very frail indeed. But when he had an offer to ride in a hot-air balloon with the actor Brian Blessed there was no question of him saying no. I wasn't so sure about it at first, but Brian really impressed me. He was a lovely warm caring man, and he promised he'd take good care of Craig. Everything went smoothly until they landed on a slag-heap and the basket tumbled over and over, though luckily, neither of them was hurt. Brian told me afterward that as they'd struggled out of the basket somewhere near Bristol a lot of little kids had run up. No one recognized Brian at all but they all recognized Craig and to Brian's horror one little girl said, "Hello, Craig, I thought you were dead." But Craig wasn't bothered at all. "I'm going to live till I'm ninety-odd," he said. Brian told me it was one of the most moving moments of his life.

A week later Craig was a guest of honor at the very first Chelsea match of the season at Stamford Bridge. Charlie and Ernie went with him. I'd let Charlie take my place. I felt he deserved to go after all his hard work. Before the match they had lunch with Bobby Campbell, his wife Susan and their son Luke. Craig had a wonderful time. He'd really missed his football.

At the beginning of September, Sharon had another baby. This time it was a boy and she and Steven named him Craig. "We couldn't call him anything else really, Mum, could we?" Steven said. That month too we finally had our week at the seaside in the Malcolm Sargent Home at Jaywick Sands—the holiday Craig had been too ill to take a year before. The weather was lovely and he got a bit of a tan. He came home looking really well.

Craig had received two exciting new celebrity cards while we were away—from Madonna and Michael Jackson. Madonna had written Craig a lovely letter, telling him how her mother had suffered from cancer. I rang the *Sun* to let them know—they always liked us to notify them of special ones—and they said they'd send someone to the house to photograph them on September 17.

The interviewer wasn't Ruki this time but a new reporter, Ingrid Miller, a lovely girl who got really upset reading all the cards—I discovered afterward that her husband had just died. Craig was in bed when she arrived with the photographer so they popped upstairs to have a word with him, then came back down to photograph the cards. While we were talking Ernie came in and went upstairs to play cards with Craig. Ingrid and Steven, the photographer, were just packing up to go when the telephone rang. It went every ten minutes these days. I'd thought of getting an answering machine but I couldn't afford to return the calls so I just put up with it. Usually the calls were from PR people wanting Craig to appear here or go there. But this one wasn't.

"Marion? How are you?" It was Diana Tait's voice. "I've just come back from holiday." There was a little pause. "I'm afraid the radiographer tells me that the results of Craig's latest scans aren't very good. I'd like you and Ernie to come in and see me on Thursday afternoon." There was another pause. "Nina will be with me."

My heart stood still. Nina was the liaison sister—one of her jobs was to arrange the Macmillan nurses when your child was dying. Calling in the liaison sister meant the beginning of the end. Suddenly I felt my hackles rise. "No way! I don't need her. I don't want her there." I shouted down the phone. "You'd better not have her there."

"All right, Marion," Diana Tait said quietly. "As you wish. I'll see you at two o"clock on Thursday."

I put the phone down and I started to shake. I couldn't think straight. Part of me was angry but another part was shocked and numb. Ingrid came into the kitchen and put her arm around me. "There's something wrong, isn't there?"

"No, no, nothing wrong." I shook my head. "Everything's fine." I mustn't let her know, I thought. I feared (although I had no reason at all not to trust her) that if I did it would be in the papers and Kate would see it and my dad would see it and worse Craig would see it and he'd lose the will to live. That was the only thing I was certain about. Craig must not find out.

I made an excuse and went upstairs and called Ernie out of Craig's bedroom. When I told him he went completely white. I was crying by now but not making any noise. The tears were just pouring down my face. I came back downstairs, leaving Ernie on the landing. Ingrid put her arm around me and looked me straight in the eye. "No story," she said. "I promise no story." As she and the photographer let themselves out Ernie and I fell on each other and sobbed. "Thursday!" I gasped. "How will we last till Thursday?"

There were three nights before our appointment and I don't think we slept a wink during one of them. I found the cancer booklet the Marsden had given us and read again how children with brain tumors die in their sleep. Every few hours in the night I crept into Craig's room and held a mirror over his mouth. I thought I was going to go out of my mind. I stayed in the house. For the very first time I couldn't face seeing people—I knew I'd break down.

It wasn't fair. I'd thought he was getting better. I'd really thought he was great. But I'd just been kidding myself. All this time that horrible thing had been lurking there ready to start growing again. That *monster* with teeth and hair and nails. I hated it. I really hated it. I wanted to tear it out of his head with my bare hands.

Thursday came at last and Ernie and I drove up to the Marsden, leaving Craig with Carol. I'd told him we were going to the poll tax office to have a fight about paying. It was the first time I'd lied to him. But I had to say something—we'd never both gone off before. One of us always stayed with him. Craig swallowed the story. He knew I was always grumbling about the poll tax.

I felt like an old lady as we walked down the hospital corridor. My legs were like jelly. Whoever invented that expression got it right. I could hardly put one foot in front of the other. Ernie shepherded me in front of him and somehow we got to Diana Tait's office. She wasn't there and we sat down to wait. By the time she came in I was

trembling from head to foot. She kissed me and then Ernie
as she always did, then she put a scan up on the screen.
"As you can see the tumor has got a lot larger," she
said. "It's growing very fast."

There was a big black mass in the middle of his brain.
I stared at it as if hypnotized, not wanting to believe my
eyes. "Isn't there an operation you can do?"

Diana Tait shook her head sadly. "I'm afraid there's
very little we can do," she said. I looked at Ernie. He appeared to be in shock.

"When will he die?" I couldn't believe I was asking it.

"I can't predict that. I don't know. As you're aware, this
tumor is very unusual."

"How will he die then?" I demanded. I had to know.
"Will it be like it says in that cancer book? Will he just die
in his sleep? Will he be in pain?"

"We'll give him morphine for the pain when the time
comes," she said gently. I felt Ernie's shudder through my
jacket.

"So you're telling us to take him home and let him die
in peace?"

She shrugged and her eyes were sad. "Well, yes," she
said. "We can give him short sharp doses of radiotherapy,
but that will only be a delaying tactic."

I'd seen kids who'd had short sharp bursts of radiotherapy and I didn't want that for Craig. I stood beside her
looking at the scan, Ernie on the other side of me. And
suddenly I got this feeling. This tremendous surge of energy. It was as though it was coming up through my feet.
One minute I'd been on the verge of collapse, the next I
felt incredibly strong and calm.

I knew what I had to do. I had to take Craig back. He
was mine. Why should I let the hospital decide if he was
going to live or die? If they wouldn't fight for him then I
would.

I glared at her. "No way," I said. "He is not going to
die." I jabbed my finger at her. "You're not having him."
I pointed up to the sky. *"He's* not having him. *I'm* having
him."

Suddenly I had an idea. "I'm going to Russia. I'm telling you, I'm going to Russia." Hundreds of people had

written to us from Russia that summer asking us to visit. Maybe that was what I was meant to do. I had no idea how we'd pay for it, We didn't have two ha'pennies to rub together, but some way, *some way,* I knew I was going to get help for Craig.

"Oh Marion, please. Please don't go to Russia. They're not as far advanced as we are."

"Lady, I am going somewhere." I was trembling now with temper. "Are you going to be behind me? Wherever I go?"

"Yes," she said. "I will, I'll be behind you." We turned to go and she kissed us goodbye. Then she touched my arm. "Marion, I didn't want this to happen either you know. I'm very fond of Craig. Of you all. I am so very sorry."

That night before I went to bed I took out my diary and under Thursday September 20, 1990 I wrote, *The very worst day of our life. Please God in heaven, let the doctor be wrong. All that I have I give to you, O Lord. Please don't take my son. I love him so very, very much. Please answer, Father. Thank you, Marion.*

The next morning it was raining again. It was true, every time we had bad news it seemed to rain. I'd been crying all night and I looked a wreck. Craig came down at about ten o'clock and lay down on the settee. He mustn't see how upset I am, I thought. He mustn't ask me what's the matter. I knew I'd have to lie to him and I didn't want ever to lie to him again. I wandered around the house like a zombie looking for something to do to take my mind off it. There were half a dozen sacks in the kitchen and I decided to open some cards. Most of the sacks were from the Post Office but there was one big plastic bag full of letters from private delivery firms—Federal Express, DHL and UPS. I hated opening the private-delivery mail. Each letter came in a plastic envelope which was really difficult to open. So I don't know what made me go for that one rather than for the Royal Mail bags. I reached in and pulled out the top letter.

It was a Federal Express envelope. I took a knife out of the kitchen drawer and opened it. Inside was another long brown envelope, and inside that was a letter. It was typed on official-looking notepaper headed: University of Virginia Health Sciences Center, Department of Neurosurgery, and it was dated August 7—six weeks earlier.

By the time I finished reading that letter, I was shaking like a leaf. God had answered my prayers.

Chapter 14

—⁓—

DEAR MRS. SHERGOLD,

I am writing on behalf of my friend John Kluge. Mr. Kluge lives here in Charlottesville. He is the wealthiest man in the United States. More importantly, he is one of the most concerned individuals living today.

Mr. Kluge called me this morning because he had been asked to send your son Craig a postcard. Mr. Kluge in his characteristic manner was taken with the situation and wanted to be sure that everything medically possible was being done for Craig. In fact, he offered to fly him here if there was any hope that anything could be done. Obviously, not knowing the particulars of Craig's case, I could not advise him.

We attempted to telephone you this morning, but found your phone to be unlisted.

I would appreciate it if you would telephone me collect so we can determine if Mr. Kluge can be of any assistance to you.

Very truly yours,
Neal F. Kassell, MD, Professor and Vice Chairman,
University of Virginia School of Medicine.

"Oh my God! Oh dear! Oh! Oh! Oh!" I screamed. I was in a complete panic, running round the kitchen like a headless chicken. Luckily Craig was sound asleep on the settee—if I'd dropped a bomb he wouldn't have heard it. Kate couldn't have chosen a better moment to knock on the door. "Kate! Kate! Come in! Look at this letter!" I waved it at her.

"Oh, he's going to think I'm a wicked mother! He's going to think I haven't even had the decency to answer his letter! What shall I do?" I was hysterical.

Kate took me in hand. I hadn't told her about the bad news but she knew at once this was important. "You've got to ring him now," she said firmly. She made me a cup of coffee and gave me a cigarette and sat me down, then she dialed the number at the bottom of the letter. Neither of us stopped to think what time it might be in America. I took the receiver from her and took deep breaths.

The phone was answered straight away. "Neal Kassell speaking." He had a wonderful drawling voice which reminded me of Chicago gangsters. For a moment I was lost for words. I'd expected to have to go through telephonists and secretaries first.

"Hello," I stammered. "This is Marion Shergold. I'm ringing from England."

He knew who I was at once. "Oh hello, Mrs. Shergold. You got my letter then?"

"I'm ever so sorry," I said. "But I've only just opened it. We've got six hundred sacks of mail coming in every week . . ."

He gave a little chuckle. "I understand, don't worry. We'd expected it would take time but we knew you'd come around to it in the end. How is Craig?"

"You're not going to believe this," I said, "but they told me yesterday to take him home and let him die. I thought I was seeing things when I read your letter. It was like a message from heaven."

"Well we'd really like to help Craig if we can but I don't want you to build up too many hopes at this stage," Dr. Kassell said. "The reason Mr. Kluge thought we might be able to do something is that we have a new treatment for brain tumors here in Charlottesville, called the gamma knife. You may have heard of it."

The name rang a bell—I had a feeling I'd read an article about it somewhere. "What is it?" I asked him.

"It's a new instrument that fires high-energy radiation beams directly into the brain. It might offer a possible treatment for Craig but that's all it is—a possibility. I'm not promising anything. OK?"

"OK," I agreed.

"Now," the professor's voice turned businesslike, "before we can make any decisions about bringing him over I must have his files—all his medical notes and scans. What I'd like you to do is to Federal Express them straight to us. We'll pay. Phone me when you know what's happening." He chuckled again. "And call collect next time."

"Oh thank you! Thank you! Thank you!" I gabbled. I put the phone down and threw my arms around Kate. "Look after Craig for me," I said.

Without stopping to drink my coffee I ran out to the car and drove like the devil up to the Royal Marsden Hospital. I abandoned the car in the staff parking lot and galloped up the stairs to Dr. Tait's office.

She wasn't there. I was told she was away and that Craig's notes could not be released without her permission. I couldn't believe it. I lost control. I pleaded. I stormed. Then I pleaded again. But the answer was a sympathetic no, so I phoned Dr. Kassell and explained we would have to wait a week until Diana Tait got back. Although he tried to set my mind at rest it was the longest week of my life.

While we were waiting I went to see Richard Hayward. Ernie suggested it. He said we should find out if Dr. Kassell was accepted by our medical profession. Dr. Hayward was reassuring. "Dr. Kassell is a fine doctor," he said. "He's a world-renowned surgeon." But he wasn't too enthusiastic about the gamma knife. He described it as a big cumbersome instrument. He looked thoughtful then said, "I have to warn you that it would be extremely risky to operate on Craig a second time, but if you would like me to try . . ." he hesitated.

I thanked him but I said no. Eighteen months before, instinct had told me Dr. Hayward would save Craig's life. Now the same instinct told me it was Dr. Kassell who had to do the next operation. Whatever had nudged him into contacting us when he did, it had to be more than just co-incidence. I was sure fate meant us to go to America.

Diana Tait returned to work on October 1. "I will send the notes on, Marion," she agreed when I rang her. "But please don't build too many hopes up on it. Craig is very, very ill you know." But how could I possibly stop myself hoping? While we waited to hear again from Dr. Kassell I tried to carry on as usual. I didn't want Craig to suspect anything was in the air. We even took him with us to a big all-day outdoor card session in Lordshill, which he coped with really well. Better than I did. I was finding it really hard to look people in the eye and pretend everything was all right.

At last, on October 16, Dr. Kassell's secretary Kim phoned to say they'd received the scans from the Marsden and Dr. Tait had faxed them a letter giving details of Craig's treatment so far. "We'll be in touch with you again very shortly to talk about when Craig should come over," Kim promised.

Two days later Linda Stein from the Children's Wish Foundation phoned. It was uncanny. I hadn't spoken to her since the summer. "Hi, honey. How is Craig?"

"Not so good," I told her Diana Tait's news.

"Oh Marion, I'm so sorry. The reason I rang was to tell you we'd arranged Craig's trip to come to Universal Studios. We thought he could come here to Atlanta first to see all the cards we have for him here. Then we would fly him to Florida. Do you think he's well enough? It would be a great tonic for him."

In all the upset of the past few weeks I'd nearly forgotten about Craig's "wish." But I was certain it would be impossible now. I explained to Linda about Dr. Kassell's letter and how we might be flying to Virginia for treatment with the gamma knife.

"Wow, that's fantastic," she exclaimed. "If you knew—in May I just wanted to pick Craig up and bring him back with us to the States. I felt so sure they could do something for him over here. Oh, it's wonderful, Marion. I can't believe it!"

Then she came up with an idea. "Look, if he's coming

to America anyway why don't we give him his wish at the same time?"

I wasn't sure. Craig really deserved that wish. He'd been through such a lot. But we didn't know how fast the tumor was growing. His condition didn't seem to have got too much worse since Diana Tait had told us the bad news, but who knew what might happen in the next few weeks? Maybe if we took time to go to Universal Studios, Craig would die before they could use the gamma knife.

"Linda, would you ask the doctors if we can do the wish?" I asked. "I'll do whatever they say.'

"Of course I will, Marion honey," Linda said. "Leave it to me."

Four days later she rang back. "Get your things together. You're flying tomorrow morning at 11 A.M."

"What? Linda, you're joking!"

She laughed. "I've arranged the flights—everything. I've spoken to Dr. Kassell. He's seen the scans and he says it's OK to go ahead and give Craig his wish before he goes into hospital—he doesn't think three weeks will make any difference. In fact, he thinks it's a wonderful idea. He said it'll do Craig good!"

Talk about panic! Ernie and I flew around throwing things into bags. I rang Carol, Kate and Dad to tell them what was happening. When Slippery Chris called around to collect some sacks I asked him to tell everyone at cards where we'd gone. Then I remembered my promise to keep the *Sun* informed so I rang them—they'd been so good to Craig. They asked if we'd mind if they sent Ruki and a photographer with us and I said no—I was very fond of Ruki and the thought of having a friend with us in a foreign country was comforting.

Craig was so excited, but so far he only knew about the "wish" part of the trip. That evening I said casually, "Craig, while we're in America we might see a doctor."

"Oh Mum," he groaned. "Not another operation."

"No, just to look at you, because the doctors are very clever in America," I said.

Our air-tickets, paid for by the Children's Wish foundation, arrived at three the next morning. Just before seven Carol called to collect us for the drive to Gatwick. The traffic on the M25 was bumper to bumper, and I was in a cold sweat thinking we'd miss the plane. But then the road ahead cleared, Carol drove like the wind, and we just made it. Ruki and Phil, the photographer, were waiting by the check-in desk in a terrible panic. I kissed goodbye to Carol, Dawn and my sister-in-law Pat—no one else was there because I still hadn't let on to the family how serious this was. Very soon afterward the plane started boarding. As the jumbo lifted from the runway, Slippery Chris's words the day before were running round my head. "Safe journey, God bless you. I hope you come back as a family."

The flight took ten hours and I barely took my eyes off Craig the entire time. Over the past few weeks he had lost even more weight, and though he was still as cheerful as ever, he looked very frail now. The stewardess obviously realized how sick he was and she lifted the arm-rest on the seat, and made up a little bed for him and he slept for most of the flight. We arrived in Atlanta in the mid-afternoon and to my relief they allowed us to by-pass customs and go straight through to the arrival lounge where Linda and Arthur gave us a wonderful warm welcome. We were driven straight to our hotel. My jaw dropped as we pushed Craig's wheelchair into the Hyatt. We'd never stayed anywhere so luxurious in our lives. The foyer was filled with tropical plants and full-size trees and there were cages of tropical birds half-hidden in the foliage. There was even an artificial waterfall. They greeted us like royalty and piled our battered old suitcases on the luggage trolley without batting an eyelid. Our room was on the executive floor (you needed a special card before the elevator would even let you out) and we had Craig's ultimate luxury, a telly in the bathroom. He lay in the bath for an hour after Linda and Arthur had gone, watching cartoons. That night as I sat in our huge pink bed and looked around at the flowers and mirrors and pictures everything felt like a dream. This morning we'd woken up on a council housing estate in South London. Now we were going to bed in a palace on the other side of the world. Even the idea of Craig's hospital appointment seemed unreal in these surroundings. It was something far ahead that we didn't have to worry about yet. I snuggled up to Ernie. "Let's enjoy these three weeks," I whispered. "We won't even talk about the operation. Let's just live for the moment."

And that's what we did. The Children's Wish Foundation made it easy for us. Everything was taken out of our hands and every day was filled so that there was no time to sit and brood even if we'd wanted to. We spent the first week in Atlanta with Linda and Arthur who treated us like their own family. Everywhere we went Ruki and Phil came too—we thought of them both as our friends now. Linda and Arthur had hired a thirty-three-foot-long stretch limo and we all traveled in it to a gym where we met the famous American wrestlers Sting and Lex Lugher, the first part of Craig's wish. After Craig had felt the wrestlers' muscles for photographers, the limo took us on to a warehouse to see some of his cards. To our surprise dozens of people were waiting outside for Craig's arrival, holding balloons and banners saying, "Welcome to America" and "We love you Craig." The warehouse was bursting at the seams with cards. They were all over the walls, in sacks on the floor, spread over tables ready for counting (the set-up for counting was just like ours, except that they counted five days a week). On the warehouse wall there was a poster saying, "May all the prayers that have been said for you be answered." Craig went round meeting the American card openers, shaking hands, saying, "Hi. Hi. Hi," over and over again. He was quite relaxed about being the center of attention. Everybody got a look-in and a word. "Anyone else wanna see me?" he asked. Arthur nudged me. "Do you know, that boy could be the next president . . ."

Afterward the card openers threw a welcome party for him with a beautiful buffet, but it was all Mexican and deep-south food and though he tried Craig couldn't eat it. The Connie Chung television show people were there filming the evening. They were making a film about Craig to put out on Thanksgiving night at the end of November and had already interviewed Craig and me (though not Ernie, who, as usual, was too shy) in the hotel. They'd even been to England that summer to film our four million cards from Russia—somehow they found the idea of *Rus-*

sians sending get-well cards hard to believe. The TV interviewer asked Craig how he felt about his reception in America. "I feel like a star," he said slowly. He smiled at me as he struggled to get the words out. "Mum always said I'd be a star and now I am, I don't believe it!"

After a wonderful Halloween party it was time to say goodbye to Linda and Arthur and move on to Florida to visit Universal Studios and Disneyworld—Linda had added Disneyworld to the itinerary when she learned that Craig was too ill to enjoy it the last time. The dream-like feeling continued. We were met at the airport by the Sheriff of Orange County, Walter J. Gallagher. He was accompanied by a big crowd of people—I thought they must be waiting for someone else till I realized we were the last ones off the plane. I was presented with flowers. Then four police motor cycles with flashing lights and sirens escorted us the whole way from the airport, stopping traffic for us at every junction. "Oh I love this," Craig said, his eyes popping. "I feel like a king."

To my delight the hotel where we were staying was called the Peabody. "That's lucky," I said to Ernie. I was born in Peabody Buildings and I was always on the lookout for good omens.

This time round we enjoyed Disneyworld much more. Amazingly Craig seemed brighter, even though his scans showed his condition was so much worse than last March. We were treated like VIPs with CBS TV cameras following us around all the time. A private meeting had been organized with Mickey Mouse, who gave Craig a huge cuddle.

"Where's Minnie then?" asked Craig. Mickey shrugged, to suggest he didn't know.

"I know," Craig said, "she's out with another mouse!" The TV crew fell about laughing. Afterward Craig was asked to go on a float to take part in the Disney parade. But he wouldn't. "No—I want to *see* the parade, not be in it!" he said.

The two weeks in Florida passed in a flash. Two benefactors of the Children's Wish Foundation, Ward and Sandy Grimer, looked after our every need and every day they came up with something different for Craig to do—a trip to a basket-ball game, another ride in a stretch limo, a visit to Wet and Wild. The surprises were non-stop. Walter J. Gallagher, the sheriff, was wonderful too and arranged several extra outings for Craig. There was a photo-call on a police motor bike, a trip to a display by SWAT (the shock troops of the American police), and a ride on a police horse. Craig was even made a deputy sheriff of Orange County and presented with a real gold star with his name on it. As a final treat on the day before we left, Craig was named Honorary Duckmaster and allowed to put the Peabody Hotel's pet ducks to "bed" in their famous "duck parade," an honor usually reserved for film stars. All the activity could have exhausted him but Linda, Ward and Sandy had scheduled everything carefully so he could sleep his three hours every afternoon, and as a result he hardly flagged at all.

And then all too quickly the fortnight had passed and it was time to say goodbye. It was a painful parting. For two weeks we had felt a part of a big happy family. Nothing had been too much trouble for Ward and Sandy and as a final gesture they had arranged for a stretch limo to take us to the airport. Everyone cried as we left, even the tough traffic cops who escorted us, and Ernie and I were both in floods of tears. Partly it was the pain of leaving our new friends, but partly too it was because the dream was over and we had to come back to reality.

Although Craig had got tanned in the Florida sun and looked better than when he had arrived, there was no point in deceiving ourselves that the holiday had changed anything. He was still a desperately sick little boy and now we had to face that again. I don't think I've ever felt so frightened of the future as I did that day as we left Orlando bound for the University of Virginia Medical Center.

Our visit to Charlottesville started badly. The noise of the plane engines as we flew in over the Blue Ridge Mountains had me shaking in my seat. For me, as far as planes are concerned, the bigger the better, and this was the smallest plane I'd flown on in my life.

But things improved once we landed. A pretty, dark-haired girl was waiting to meet us.

"Hi, I'm Mona. I'm one of Dr. Kassell's assistants," she smiled. "I've a car outside to take you to your hotel." The drive to the hotel was wonderful. I felt as though I'd stepped back in time into an English colony. The countryside was so pretty with all the red and gold leaves falling. It reminded me of Guildford. I'd had no idea America could be like this. Where were the billboards. Where was the K-Mart?

Even our hotel, The Boar's Head, was like a traditional English country hotel, that had been picked up and dropped into the Virginia countryside. It was set in beautiful parkland complete with swans on a lake. The manageress came out to meet us as we got out of Mona's car. "Please call me Sandy," she smiled. "I want you to feel that from now on you are our family." After pressing a big bag of cookies and chocolate on us, Mona left. "Get some sleep," she advised. "Dr. Kassell wants to see Craig at six-forty tomorrow morning." I thought I'd misheard at first. Obviously American working hours were different to ours.

When Mona returned the next morning it was only just starting to get light, but we were ready and waiting. Ernie and I had hardly slept, though Craig had gone out like a light and hadn't wanted to get up. Mona drove down the road for about ten minutes and then suddenly we rounded a corner and saw a huge collection of modern white buildings—the University of Virginia Medical Center. Behind it the blue mountains rose into the morning mist.

Mona led us through an impressive entrance with big white pillars and along a corridor to Dr. Kassell's office where she knocked on the door. it was opened straight away by a handsome silver-haired man. He held out his hand. "Mr. and Mrs. Shergold?"

Neal Kassell was nothing like I'd pictured him. Some consultants can be a bit stand-offish but Neal Kassell looked really warm and human. I guessed he was in his early forties and behind his tortoiseshell glasses he had friendly brown eyes.

"And this must be Craig," he smiled. "How are you, Craig? Won't you come in? How was Disneyworld?" His voice still reminded me of gangster movies but there was nothing at all gangster-like about Neal Kassell. Within seconds of meeting him I knew that this was a man I could trust with my son's life.

When we were all sitting down Dr. Kassell explained about the tests they would do over the next few days to find out more about Craig's tumor. "We had the scans from London but they're nearly three months old now so we need to do more," he said. "We'll also do eye tests and co-ordination tests which you'll be used to. Then, I want to find out if the tumor is feeding off a blood vessel. To do that, we'll have to carry out an X-ray called an arteriogram."

Craig didn't flinch but Dr. Kassell must have seen my face drop. He explained that if the tumor *was* feeding off a blood vessel they could cut off its blood supply and reduce its size before they used the gamma knife, so it was really important to find out. The procedure would involve putting a catheter into a blood vessel in Craig's groin and passing it up through his body into his brain.

"Anyway," he smiled at Craig, "that's later. First I want you to have some tests. Are you ready to go?"

I wanted to ask Dr. Kassell if we would be meeting his generous friend Mr. Kluge but I was a bit too much in awe of him to bring it up.

It was a long day. We trailed from clinic to clinic doing one test after another. It wasn't until seven o'clock in the evening, when Craig actually fell asleep in the middle of an eye examination, that the doctors decided to call a halt. Another two days of tests followed including another MR scan. During those two days, while Craig was visiting as an out-patient, we got to know many of the people who worked in the hospital. Everyone was so anxious to make us feel at home. Kim, Dr. Kassell's secretary, and Lisa, his medical assistant, both invited us to their homes and Kim even asked me to her baby shower—she was expecting a baby in April. The kindness of all the Americans still amazed me. They treated us like long-lost friends.

Both Kim and Lisa sang Dr. Kassell's praises. He was a wonderful boss, Kim said, though he was sometimes a bit unconventional. I'd noticed myself that he never wore socks. Kim told us no one knew why. She said it was quite a joke with the nurses.

Craig was admitted to hospital for his arteriogram on Monday November 19. A nurse took us to the children's ward. She said her name was Nurse Nicely ("Straight out of Disney!" I whispered to Craig) and she said she would be looking after Craig in his own private room. It was like a luxury hotel room. Craig looked around him in amazement. "Oh yeh!" he said. His bed had a control panel with so many knobs and switches and dials to angle the bed that it was like the flight deck on Concorde. Craig did nothing but play with the controls for the first hour. There was even a telly hanging from the ceiling above his bed which moved by remote control so he was able to watch it while lying flat on his back.

Although this was to be only an arteriogram Dr. Kassell had warned us it carried a risk. We didn't realize how much risk until the next morning when another doctor brought us the consent form to sign. He took all three of us into a small office and spelt out the dangers bluntly. He told us, "this could affect Craig's sight. It might cause a hemorrhage, or even a stroke. I have to explain all the possibilities so that you know exactly what it is you are giving your consent to." I was getting lower and lower. I felt so guilty. I'd told Craig when we came here it was just for a check-up. Now he was faced with further treatment when he'd begged me not to make him have any more. I looked at him. "Well?" I asked. He shrugged. "If it's got to be done it's got to be done."

They needed to take a blood sample before the op. With the Hickman line in place that had been easy, but now, because the chemotherapy had burnt all his blood vessels, they had to make several attempts. First from his arms, then from his hands. "You poor darling, the nurse said as he bit his lip, trying to pretend it didn't hurt. "I tell you what, we'll get Dracula in." Craig giggled thinking she was kidding but Dracula turned out to be the nickname of the best blood nurse in the hospital. He was brilliant and he managed to get blood out of Craig's foot.

Sandy, the operating room nurse, was very kind and sympathetic. Just before Craig went into surgery at eleven she gave him a blue silk Christmas bell she'd made for him to hang on our Christmas tree when we went home.

After he went down we waited in the coffee bar, willing ourselves to stay calm. Lots of people seemed to have heard about Craig—we were the only English people in the hospital—and even the assistants behind the coffee bar asked after him and wished us luck. There was a balcony called the smoking shelf nearby and I wandered out for a cigarette. An old man was sitting out there puffing on a roll-up. He was a real old hill-billy with only one tooth in his head. We started talking and he was chatting away to me about living in the mountains and about shooting bears. I told him about Craig and he rolled another cigarette, then he said, "You know what you have to do, don't you?" I looked at him, puzzled. "You have to pray to the mountains," he said pointing to the blue peaks on the horizon. "I've got cancer myself and I pray to the mountains every night." He gave me a gummy smile. "And I'm going to be OK ..."

The nurses had told us the procedure would take about an hour and at half-past twelve we went back to the recovery room. We arrived just in time to see Craig emerge from surgery. As we watched, a doctor pulled the catheter out of his groin and a jet of blood shot across the room. The doctor clamped a pressure pad over his groin and it stopped. "Don't worry—just routine," Sandy smiled at us over her mask. Ernie looked as though he was going to pass out but I smiled back—blood didn't bother me and somehow I felt safe with these people. I just knew it was going to be all right. They were thrilled with Craig. "He's been really brave," the doctor told us. "He'll have to lie flat for a while but he'll be out in a couple of days."

The following day Dr. Kassell arranged for us to see the gamma knife. It looked just as Dr. Hayward had described it—a big cumbersome machine with a huge metal helmet which looked like a torture chamber. Dr. Kassell told us it worked through a beam of radiation. He also told us that with some tumors the gamma knife could hit a tumor today and the patient could walk out of the hospital tomorrow, and not even need radiotherapy as a follow up. But he still hadn't told us if they could use it on Craig. He wouldn't be able to tell us that until Saturday. First he had to assess the results of all the tests.

Although it was only twenty-four hours since his arteriogram Craig was already up and about by the afternoon. He told us he'd been telling Dr. Kassell jokes and the doctor had recorded some of them on his audio recorder so he could play them back to Mr. Kluge when he saw him next. "He told me we'd be meeting Mr. Kluge one day and when we did I'd have to tell him the jokes myself," he grinned.

The following day Craig was discharged and we took him back to the hotel. It was Thanksgiving Day. People had been talking about Thanksgiving Day all week. A lot of the nurses had the day off and were going home to their families. It seemed to be a time for family reunions and get-togethers, and every time someone had mentioned it that week I'd felt more and more homesick. We really loved America but we'd been away nearly five weeks and I was missing Dad and Kate and Steve and Sharon and my grandchildren so much. We had no idea when we'd see them again. It was lovely to have Craig back with us but, even so, I felt very low as we watched the preparations in the hotel for Thanksgiving dinner.

And then the phone rang. It was Kim. "Hi, Marion. Dr. Kassell has booked a table in the hotel restaurant for you tonight for a Thanksgiving meal. Have a really lovely time. Dress up. Enjoy yourself. You're going to love it!"

We hadn't eaten in the hotel restaurant before. We'd been eating in McDonald's or Shoney's, another fast food restaurant, because although Mr. Kluge was paying our hotel bill we didn't want to take liberties with his generosity.

We were given VIP treatment. Sandy, the manageress, led us into the crowded candlelit restaurant, past the inglenook fireplace with its roaring fire, to a table overlooking the lake. As we passed them, the other diners looked up and whispered—Charlottesville was only a small town and the news of Craig's visit had been on the local TV.

That night we had the works. Roast turkey with beautiful fresh vegetables and pumpkin pie. Even Craig tucked in and tried everything. People kept coming up to wish him luck and I realized suddenly that I didn't feel homesick anymore. It was as though we really belonged here in this wonderful country. I held Craig's and Ernie's hands across the table. "When we get back to England we're going to celebrate Thanksgiving Day every year for the rest of our lives," I promised.

The following day I woke up with one of my witchy feelings. I knew that Dr. Kassell was going to send us home, I just knew it. I wondered whether to tell Ernie but decided against it. It was a cold day and we spent it indoors in our room playing hangman and Snakes and Ladders with Craig and watching TV. By the afternoon, when Craig fell asleep, the feeling had grown so strong I had to say something. "Dr. Kassell won't be using the gamma knife on Craig," I said to Ernie.

He gave me a funny look. "How do you know that?"

I said, "I just know. He'll be sending us home. He'll say he can't do any more. Believe me, we'll be home for Christmas." Ernie wouldn't listen. "No, Mal, he'll be fine," he said. And he refused to discuss it. Ernie won't argue. It's the most maddening thing about him. He just wouldn't accept what I was saying.

The next morning we went in for our appointment with Dr. Kassell with our hearts in our mouths. Kim said he was waiting for us in his office, and we left Craig telling jokes to Kim and Lisa and went in. Neal Kassell looked very serious. He waited till we'd both sat down, then he said, "I'm so sorry but things are worse than I thought. Craig really is a very sick little boy." I gulped and looked at Ernie but he wouldn't meet my eyes. "The tumor is not feeding off a blood vessel," Dr. Kassell continued. "It's bad news because it means we can't reduce it in size before surgery, and at the moment the tumor is far too large for the gamma knife."

Because of my premonition I didn't feel any shock—just a sort of numbness. Dr. Kassell seemed upset. He was pacing up and down the room. He'd spent a lot of time with Craig in the few days since we'd been here and I think he'd become genuinely fond of him. "Isn't there anything at all you can do?" I asked.

There had to be. I knew there had to be.

Dr. Kassell hesitated. "There is one possibility," he said. "We could carry out another surgical operation to reduce the tumor to a size where we *could* use the gamma knife.

We could try to remove about a third or possibly a half of the tumor that way. But the operation would carry a lot of risks. It could go tragically wrong. The tumor is in a very bad place."

"What sort of risks?" Ernie asked. His voice sounded strangled.

Dr. Kassell stopped pacing. "Listen, both of you. There is no way I can make this easy. Craig could die on the operating table, or very soon afterward." He looked away. "If only I'd got to him sooner." I wasn't sure if he was speaking to us or to himself. He looked at us again. "Even if he doesn't die, the operation could make him blind or deaf or leave him in a coma." I swallowed hard. I'd heard all this before when we were in Great Ormond Street. Last time we'd decided to go ahead. What were we going to do this time?

"What will this operation mean?" I asked. "If it's a success will he have a fuller life—will he get back to how he was before? Will it cure him?"

"No," Dr. Kassell shook his head. "It would be wrong for me to hold out that hope for you. I would have to be very optimistic to promise you that and I don't think I could be. The most I think it could give him would be another six to nine months of life—but I don't know. I really don't know . . ."

Poor Ernie had turned bright red and was gulping. I felt numb. Dr. Kassell looked at the floor.

"Have you got children, Dr. Kassell?" I asked suddenly.

He nodded. "Yes, I have three daughters."

"Would you operate on one of them?"

He looked taken aback. "Marion, I don't know. I really don't know." He shook his head. "I do think that only you and Craig can decide if it's a risk you want to take. Please. Go home for Christmas. Speak to your family and the English doctors. Have a nice Christmas and think hard about what I'm saying." Then he added quietly, "If you decide to go ahead then I'm willing to operate in the new year."

Chapter 15

—✺—

WE WALKED slowly out of Dr. Kassell's office to the secretary's desk, where Craig was still joking with Kim and Lisa. "Craig," I said, "we're going home for Christmas."

His face lit up. "Cor, Mum, that's great."

Ernie tried to smile but it was a big effort—he looked very down. I knew he'd read the same message into the doctor's words as I had. Dr. Kassell didn't expect Craig would even live until Christmas.

But to my surprise I felt a sense of relief. It was as if this was meant to be. I was certain now there was some greater power behind all this. And that power was going to look after us. My first premonition had come true. Now I felt even more strongly that Craig was going to be all right.

As I played and laughed with Craig in the bedroom that night I sensed Ernie looking at me puzzled. I knew he couldn't understand why I wasn't as depressed as him. But my peace of mind didn't last. That night I woke up in bed in a cold sweat. The sheets were wringing wet and I felt as if I was dying. I crept out to the bathroom and as I got there I felt a sharp pain shoot down my arm and back. I doubled up in agony and fell on to the toilet seat. What on earth could it be? I didn't dare cry out in case I woke Craig. At last, after what seemed like hours, the pain died away and I started to sweat again—it just rolled off me. I

208

wrapped myself in some towels and sat it out until I felt well enough to crawl back into bed next to Ernie.

Next morning I felt better and decided not to mention it. Poor Ernie had enough to worry about already. It was just something to do with my time of life I told myself—or maybe my weight. I'd put on five stone now. I promised myself I'd try and diet.

Kim wasn't able to book us a flight home until Thursday and we decided to fill in the remaining five days by hiring a car and taking Craig to see the local sights. We toured the lovely Skyline Drive in the Blue Ridge Mountains and visited Thomas Jefferson's house, Monticello. And Craig was thrilled when we discovered Jellystone Park, home of Yogi Bear and Booboo.

We arrived back in England on Friday, December 1, and were given a wonderful welcome by all our friends. I felt so relieved to be home. It was great to see my family again, especially little Kylie and Craig. A few days after we got back I decided to go and see the lady doctor in our local surgery to talk about what Dr. Kassell had said. The arguments had been going round and round in my head. Was the risk of the operation really worth taking, just to give him a few extra months? While I was in America I'd felt so certain that everything would be all right but now, gradually, my confidence disappeared. Ernie wasn't much help. He wouldn't discuss what we should do. His mind was made up. "There's no question about it, Mal—we've got to go back ..." But I did feel it had to be a mother's decision.

I hoped that this doctor, who was a mother herself and an old friend, could help me make it. It was the first time I'd been up to the surgery since I'd taken Craig there nearly two years before. This time I left Craig with my dad, unplugging the phone as I always did with Dad, because he can't hear properly and he shouts down the phone so people can't understand him either.

My GP was very welcoming. She listened sympathetically as I explained my dilemma. "The thing is I'm so frightened of him going through the pain he went through in GOSH. It was so terrible—and if there's no hope of it curing him, is it fair to put him through it again? And what if he dies during the operation? I'd never forgive myself." I broke down. "Please tell me, what should I do?"

She came over and put her arm around me. "Only you can decide, Marion. I can't tell you," she said softly. "But I know what your answer's going to be."

"I wish I knew. I haven't a clue." I felt as confused as ever.

She turned back to her desk and took out a piece of paper. "I told my daughter you were coming in and she asked me to read this to you," she said. "It's from the book of Mark." She started to read: *If you do not doubt in your heart and believe that what you say will happen, it will be done for you. For this reason I tell you: when you pray and ask for something, believe you have received it and everything will be given you.*

I stared at her, sensing that somewhere in the lines she had just read lay my answer. After a moment she said, "And how are *you* feeling, Marion? How are you coping with the strain?"

"Well to tell you the truth," I said, "I had a very funny turn when I was in America." I'd forgotten about it until she asked me.

"What do you mean by 'a funny turn'?"

I started to tell her and all at once, as I was speaking, it happened again. I felt a pain shoot down my arm and I started to sweat. At once it was panic stations. The doctor thought I was having a heart attack. She called for an ambulance but I was frantic because Grandad and Craig were alone in the house and the phone was cut off. "I've got to go home first," I said.

"But you can't drive like that, Marion—"

"I can. I promise I'll be all right." I gave her a big smile, pretending the pain had gone. "I feel better now, honest. I'll drive home to see Craig and the ambulance can pick me up from home."

In the end she gave in. I think she realized that if she didn't let me have my way it would make me worse.

When I got home Kate had arrived with her kids, Sami and Zeki. I sent Craig up to his bedroom to play with them and took Kate into the kitchen to explain what had happened.

"Don't tell Craig," I said. "We'll just tell him Mummy's got to go out again."

Poor Kate was so frightened. She'd not got over losing Mum. "Oh Marion—please don't let anything happen to you too."

I gritted my teeth. "Don't make a fuss in front of Craig. I'm all right. It's indigestion. Don't you dare let him know there's anything wrong with me, 'cos he'll give in. I know he will."

Craig was upstairs with Dad when the ambulance driver knocked on the door. Kate came with me to the hospital and stayed while they ran tests on three different machines. One machine said I'd had a heart attack and two said I hadn't. They wanted to keep me in but I wouldn't let them. "No," I said, "I'm all right. If two machines say I'm all right, then I am. I'm going home."

I wasn't all right, I knew it really, but I couldn't give in. Craig needed me.

A few days later I was called back to St. Helier Hospital for follow-up tests and they put me on a walking machine. It was too much for me and I collapsed with an asthma attack and had to be helped off, gasping for air. After half an hour they said I could go home. But instead of going straight to my car I went to the chapel to look for the visitors' book—my hotline to God. I opened it and wrote. *Please God, help me. Give me the strength to get back to America with Craig.*

I was still kneeling there ten minutes later when the hospital chaplain came in. He put his arm around me and guided me to a seat and I collapsed against him and blurted out all my problems. He knew all about Craig. "Keep up your faith," he said. "Pray and God will answer."

"Oh, but it's so much," I sobbed. "I don't think there's a mother in the world who'd change places with me."

"No," he said gently. "Perhaps that's why you've been chosen. You're strong. You've had the strength to come so far. With God's help you can keep going."

His words touched something deep inside me just as, a few days before, the words of my family doctor had done. It had been a long time since I'd asked God for help the way I had when Craig was in Great Ormond Street. That night I knelt by the side of my bed and prayed, "Please God, help me. Help me, tell me what to do next." I climbed into bed and the last thing I remember seeing before I drifted off to sleep was my mum's face smiling at me. It was as clear as if she was standing at the end of the bed. When I woke up the next morning my prayers had been answered. I knew what I had to do. The moment had come to tell Craig the truth.

That afternoon while Craig was sitting in his chair in the front room I sat on the floor at his feet. Taking hold of his hand I said, "Craig, do you want to go back to America?"

"Yeh!" he said.

"You do know you've got to have a very serious operation?"

Another "Yeh."

"Craig I've got to talk to you about it." I took a deep breath. "If this operation goes wrong—you know you could die."

I'd not felt the need to say this to him before the first operation, but then he'd been only nine. Now I was talking to an eleven year old. I knew I had a duty to spell it out to him, to involve him in the decision.

He gave a little chuckle. "I won't die, Mum. Don't *worry!* I won't die."

"Do you really want to go?"

"Yeh I do. I like that old Dr. Kassell. I have faith in him. He's going to get me well."

But there was something else I had to ask him. It had been preying on my mind.

"Supposing you were like a cabbage, Craig. You know, those people who stare at you and they can't talk anymore, they can only see you. You've seen people like it in the hospital. Would you blame Mummy?"

He shook his head. "I wouldn't blame you for anything, Mum. I'd blame this wicked cancer."

I squeezed his hands. They felt icy cold. They'd been like that ever since the day after his first operation.

I had one final question. "If you were to have this operation, Craig, you'd most likely have all that terrible, terrible pain you had in GOSH all over again. Do you really want to have to go through that?"

"Mum," he said, "no pain, no gain." He gave me an impatient grin. "I want to go—all right?"

And that was that. There was no more discussion. Now it was no longer a question of *if* we went but *when.* I felt the tension that had been tearing me apart lift away. The decision had been made. I was sure I would have no more "funny turns."

As soon as they heard we'd be going back to America our wonderful friends from "cards" rallied round to raise funds for our stay. Fred and Thelma and Mac and Jean ran race nights. Jacky organized a karaoke evening. Cis and Bev, the Brownie and Girl Guide leaders, ran raffles. There was a jumble sale, tombola stalls, and sales of home-made cakes. Even the OAPs from Thelma's bingo club saved their pennies for us. It still hurt my pride to accept them but without their generosity I knew we couldn't go. Craig's hospital bills would be paid by Mr. Kluge, but we'd still need money for our hotel expenses, and for food and phone calls and taxis while we were in America. I'd discovered in November that money didn't go very far in Charlottesville. We couldn't afford to be proud.

Once more I thanked God for the card people. They'd helped Ernie and me so much during those last dark months. On card nights everyone always asked how Craig was. And not one session went by without them singing "He's Got the Whole World in His Hands" just for Craig. We were still having two card meetings a week. The meetings had carried on without us during the whole five weeks we were in America and I felt duty-bound not to miss one after we got back. If I had to skip one because Craig was poorly then Ernie would go. Sixty sackfuls were still arriving every week. They all had to be opened in case there were donations to Craig's fund inside, but we had stopped counting them back in October when the count reached thirty-three million. Guinness wasn't going to update Craig's record again so there didn't seem any point in carrying on.

Guinness did want us to help with their exhibition though. They were staging a display of Craig's cards at the

Guinness Museum in the Trocadero in London and invited Craig along to open it on December 12. Suddenly Guinness seemed quite proud of him. They'd even been doing some calculations and had worked out that if all the cards Craig had received were put in one big pile it would be ten times higher than Mount Everest.

Not all the envelopes addressed to Craig contained get-well cards now. There'd been a bizarre development while we were away. People had got the idea that Craig was collecting business cards and they were sending them in by the thousand. Parcels of business cards were arriving every day from all over the world. It started to get me down a bit. The get-well cards had never bothered me. No matter what chaos they'd caused I'd coped because I knew we were achieving something. But the business cards weren't achieving anything. The recycling people didn't want them, so we weren't even making any money for cancer funds by opening them.

One newspaper suggested it was a malicious hoax but I didn't believe that. I felt it was more likely to be an accident. Somewhere a person copying a chain letter in a hurry had changed "get-well card" into "business card" and the mistake had multiplied. I tried not to lose sleep over it but it was an extra stress I didn't need when I was trying to concentrate all my energies on Craig.

I took Dr. Kassell's advice and set out to give Craig his best Christmas ever. I had plenty of help in my mission. Soon after we got back, the Rolling Stone Bill Wyman invited Craig for lunch in his restaurant, "Sticky Fingers." He'd held a Halloween Party in aid of Craig's Marsden Fund and wanted to present Craig with the check.

I was really in awe of meeting Bill Wyman—it's not every day you get to meet a legendary rock star—but I needn't have worried. Bill turned out to be a very normal, exceptionally generous man who was only concerned with our comfort and was genuinely shocked to see how ill Craig was. I was pleased that instead of showing him pity, he jollied him along. "Come on, what'll you have, Craig? Guinness? Vodka and tonic?"

I hadn't realized Bill came from Eltham, just a few miles from Carshalton. *And* he grew up on a council estate just like ours. He reminded me so much of Kevin I felt he could have been my brother. "Are you going to eat with me?" he asked Craig.

"Oh Mum, do I have to?" Craig pulled a face. I couldn't tempt him with food at all now. (Dr. Kassell had explained that the tumor had damaged his appetite center).

"Bill, he might have a little pick," I said. But Craig was too tired to even try—he kept looking for somewhere to rest his head. Bill promptly took off his lovely woollen scarf and folded it up and put it on the table. "Here you are, mate," he said to Craig, "here's a present for you. Put your head on that. But no bloody dribbling on it, mind, 'cos my mum brought me that." Craig had started dribbling out of one side of his mouth since we'd got back from the States and he was starting to get embarrassed about it but Bill saying that made him laugh and he put his head down on the scarf and dozed.

Halfway through dinner he suddenly sat up and said, "The potatoes look nice, Mum."

Bill said, "Come on, then, have one of mine," and offered him a couple off his plate.

Craig had a nibble, then smiled. "Your cook's all right," he said and he tucked in.

"Are you ready for photos, Craig?" Bill said when he'd finished. A photocall had been arranged for the handover of the Marsden check. Craig still looked only half-awake but as soon as he saw the gang of pressmen outside the restaurant his smile sprang into place. "How can he turn it on like that?" Bill looked amazed. "He's more professional than some stars!" The photographers snapped away for about five minutes then Bill held up his hand. "Right. That's it. Finished. This child's ill." And they went off as meek as lambs.

Craig really enjoyed himself that day. He wasn't into Rolling Stones music—he'd have had trouble telling you one of their records—but he liked Bill because he was so down to earth and treated him like a normal kid. Before we left, Bill presented him with a leather bomber jacket, with *Sticky Fingers* and *Rock and Roll* written on the back—he'd asked the Marsden for Craig's measurements to make sure it would fit, which really touched me.

There was a postscript to that day. Two days before Christmas a private messenger from Harrods arrived with a great big Ninja turtle for Craig and a big wicker basket full of fruit, sherry and port for the family. The card just said, *Love Bill.*

During the run-up to Christmas we were invited backstage at the Strand Theater in the West End to meet Marti Caine who was appearing in panto in *The Snow Queen.* She was another star who was completely natural, and just as funny offstage as on. "Oh, this costume!" she groaned as we walked into her dressing-room. "It's so heavy— don't come near my armpits, Craig, whatever you do."

Craig roared.

"I hear you've just been to America," she said to him. "How was it?"

"Great." Craig smiled.

I knew Marti herself was being treated for cancer in America, and had just had months of chemotherapy. Now she winked at me.

"You're not going to give up, Mum, are you?"

I shook my head. "No. I'm *not.*"

She smiled. "No, you don't look like you're the type to give up," she said. "Bloody well fight it. Look at me. I'm all right."

We'd had a phone call from the Greeting Card Association of Great Britain. They wanted to give Craig something for Christmas in recognition of all the trade he'd brought them. Did I have any suggestions? "Well, he'd love a little pool table," I said. I was thinking of a collapsible one, the sort you could pack away under the stairs when you weren't using it. The Thursday before Christmas there was a knock on the door and two men stood there with the pool table. It was over six feet long and about four feet wide. "Where the heck are we going to put it?" I asked Ernie. "They must think we live in a palace."

We decided to move the dining table out into the garage. "We'll just have to learn to eat off our knees," I told Craig. Steve James, the snooker player, came to make the official presentation and give Craig a game which, of course, he let him win. "Watch out Stephen Hendry," he joked.

But anyone could see that neither Stephen Hendry nor Steve had any worries. Craig's coordination was getting worse every day and that pool table caused him more frustration than fun in the next few weeks. His left hand had got so shaky that hitting the balls at all was a matter of luck rather than judgment.

He was getting steadily worse in other ways. I cringed now whenever I put him in the bath—he was just a little bag of bones. His walking was getting worse too. Six months ago he'd been able to walk around without his wheelchair for five or ten minutes at a time. Now he could hardly walk more than a step or two on his own.

It was Christmas Day that really brought it home to us. Last Christmas, when we'd just got back from France, he'd been so bright. His hair had been growing again. He'd been eating. The future had seemed really hopeful. Now, a year on, everything looked bleak. It rained solidly all day and Craig was really ill. While we were in America I'd bought Craig a little golden boxing glove on a gold chain. His favorite film of all time was *Rocky* so I thought it would be the perfect Christmas present for him. He opened it slowly and gave me a big thank-you kiss. "That's because you're the best fighter in the world," I told him. He gave a little grin and let me fix it around his neck, but his mind seemed to be on other things.

He managed to open most of his presents but then he just sat, looking far away. I'd cooked a turkey with all the trimmings but Craig didn't want any and when we looked at him, Ernie and I couldn't face food either. After Craig went up to bed we sat pushing the food around our plates, neither of us mentioning the terrible change we could see in him. When we went to bed that night I think both Ernie and I secretly feared we had just spent our last Christmas with Craig.

It was a very sad holiday altogether. Craig's Aunty Joyce died soon after Christmas. We'd known for some time she had lung cancer but still it came as a blow. Joyce and Fred, Ernie's brother, had done so much for us. Joyce had always told Craig that he'd given her the inspiration to keep on fighting.

Craig seemed very depressed after she died. By the end

of January he was spending more and more time in bed and his speech had slowed right down—he was slurring his words badly and often he didn't finish his sentences. Mrs. Dinnage was still coming to give him lessons, but now she only stayed an hour—the caravan was too cold to work in, so they'd sit in the front room and spread his books over the coffee table. Incredibly he was still able to perk up for TV appearances and interviews, and there were still plenty of them. In April the Royal Marsden was planning to launch a mobile exhibition of Craig's cards called The Craig Shergold Roadshow, which would tour the country raising money for the Royal Marsden Appeal. They needed Craig to promote the idea and he went up to the BBC studios in Manchester to be interviewed about it on *People Today*.

He was very chirpy that day. He told Adrian Mills his ambition was to visit Las Vegas, then he showed him a card he'd just received from some American Marines in the Gulf, which he was really proud of. It was written on a troops' ration apple-sauce wrapper with the message, *Get well soon. HANG TUFF!!* For five minutes he chatted cheerfully. I don't think anyone in the studio suspected just how ill he was. He even made a joke about how long I took to put my "war-paint" on. "She goes in front of the mirror . . . six hours later she comes downstairs and she don't look no better than she did," he told Adrian. His voice now sounded like one of those old-fashioned gramophones that had wound right down, but his sense of humor still shone through.

After the program he visited the set of *Coronation Street* to meet the cast, and during lunch was offered his first taste of black pudding and, judging by the face he pulled, his last. Afterward, though, going home on the train from Manchester, it was as though a light had been switched off. He was so tired he actually dozed off to sleep in the middle of a sentence. I nearly rang Dr. Kassell when we got home. But something stopped me. Not yet, I told myself. Not yet. I was so aware that this operation might mean the end of everything. I wanted to make the very most of the time we had left. To give him every possible second of life that we could steal.

I decided my aim now would be to make every day special for him. If I could make him laugh or enjoy doing something different then it was all I asked for. I didn't set my sights high. Little things were enough. I'd take off Julie Walters doing the Imperial Leather soap advert—that always made him chuckle. I'd push his wheelchair into the kitchen so he could help me make the Yorkshire pudding or stuff the chicken. And every day I invited his friends in to play cards with him, Lee, Holly, Gillian, Vicky, Boyson, Frank. Every day turned into a party. I'd write names on pieces of paper and pin them to the kids' backs and they'd have to guess who they were—Margaret Thatcher, Elvis Presley, the Wizard of Oz . . .

At the beginning of February a photographer, Anthony Grant, asked Craig to be on the cover of a new book which aimed to raise money for the Royal Marsden and an American cancer hospital. The book was going to be called *Take Two* and would be a collection of photos of famous people posing as their heroes. Anthony told me several big names had already agreed to help. Jeremy Irons was going to be Vincent Van Gogh, and John Cleese had offered to pose as Lady Jane Grey! "Does Craig have a hero?" Anthony asked. "Some character in a film he'd like to dress up as?" That was easy. Nothing had changed. Craig's favorite film was still *Rocky*. Anthony said that was a great idea. When we went up to his studio Anthony had been to Lonsdale's for some stars-and-stripes boxing gloves, boots and shorts, and had draped an American flag across the studio wall. I helped Craig get changed— Anthony agreed he could keep his own little gold boxing glove on its chain around his neck—and he got into a fighting pose in front of the flag. I worried he wouldn't be steady enough on his feet to stand still as long as Anthony wanted but he managed it. The result is one of our most treasured photographs.

By the middle of February Craig couldn't walk at all without support, and his dribbling had got worse. I had to put a towel on his shoulder and change it every couple of hours. Sometimes I'd catch him staring into the distance, his face full of pain, spit running down his chin and I'd be reminded of a Down Syndrome child. Just looking at him made me want to cry.

Then, on Monday, February 25, he woke up complaining that he couldn't feel anything on the left side of his face and I knew then we couldn't put it off any longer. If we wanted the operation done at all I had to ring Dr. Kassell before Craig got too ill to travel.

I decided to wait until one o'clock to ring, when it would be eight in the morning in Virginia. But at midday I received a transatlantic telephone call.

"Hi, Marion, this is Kim, Dr. Kassell's secretary. Dr. Kassell wants to speak to you. I'll put you through to him."

I couldn't believe it. It had to be telepathy.

As soon as he came on the line I blurted out, "Dr. Kassell, I think the time has come. We're ready to come back."

"How is he, Marion?" Dr. Kassell's voice was concerned. "Describe his condition to me." He listened without comment as I described Craig's speech and walking difficulties, but when I told him about the dribbling and the sudden numbness in his face I heard him murmur, "Oh dear."

"Marion, that's a very bad sign. We'd better get you out here as quickly as possible. How soon can you come?"

"Tonight!" I said.

He gave a short laugh. "Fine. We'll get things moving this end. Kim will fix everything. She'll let you know the arrangements as soon as she's made them. Give Craig my love. Oh and tell him Mr. Kluge sends his regards."

"I will," I promised. How many surgeons sent their love to their patients? I wondered. On impulse I said, "Craig has great faith in you, Dr. Kassell. He's certain you're going to get him well."

There was a pause at the other end. "You have to remember what I told you, Marion," he said quietly. "I'm not promising you anything."

"I know," I said. "I know."

I put the phone down and ran up the stairs to Craig's bedroom. "We're going to America!"

His face lit up. "When?"

"Very soon!"

"Great!"

"Are you frightened?"

Struggling with each word he said slowly, "I'd be a liar if I said I wasn't a little bit frightened ..." Then he smiled. "But I won't know anything, will I? I'll be asleep."

I gazed down at him, propped up high on his five pillows to let the shunt do its work. His face was all swollen and distorted, his eyes dark and bruised. He looked as though he'd just done three rounds with Frank Bruno. I wanted to kiss him and hug him tightly to me, but I knew his poor frail little body couldn't stand it. I felt tears starting down my face. Craig was watching me.

"Mum, come here," he said, and he held his arms out to me. I put my head on his chest and he cuddled me as though it was me who was the child and not him. "Stop worrying," he said. "Doc Kassell is going to get me well."

I choked.

"I mean it," he said. "I am going to be fine. I won't die. I love you and Dad and Steve and Grandad too much. All right?"

His words calmed me. I dried my eyes and sat up, feeling ashamed of myself. He was so brave. And I was the one who should be comforting him. He smiled, realizing the storm was over. "Go down now," he ordered. "Let me sleep!"

The airline tickets were delivered the next day, Tuesday, by Federal Express. We were to travel from Heathrow on Wednesday morning and our flight would take us to Charlottesville via New York and Washington. Kim rang again to say Mr. Kluge would not only be paying Craig's hospital fees but would also foot the bill for our air fares and hotel bills.

In the few hours we had to get ready we ran around in a frenzy. While Ernie packed our cases with our warmest clothes—Kim had said it was very cold in Charlottesville—I drove to and fro in the car. To the hospital to collect Craig's scans. To the surgery to fetch his drugs. To the bank to change pounds into dollars. To the supermarket to buy boxes of Cadbury's chocolates for the

American nurses. To Mothercare for a present for Kim's baby, due soon.

Ernie rang up work to tell them he was taking indefinite leave. "I hope your job's still waiting for you when you come back," I said nervously. "Sod the job," he said. "Craig comes first." The tom-tom drums had been beating and our phone rang non-stop. Not just friends, but the Press wanted to know what was happening. Even Linda and Arthur rang from Atlanta offering to keep us company during the operation. "We just want to bring you a little comfort and be there if you need us," Linda said. "We can't bear to think of you in a strange country with no family around you." I accepted gratefully.

On Tuesday night with our bags packed and ready we held a last emotional card night. Craig was on top form, making everybody laugh. Everyone sang "Nothing Could Be Finer Than to Be in Carolina" because no one could think of a song about Virginia. Then someone remembered "Country Roads" so we all sang that. And someone else shouted "Lonesome Pine" and everyone started chanting "In the Blue Ridge Mountains of Virginia . . ."

It was a real party atmosphere—with everyone trying to hide their fears and be jolly for Craig's sake.

If you searched the world over you wouldn't find a better crowd of people, I thought. Over the eighteen months we'd become one big family and like any family saying goodbye, everyone wanted to give Craig presents and messages of good luck—there was a lucky white rabbit from Lol and Pat, and a "Superted" teddy from Gillian and Vicky. John and Eileen pressed money into his hand "to buy an American burger." Cis and Bev did the same. Tony and Jean promised they'd make sure everyone carried on doing the cards while we were away, "So you won't have too many waiting when you get back."

Just before nine o'clock Ernie and I took Craig by the hand and ran out through the rain to the car. As we piled inside everyone crowded in the doorway and broke into a chorus of "Good Luck, Good Health, God Bless You." Then as we drove away Louise, Vicky, Karen and Gillian, four little girls who helped every card night, ran by the side of the car keeping up with us as long as they could, tears streaming down their faces. I rubbed Craig's cold hand and forced a smile. "See? You can still get the girls chasing after you."

He shook his head at me, grinning. "Oh, Mu-u-um!"

The flight left Heathrow at eleven-thirty. Carol drove us to the airport. This time the whole family had turned up to say goodbye. The only one missing was poor Steve who had chickenpox and didn't dare risk passing it on to Craig. The television cameras were there too but Stuart Maister, the reporter, was very sympathetic and we didn't feel they were intruding. Craig performed like an old trouper for the camera. "I just can't wait to have my operation and get well," he told Stuart. "I'm going to come back fighting and running and doing everything I used to do." Grandad got very emotional then. It was his birthday in four days' time and when Craig started singing "Happy Birthday" it was just too much for him. "Don't worry. I'll be back," Craig kept saying as Grandad dabbed his eyes with his handkerchief. "I'll be back . . ."

I tried to be brave even though inside I was torn apart. Leaving everybody was terrible but I'd got better recently at hiding my feelings. Craig always teased me without mercy if I cried in public and I knew what I could expect to hear if I broke down now. "Oh no! She's off again . . ."

The three-leg flight to Charlottesville took nineteen hours. Craig slept for most of the journey, playing cards with Ernie whenever he woke. I watched the two of them out of the corner of my eye—anyone would have thought they hadn't a care in the world. Would Ernie be playing cards with Craig the next time we crossed the Atlantic? I wondered. Suddenly I had a sharp vision of poor Margaret taking Philip's little body back with her in the plane to Gibraltar. I shuddered. I couldn't face that. If Craig died in America I knew I would never come home.

Chapter 16

—⁓—

BECAUSE OF bad flight conditions it wasn't until very early on Thursday morning that we arrived, by a tiny ten-seater plane, at Charlottesville's little airport. There was a light covering of snow on the ground as we walked out to the airport parking lot where a taxi was waiting to take us to The Boar's Head. The night porter greeted us like old friends and took us inside to the lounge where Linda and Arthur were waiting up for us. As they stretched out their arms in welcome I had a sudden comforting feeling of having come home.

Craig was very tired and looked really ill after the long journey. Our hotel room was filled with flowers and fruit and cards of welcome from the hotel staff, but he didn't even notice them. He was asleep before his head hit the pillow.

But the following morning, to our surprise he woke at nine, fresh as a daisy, and even ate breakfast with us. "Sausage and egg, sunny-side up, please," he grinned at Liza, the waitress. At ten-thirty we lifted him into Linda's and Arthur's rental car and took him to the hospital. Dr. Kassell, Kim and Lisa were waiting for us at the desk in the passage outside his office and Linda and Arthur left us with them and went off to get coffee.

Dr. Kassell greeted us all warmly, then he bent down

and looked into Craig's eyes and felt his cheeks, checking how much sensation he had in them.

"I'm just going to talk to Mum and Dad a minute," he said to Craig. "You'll be all right with Lisa and Kim, won't you?"

"Yeh," shrugged Craig. "Great." He loved being with those two—they always had fun together.

Dr. Kassell showed us into his office. I handed him the big brown envelope containing Craig's latest scans and he put them up on the screen and examined them. When he turned back to face us his face was grave. "I'm afraid things don't look good," he said. "If you give us the go-ahead then we'll go for it. But I have to say, I really don't rate his chances very highly. You do understand what I'm telling you, don't you?"

Ernie looked shaken. "What do you think his chances are then, doctor?" he asked.

Dr. Kassell hesitated. "I estimate the chance of him not coming through this, one way or another, is about 20 percent." He studied our faces. "You know, you can still change your minds."

I got the feeling that Dr. Kassell really didn't want to do this operation. But there was no way we were going to change our minds now. We were committed to it. "Dr. Kassell, I've explained everything to Craig," I told him. "He knows the danger and he wants to do it. He has so much faith in you. And we have too. God is with you. Craig will be all right. I know—"

Dr. Kassell broke in, "Fine. Fine." Then he gave a little sigh. "Marion, I only wish I had the same faith as you. Still," he smiled, "Craig is well loved and that's on his side."

As we turned to leave he called after us, "By the way, I nearly forgot. Mr. Kluge sends you all his best wishes."

Craig was whisked off for tests and the next three hours were taken up with scans and assessments. Late in the afternoon Dr. Kassell called us into his office again. He looked worried. "I'm going to admit Craig tonight," he said. "The operation is scheduled for tomorrow."

"Is it that urgent?"

He nodded, "It's that urgent."

Briefly he outlined what the operation involved. Dr. Kassell would lead the operating team, helped by Dr. Jane and two assistants. The plan was to try and reduce the size of the tumor by up to 50 percent. This time the team would approach the tumor from a different angle. Two years ago Dr. Hayward had opened Craig's skull down the back. This time Dr. Kassell planned to take out a disc of bone from the top of his skull. It was riskier but it would make the tumor more accessible.

Dr. Kassell shook Ernie's hand, then he turned to me. "Let's hope everything turns out for the best," he said. "I'll see you tomorrow."

We took Craig up to the children's ward and settled him in his bed—Nurse Nicely had been assigned to look after him again so he'd feel at home. He was very cheerful, and was cracking jokes with Linda and Arthur. He loved their company and the way Arthur called him "Goofy" because of the "Goofy" slippers he'd given him on the last trip.

A registrar brought us the consent form and Ernie signed it as he always did. I don't think I could have held a pen by that stage. The stress was getting to me. My arms and legs were trembling. But I was alert enough to notice that we were giving consent for blood transfusions if necessary. "Please make sure the blood's good," I begged the registrar. "Make sure it's not infected with AIDS."

He raised his eyebrows and smiled. "I'd never have thought of that!" he said. I felt embarrassed, but I'd had to say it.

At eight, visitors were supposed to leave, and Ernie, Linda and Arthur stood up. I planned to stay the night in Craig's room—there was a leather convertible chair which pulled down into a single bed. But when Craig realized my intention he grabbed my arm. "Mum, I do love you but please can Dad sleep with me tonight?"

I was hurt. "Why?"

"I know you. You'll be touching me all night, asking me if I'm all right. Linda and Arthur will look after you." He appealed to them. "You will, won't you?"

"Of course, honey," Linda smiled.

Arthur cuddled him. "Goofy, you're a star."

It was so hard to leave him. But I knew Craig was right.

He knew me better than I knew myself. And tonight he needed all the sleep he could get.

I spent a terrible night. At four o'clock in the morning I woke to find myself out of bed pressed against the bedroom wall, shivering and screaming. But my mind was blank. I hadn't a clue what my nightmare had been about.

At ten to six the phone on my bedside table jolted me awake. It was Ernie.

"He's going down to surgery at seven-thirty, Mal."

"Give me ten minutes," I said. "I'll be there." I knocked at Linda's and Arthur's door. Minutes later Linda came into my room. "Before you go to the hospital, Arthur and I wanted to give you this." She handed me a beautiful photograph album. She'd covered it herself in a lovely blue flowered print material with a lace trimming. There was a photograph of Craig in Atlanta stitched on the front and inside the cover she'd pasted a card with a flowered border. On the card in her neat sloping handwriting, she had written a message.

Some people come into our lives and quickly go. Some stay for a while and leave footprints on our hearts and we are never, ever, the same.

I hugged her, tears brimming.

"Come on," she put her arm around me. "It's time to go."

"Hi, Mum," Craig said as we walked into his room. "I'm having my op this morning. Dr. Kassell's been in to tell me and I've been washed in disinfectant. Ea-rghh!" He was so happy and chirpy. "I'm not scared, Mum, honest," he said. "I *am* going to beat this cancer."

Linda and Arthur had brought him a big fluffy gray elephant and he cuddled it and said he was going to call it Arthur. Then Linda slipped something around my neck. It was a beautiful elephant pendant with a ruby eye and a gold collar. "Honey, for luck," she whispered. "We love you."

The minutes ticked away. At seven-thirty on the dot two smiling nurses came into the room to take him down to surgery. We walked on either side of his gurney as they wheeled him down the corridor and into the elevator.

Linda and Arthur stayed behind in his room to let us have those precious moments with him on our own.

One of the nurses worked it so we could stay with him until the last possible minute. "Act normal," she whispered as we walked into the pre-med room. "You're not supposed to be in here."

Craig looked up at her. "What's your name?" he asked. "Nurse Butter," she replied. Craig laughed. "Can I put you on my toast?" and she laughed back. Then he started to sing and I bent down to listen. I should have known. It was our song, "I Just Called to Say I Love You."

"I've seen kids more nervous than this going in to have their appendix out," Nurse Butter whispered to me. He heard her and grinned. Then he saw me watching him and his face changed. "I'll be all right, Mum, don't worry."

"Come on then, Craig—in we go," Nurse Butter said, and he started to sing again. He was still singing when she pushed his gurney over the yellow line and through the swing-doors into the operating room. Ernie and I held each other's hands and stared after him. I had an irresistible urge to run through the doors and bring him back. One of the nurses must have guessed what I was thinking because she grabbed my arm.

"Honey, your kid has guts. God is within him. He'll be fine, don't worry. He wouldn't want his mom upset." I gave her a grateful kiss. "We'll be waiting in the West Visitors' Lounge," I told her. "Please call us if he needs us."

The hours that followed were the longest of my life—even longer than the hours we'd spent waiting at Great Ormond Street. This time I knew more about the dangers. This time his chances of dying or worse had been spelt out for me by Dr. Kassell, 20 percent. One in five. They were bad odds to risk your life on. Ernie had worked it out. "You'd have a better chance playing Russian roulette," he told me.

After a bit he got up and started to pace up and down the room. Linda and Arthur watched him, looking concerned. I was so grateful to them for being there. Linda was such a tower of strength. Yet Linda's own daughter Susan had been almost the same age as Craig when she died. How could she bear to go through this?

From time to time I prayed silently. I knew we weren't hoping for a cure this time. Dr. Kassell had been blunt about that. The only hope this operation offered was a little more time. But as the morning wore on I couldn't help praying for more than just a few extra months. Praying that the American doctors would do what the English doctors had failed to do and get rid of the tumor completely. It was a foolish dream and I tried to nip it in the bud. If I hoped for too much I might get nothing, I told myself. Even six months was better than no time at all. Better than being told that he hadn't woken up. That his heart had stopped beating during the operation. That I wouldn't ever again see his face break into that loving, cheeky smile . . .

By midday my mood had hit rock bottom. The thought of Craig dying on the operating table haunted me. My head throbbed. Ernie had stopped pacing up and down but he looked ill with worry. He cuddled me to him. "Try and have a nap," he said. But I didn't want to try. It was as though my body had shut down. I didn't want sleep or food or drink or even cigarettes. All I wanted was Craig. I felt a million years old. I must have looked it too. I'd run my fingers through my hair so many times that it was standing on end and I knew there were great streaks of mascara under my eyes.

No one had told us how long the operation might take. I don't suppose anyone knew. We'd been in the visitors' lounge for about six hours when suddenly I felt a piercing, sharp pain in my head. A moment later an amazing sense of peace came over me. I looked around at Ernie. He had his head buried in his hands. Linda was still sitting quietly on the next bench. Opposite me, though, Arthur was starting to look edgy and nervous. "Arthur," I said, "how about coming outside for a cigarette?" He looked relieved. Neither of us had smoked all morning. "Sure, honey. Are you all right?" He followed me out on to the balcony.

"You're very chirpy suddenly," he said, as he lit my cigarette.

"Arthur," I said, "I want to tell you something. And I want you to look at your watch so you'll remember the time when you heard it." He gave a puzzled frown, but he looked at his watch.

"Right. Listen, Arthur. I've got a terrible pain in my head but Craig's all right, I know he's all right." Arthur gave me a funny look. Perhaps he thought I was cracking up. I didn't say any more. How could I tell someone as sensible and down-to-earth as Arthur that I had heard Craig's voice telling me clear as a bell, "Mum, they are sewing me up. I'm fine."

We smoked a couple of cigarettes, then went back in to the visitors' lounge. There were one or two other people waiting there now and in the corner a few student nurses were being given a talk by one of the ward sisters.

At three o'clock Stuart Maister, the ITN reporter, came running in with Frank, his cameraman. I was sitting quite calmly now but my poor Ernie was pacing up and down the room again. Stuart looked excited. "Marion! Ernie! Where've you been?"

"We've been here all day," I said. "We haven't moved."

"Have you see the doctor yet?"

"Stuart, I don't expect the doctor to leave surgery to come and talk to us. Go and talk to those young nurses— give yourselves something else to think about."

Stuart and Frank turned on their heels and ran out. "I think I've embarrassed them," I said to Linda. But I'd misunderstood.

Minutes later the lounge door swung open again and Stuart and Frank reappeared. This time they were accompanied by Dr. Kassell. He was wearing a white coat over his green surgical suit and he was smiling.

He walked over to us. "We have some terrific news for you." He stopped in front of the bench where I was sitting and smiled down at me. "OK. As best we can tell we really didn't hurt him. And we got at least 90 percent of the tumor out and maybe a lot more."

90 percent! They'd only been going to remove 50 percent. 90 percent was even more than they'd taken out in England! Did this mean my dreams might come true after all? I jumped up wanting to throw my arms around this wonderful man and hug him to death. At the last minute, though, I remembered my manners and settled for a quick peck on his cheek. He gave a little chuckle. My legs had turned to jelly. I collapsed back on to my seat and Linda

came and sat down next to me and put her arm around me. Ernie ran his hand through my hair, his eyes shining.

"So far so good," Dr. Kassell continued. "Now that doesn't mean that he's not going to have a complication of an infection or a blood clot but we got really an amazing amount of the tumor out. I'm very pleased with him."

Then he looked me straight in the eye. "You know, I'm pretty sure within a couple of days we're going to have some even better news . . ." He didn't say any more, and I didn't ask him what he meant, but I felt my heart lift even higher. Dr. Kassell wouldn't give us false hope. I was sure of that.

"When can we see him?" I asked.

"You can go to him now. He's fine." Dr. Kassell smiled. He turned to go.

Suddenly I remembered something. I called after him, "Oh, Dr. Kassell. What time did you finish the operation?" He thought for a moment. "We started to sew him up at around one forty," he said.

I looked at Arthur. "What time did I tell you I had the pain in my head?"

Arthur looked shaken. "It was one forty-two," he said.

I looked up to heaven. "Thank you, God," I said silently. "Thank you."

Craig had been taken to the Nerancy Neuro ICU, the brain surgery intensive-care unit on the sixth floor. Stuart and Frank came with us in the elevator but didn't attempt to follow us into the unit, for which I was grateful. Two nurses sitting at the central monitors smiled at us as we walked in and pointed to his room.

At the door another nurse came out to greet us. "I'm Natalie," she said. "I'll be looking after Craig for the next few days." We followed her inside.

Craig was lying quietly on his back, surrounded by machines and drips. His head was wrapped in a white helmet of bandages. There was a plastic tube in his mouth, and his lips were shiny with cream. His eyes were closed, his beautiful black curly eyelashes resting on his cheeks so he looked like a sleeping baby. I whispered to the nurse, "Is he all right?"

"He's fine," she smiled. "But why are you whispering?"

"Because he doesn't like my voice because of the pain."
I was still whispering.

"What pain?"

"The pain in his head," I mouthed.

She smiled again. "Honey, we've taken the pain away.
Come, talk to him."

I went up to the head of his bed. Ernie followed close
behind me. "Craig?" I said softly. There was no response.

"Craig? Craig? It's Mummy. Please open your eyes."

I thought I saw him stir slightly.

I touched his cheek gently and his eyes flickered open.
He struggled to focus them. I spoke slowly and clearly.
"The cancer's gone, Craig. It's all gone. Dr. Kassell has
taken the tumor away. You're going to be well now." Craig
took a deep breath and held it for a moment, then he let
it all out at once in a big sigh. "Thank God," he said.

"Wait a minute, honey," the nurse said. "He can't talk
properly with this in." She took the tube out of his mouth.
"Now. Talk to him again," she said.

Ernie and I took it in turns to speak to him. Then I
started to sing—the only song I could possibly sing at that
moment.

He opened his eyes and smiled.

"Does it hurt, Craig?"

"No," he whispered.

I picked up his hand and squeezed it tight. And as I did
so I felt something I hadn't felt for two whole years, not
since the day he'd left his ward in Great Ormond Street
for that first operation. I looked up at Ernie. I was so
happy I was shaking.

"What's the matter?" he asked.

I smiled at him, and tears ran down my cheeks.

"His hands are warm," I said. "Feel them . . . His hands
are *warm!*"

It was like a signal from heaven that our long nightmare
was over at last.

Chapter 17

---~m~---

VISITORS WERE only allowed to stay for ten minutes at a time in the intensive-care unit and we were asked to leave and to come back in an hour. We wandered downstairs still brimming with excitement. I wanted to tell the world. I did tell the world!

Television crews from England, America, Germany and Sweden were waiting outside the ICU for us and they fired questions as we came out. I gabbled answers as they followed us down the corridor. I can't remember what I said. I don't think it made much sense. I just remember saying, "My Craig's well! Thank God," over and over again. I must have looked like a Cheshire cat—my jaw was hurting from smiling so much. As we wandered through the hospital, people kept cheering and clapping. Everyone seemed to know about this little boy from England. Stuart Maister and Frank stayed with us chatting after the other TV crews dropped away. We had grown so close to them in the past twenty-four hours that they felt like a part of the family.

We walked into the cafeteria area—a big hall with lots of different food bars—to get a coffee. On our last visit I'd made friends with the staff here, sharing cigarettes and swapping stories about waiting on tables. Now as I turned the corner there was a shout. "Here's the English lady! How is he, ma'am?"

"He's fine!" I yelled back. "It's a miracle! I want to shout it from the top of the hospital!"

"You do that, ma'am," the big black guy who worked in the burger bar grinned. "Hey!" he shouted to the staff on the counters further down. "The English boy has made it!" A moment later the assistants from the deli, patisserie, and salad bar were swarming round us. They'd all shut up shop! Before I knew what was happening I felt myself being lifted into the air while all around me people screamed and whooped. "Shout it out, lady," someone yelled. It was like a carnival! What a wonderful crowd. Stuart bought coffees and we toasted Craig, Dr. Kassell, the card people, America, Mr. Kluge . . . Oh, did we rejoice! God was with us. The world was with us. Ernie and I were the happiest couple in the world. If we could have bottled the way we felt that afternoon we'd have been millionaires.

Stuart told us he'd already phoned the good news through to England and the story would be on English TV in a couple of hours' time, so very soon our family and all our dear friends would share in our joy. Stuart and Frank had to leave us—Dr. Kassell was due to give a press conference, but they promised to return.

Linda and Arthur sat with us waiting for the minutes to tick away till we could go back to the ICU. I ran round chatting to people—I just couldn't sit still. Suddenly at a corner table I recognized the old hillbilly who had told me to pray to the mountains back in November. His sister had brought him in for a check-up. He held his arms out to me. "Honey, your prayers have been answered." He was overcome. He told me his last check-up had shown he was clear of cancer too. When I heard that I kissed him—one tooth and all! Meeting him was the icing on the cake.

At four-thirty we were allowed back into the ICU for another ten minutes. Natalie, Craig's day nurse, was still sitting beside his bed. "He won't be left on his own for a second while he's in here," she promised. I picked up his hand—it was still warm. He opened his eyes as he felt my touch and his face looked so peaceful—the tense look that had been there for so many months had completely disappeared.

"Do you know where you are, Craig?" Nurse Natalie asked gently.

"In the University of Virginia hospital." There was no slurring. Craig's voice was still slow, but it was clear as a bell.

"Do you know the date?"

"March the first."

"And who is your doctor?"

"Dr. Kassell."

The nurse raised her eyebrows at us. "There's not a lot wrong with him!"

Craig closed his eyes again and Ernie and I sat quietly beside his bed taking it in turns to hold his hand. A tube on his pillow was draining blood from somewhere under his bandage into a little round container. Behind us the monitors bleeped and flashed. The ICU had every modern appliance imaginable. Electric stockings on his legs to keep the blood circulating. Heat lamps which shone on his body to keep him warm. A TV camera on the ceiling which relayed Craig's every move to a monitor at the central nursing station. Compared with the English hospitals I had known it was like jumping into the twenty-first century.

After ten minutes Nurse Natalie touched me gently on the shoulder. "Honey? I'll look after him now. Please go. He'll sense you're here if you stay and he must rest. You can see him again in the morning." The expression on her face told me she knew exactly how I was feeling. I gave her a big hug and she smiled. "We'll call you if we're worried but he's fine. Go, have a wash and brush up and, lady, celebrate! Your son has been born again!"

Stuart Maister and Frank were waiting outside the ICU for us. They told us the press conference had gone very well. Dr. Kassell had been really optimistic. "He said a lot of nice things about Craig, and about you and Ernie too," Stuart said. "Like what?" I asked. "He said Craig was a very strong character and you were a strong family and the fact that you and Ernie loved him so much really helped. 'Love is a great healer,' he said. He mentioned the cards too. He said he felt sure that all the people who were out there rooting for Craig had helped him to pull through."

I smiled. "I could have told you that. Did he say anything about the operation?" I thought maybe Stuart could give us a clue what Dr. Kassell had meant by talking about "even better news" soon.

"Yes he did. He said that the tumor was made of a very hard material like mother of pearl so they couldn't just cut it out—he'd had to scrape away at it for hours with a tiny instrument chipping little bits off."

"Did he mention using the gamma knife?"

Stuart nodded. "He said they may not have to use it. It depends whether the 10 percent that's left is benign or malignant. They have to analyze the tumor in the laboratory to find out—but he sounded pretty hopeful to me."

I gaped at him and Stuart chuckled. Then he looked at his watch. "Look, we've got to disappear and put the story together now. Why don't you all go out for a meal? We'll buy the champagne."

"Come on, Marion," said Linda. "Let's party! Boy have we got something to celebrate."

"Wow—a new woman!" Ernie kidded me when I came out of the hotel bathroom an hour later. But it wasn't just the change of clothes and the fresh make-up that had perked me up. It was hearing Stuart say that magic word "benign." When Craig had woken up after the operation I'd told him, "The cancer has gone." But I didn't know what had made me say it. No one had said that to me. It had just been a hunch—another witchy feeling. Now the feeling was getting stronger and stronger. It was affecting Ernie too. He looked ten years younger.

Linda and Arthur took us to a Mexican restaurant called Paco's which claimed to make "the best cocktails in Virginia" and Arthur insisted I have a pina colada to celebrate. It was lovely, but I didn't need it. Even Stuart's champagne was wasted on me that night—I was already drunk with joy.

The news of Craig's operation had been on TV and as soon as we sat down people started to come up to the table to congratulate us. I was overwhelmed. Everyone was behaving as if we'd just won an Oscar . . . Someone tapped me on the shoulder and then lifted me up in the air and swung me around. It was Glen, Craig's favorite waiter from The Boar's Head. It turned out he had an evening job at Paco's. Later on he organized a group of twelve waiters to come over and serenade us with a song of congratulations, barber-shop style! It was a very happy foursome who drove back to the hotel that night, and for the first time in months both Ernie and I slept like babies.

Our celebrations came to an abrupt end the next morning when we arrived back at the hospital to learn that Craig had developed a huge blood clot on the brain which would have to be drained immediately. Dr. Kassell was waiting to carry out the operation. He looked worried. "The puzzling thing is the bleeding doesn't seem to be coming from the area where we operated," he said. "Craig hasn't been in contact with anyone with chickenpox recently, has he?" My heart sank. Steven! I thought.

Dr. Kassell told us that chickenpox could sometimes cause this type of bleeding in the brain but he was reassuring. Although it was such a large clot he was hopeful it could be dealt with. He said that complications like this were fairly regular after major brain surgery. Once he'd told us that I really didn't get in too much of a panic. God was not going to give us a miracle yesterday and take it back today. Of that I was absolutely certain.

At midday Dr. Kassell came back out of surgery and reported to us again. "OK. We got it," he smiled. "Go and see him. I'm sure he'll be fine now."

Craig was asleep when he came back to the ICU and he slept for most of the afternoon but he woke easily when the nurses tried to rouse him and responded well to their questions. They bent the rules for us and we were allowed to sit by Craig's bed for an hour at a time on condition I didn't say a word!

At two o'clock Steven telephoned from England sounding very worried. He'd just seen a news flash on TV saying that Craig had a blood clot. "Steve, don't worry he's fine," I said. I didn't mention the chickenpox scare—Steve didn't sound too well himself and he would be devastated if he thought he had put Craig's life at risk.

Stuart and Frank were putting together an item to be broadcast in England on Sunday and Stuart asked us to

give another interview in the West Visitors' Lounge. I put
some more make-up on and put my hair up so I didn't
look such a wreck as the day before. I knew everybody at
home would be watching and they'd be reassured if they
saw me with all my war-paint on. Even Ernie overcame
his shyness and agreed to be interviewed for the very first
time. "We feel better," he told Stuart simply. "We feel
we've made it ... I think we'll start getting a few days'
sleep now. I feel happy!" And he hugged me.

All day, telegrams, flowers, videos and toys flooded in
to the hospital for Craig. By Saturday evening his bed was
surrounded with get-well cards, banners, balloons, videos
and fluffy animals. Some of the greetings were from our
friends and family (my favorite was the telegram from
Penny and Viv at the Marsden Appeals office which said
simply, *We just called to say we love you!!!*). But just as
many were from strangers. Tom Doran, the hospital's public relations officer, told me that because of the fame of
Craig's get-well card appeal, every TV channel and newspaper in America had carried the story of his operation.
Late on Saturday afternoon a huge bunch of balloons arrived from Kim. Each balloon carried a different message.
Congratulations! Get well! Good luck! We were tying
them to the end of the bed when a nurse came in carrying
a teddy wearing a vest printed with the words, *Someone in
UVA loves you.* That "someone" turned out to be Lisa. I
was really touched by the way those two girls had got so
involved with Craig.

Toward evening Craig woke up as alert and bright as a
button—it was hard to believe he'd had two brain operations in the past thirty-six hours. I was showing him the
telegrams when Craig's night nurse, Janet, came in. He
had a sheet draped loosely over him and it had slipped
halfway off his bottom. Nurse Janet said, in a pretend
shocked voice, "Craig, you are showing your fanny."

Craig gave her a pitying look. "I haven't got a fanny,"
he said. "Only girls have fannies."

Nurse Janet looked puzzled and I had to explain as del-
icately as I could the English meaning of the word. She
roared with laughter. "I can see we're going to have to
watch this young man," she said.

Craig's condition went on improving. He'd stopped dribbling, and his speech, though slow, was much clearer. On Sunday morning he greeted us with a wide smile that said, "It's great to be alive." I went down the corridor to ring Kate and tell her the good news. Our whole family was in her house hoping I'd call. "My phone's been a real hot-line," Kate said. "Everyone wants to know how he is." Ernie's brother Reg had told her that the British Legion club in Mitcham had stayed open until one o'clock in the morning because everyone in the club was watching the telly for the news flashes on Craig.

I arrived back in the ICU at the same time as Dr. Kassell. "Hello, Champ, how are you?" he asked Craig and was met with a great big beam. Dr. Kassell sent Craig down for an MR scan and the result, an hour later, was reassuring. "There's been no more bleeding, so I don't foresee any more problems," he told us. In fact, Dr. Kassell was so pleased with Craig that he gave permission for the British TV cameras to come in briefly and film him for the first time. I was pleased. I knew once our family at home could actually see how well he looked it would reassure them better than any words of mine could do. Dr. Kassell kept popping in and out all day. I was really moved to see how delighted he was with Craig. I'd always thought doctors weren't supposed to get too close to their patients. But Dr. Kassell seemed to look on Craig almost like one of his own family.

By Monday morning Craig wasn't even drowsy. He spent the morning playing hangman with Ernie and chattering non-stop. He wanted to hear all the news that Kate had given me—how Kylie and Craig and Zeki and Sami were, whether Steve had lost his spots yet, if Grandad had enjoyed his birthday . . .

The pathology report after the operation in Great Ormond Street had taken over a week to come back, so on Monday afternoon when Dr. Kassell came in to see us again, we weren't expecting it to be anything other than a routine visit. Lisa was with him and she was beaming but she was a cheerful girl and I didn't think anything of it.

"Craig, Marion, Ernie. We have some good news." Dr.

Kassell's smile was as broad as Lisa's. "We have the pathology report back from the laboratory and it confirms what we suspected when we saw it. The tumor is benign."

I didn't trust my ears. I wanted him to say it again. "Are you absolutely sure?"

He nodded.

"Craig, did you hear that?" I asked.

Craig's eyes were sparkling.

"How?" I asked. "How could it change?"

He shrugged. "I really don't know, Marion. It's something of a mystery. Whatever the reason it's the best news we could possibly have. There's a very good chance that the remaining 10 percent will lie dormant and not return." He smiled. "The tumor has done some damage—it's squeezed the brain stem until it's like a ribbon—and we're going to have to run tests to find out how much of the damage is reversible. But the signs are good." He smiled. "I'm optimistic that Craig will lead a very happy, long, successful life."

It was what we had all been praying to hear. Ernie put his arm around me. "You mean he's cured?" He still couldn't believe his ears.

Dr. Kassell nodded. "It's certainly possible. I'd even say it's likely. It's something that's going to have to be watched in the future. But even if it does start to regrow I foresee no reason we can't operate again."

Craig beamed. "Doc Kassell, you're the best doctor in the world." Then he took a deep breath and speaking very slowly and carefully, he added, "You're supercalifragilisticexpialidocious." There was a stunned silence. Craig grinned up at us, really pleased with himself.

Dr. Kassell seemed lost for words, and a moment later he hurried out. Lisa looked uncertain whether to follow him. Then Kathy, one of the nurses who sat at the central nursing station, came in looking puzzled. "Did something happen in here just now?" she asked.

"Craig said a tongue twister," I smiled. "Why?"

She laughed. "Oh! That explains it. I thought I was seeing things."

"What do you mean?"

"Well, Dr. Kassell just came shooting out of Craig's

room and as he went past my desk he gave a little skip and clicked his heels together in the air—you know, like those Cossack dancers do?" She shook her head. "I've never seen him like this before. Never."

Later that afternoon Craig's eye doctor, Dr. Newman, came into the ICU. He was a lovely man who wore a bow tie and reminded me of Groucho Marx. I'd been puzzling all afternoon about what Dr. Kassell had told me and I asked Dr. Newman if he could explain it. "How could the tumor be benign?" I asked him. "It was cancer—does it mean that the radiotherapy killed the cancer? That it did work after all?" He shook his head. "I don't think so. If the radiotherapy had worked I doubt it would have started growing again the way it did. It's always possible there were two tumors, one cancerous, the other not. Like twins. But that's speculation. We just don't know." He smiled. "It's gone. That's the important thing."

Craig recovered from his operation faster than I could have dreamed. On the Wednesday after the operation he was transferred from the intensive-care unit back to the children's ward. That same afternoon he walked unsupported for the first time in three months. "Don't you dare hold me," he told Ernie as he took five slow, wobbly steps down the hospital corridor. He hadn't experienced any of the terrible pain I'd been dreading so much; in fact, he hadn't even needed an aspirin. And his speech was getting clearer and faster every day. Craig was thrilled by that. He loved getting his tongue around tricky words again. "Supercalifragilistic . . ." was just the start. That week he practiced his new skills at every opportunity. "It's been a long time since I've been able to say, 'Sister Susie sitting on a thistle . . .' " he told Vera his physiotherapist.

Only eight days after the operation Dr. Kassell announced that we could take Craig back to the hotel. "Hospitals are for sick people," he said. "He could pick up an infection here. He's safer outside—in fact, he's safer playing in the traffic than he is here."

Craig was overjoyed. "You're the best doctor there is," he said. Dr. Kassell looked embarrassed. "No, no. There's plenty of doctors like me," he said. "There's only one patient like you!"

We still had to take Craig back as an out-patient for physiotherapy, speech therapy and occupational therapy. But for the rest of the time he was ours again. The responsibility frightened me a bit, especially as Linda and Arthur had to leave us to go to Washington on CWF business. They had been such a tower of strength, I wondered how we'd ever cope without them. But help was at hand. Ruki had arrived from London a few days earlier to cover Craig's story, and she appointed herself as our guardian. Nothing was too much trouble for her and for a week, as well as giving moral support, she organized our laundry, our taxi bookings, and took telephone messages for us.

The Press interest in Craig's operation, both worldwide and local, was tremendous. Even the *Washington Post* sent their photographer, James Parcell, and Craig made the front page on Wednesday, March 20. The picture they chose showed him laughing, with both thumbs up in a victory salute. But my favorite photograph was one they didn't use. It shows Craig staring at something faraway, his face lit by a light shining from above. There is something spiritual about it. It's a picture of a little boy who has suffered and survived.

Craig's recovery wasn't going to continue on its own. There was going to be a lot of work to do to help it along. We learned about it over the next few weeks as he attended the John Kluge Children's Rehabilitation Center (named after Craig's benefactor). Sue, his physiotherapist, explained that because parts of Craig's brain had been damaged by the tumor, and possibly by the operation itself, other parts would have to learn to take over from them. His muscle control, especially down the left side of his body, had been badly affected, which was why he was so shaky. His hand, too, was causing problems—he had very little feeling in his fingers. To improve his sense of touch Joan, his occupational therapist, hid money in a sort of play-dough material and made Craig feel through the dough till he found it. She also used a big box full of dried beans which Craig had to rummage through feeling for different objects. Sue hoped that physiotherapy would help his walking too. Since the operation he had walked with high jerky steps, but she felt that with the correct exercises it would soon look more normal.

Something else which had been damaged by the tumor was Craig's appetite center. We were warned that learning to eat the correct amount so he wouldn't get too thin or too fat would be difficult and his weight would probably yo-yo up and down while we tried to get it right.

Both his eyes and his ears had been affected, but not as badly as they might have been. Craig was having to learn to focus on objects all over again but he was adjusting quickly and it was unlikely he'd need glasses. His hearing was more of a problem—he could hear individual sounds coming from in front of him but not from the sides or behind and he found it difficult to hear properly when there was any background noise—it seemed to confuse his brain.

There was also a possibility that Craig's growth might have been stunted because of damage to the pituitary gland. Dr. Kassell told us he would have to come back in September to visit the UVA growth clinic and have the situation assessed. Then, if necessary, he would be given injections of growth hormone.

The most obvious damage of all had been to Craig's speech center. The improvement in his speech had been so quick and dramatic after the operation that I'd expected it would soon get back to normal. But after a week I realized my mistake. Although the slurring had gone and his speech had speeded up it was still slow. There was still a drawl, and a hesitation before each word—he sounded a bit like someone who'd had a stroke. Even Polly, his speech therapist, couldn't predict how much further it would improve. "Keep him singing," she advised. "It'll help a lot." That was one exercise that was no problem!

I wasn't seriously worried about any of his difficulties. Nothing could dampen my joy at having him back. Of course, learning to speak and walk and eat again would take time. But thank God that was the one thing we had plenty of. For the first time in two years, time was on our side.

Three weeks after the operation we met Craig's guardian angel Mr. Kluge for the first time. Ernie and I had been longing for this day since the first time we came to Charlottesville. We so wanted to say thank you. Dr. Kassell had always promised we'd be seeing him one day but time had passed and nothing was mentioned. Then, twelve days after Craig was discharged, Dr. Kassell told us it was on. Mr. Kluge would meet us the next day in Dr. Jane's consulting-room.

All the media had been screaming to meet him too. It was all they needed to make the fairy story complete. But Dr. Kassell said Mr. Kluge didn't want our meeting to turn into a circus so it was to be kept very hush-hush with only one local TV company and a reporter and photographer from the Charlottesville paper, the *Daily Progress,* being invited. I felt really sad that Ruki and Stuart had missed the big occasion. Ruki had only gone back to England the day before. She deserved this story and I felt she would have helped me not to feel so nervous.

I really was terrified. I told Dr. Kassell and he smiled. "Have you ever thought he might be nervous of meeting you too?"

Arthur and Linda had returned from Washington and the next morning they drove us in to the hospital. The rain was belting down. I slipped my hand into Ernie's. "It always rains when something important happens in our lives." Ernie just smiled. Now the big moment was upon us my stomach was turning over. How do you show your gratitude to the man who paid to save your son's life? What words could express what Craig and Ernie and I felt? "Thank you" seemed so inadequate.

Dr. Jane's consulting-room was next door to Dr. Kassell's office. It was very comfortable with sofas and armchairs covered in pink and gray silk and photos of Dr. Jane's family on the walls. The TV camera and reporters were already there when we arrived and we sat down on the sofas and waited. Then suddenly television lights lit up the room and we sprang to our feet as a gray-haired man walked through the door. I guessed he was in his seventies and he had a warm open smiling face which reminded me a bit of Bob Hope. I felt myself relaxing. He was so much gentler and kinder-looking than successful businessmen usually looked.

Dr. Kassell followed Mr. Kluge into the room and introduced him to us. Mr. Kluge held his hands out to Craig, and Craig took them and said simply, "Thank you. Thank you very much. I can't say a big enough thank you. I'd kiss you all over if I could."

"Craig, I don't think anyone has ever said anything so nice to me before," Mr. Kluge leaned over and kissed him.

I took Mr. Kluge's hand and kissed his cheek. "Mr. Kluge, thank you. How can we possibly thank you enough?" I asked.

"You don't have to say thank you, my dear," he said softly. "This has to be the best thing that I have done in my life. I thank God I was in the position to be able to do it."

I gulped. Everything I'd been planning to say stuck in my throat. I just couldn't speak. Neither could Ernie. I could see him fighting to stop himself cracking up. And then, suddenly, I saw a tear roll down Mr. Kluge's cheek too. Craig looked at the three of us and started to laugh. "Oh here they go," he said. "Here they go."

Mr. Kluge smiled. "Please sit down," he said. "Craig, won't you come and sit next to me?" Ernie and Craig sat on either side of him on the sofa while I sat in the armchair and we started to talk. Before long I had all forgotten the Press was there. Mr. Kluge had a skilled way of putting people at their ease and we were soon chatting and laughing as though we'd known each other for years.

The meeting went on for over two hours. While we talked Dr. Kassell popped in and out and at one stage we were taken next door to meet Mr. Kluge's nine-year-old son John. We learned so much that afternoon. We found out that although Mr. Kluge supported several charities and had funded the Rehabilitation Center at the UVA Medical Center he had never given money to an individual before. He told us he had made it a rule because he got so many begging letters and it would mean making impossible choices. One of the reporters asked why he had broken his rule for Craig.

"I saw his picture and a story about his appeal in a newspaper and I was going to send him a card," he said. "But then it was as if God touched me on the shoulder and told me I had to do something more. I had this very strong feeling that his medical condition was being neglected, and all my life I've followed my intuition." He shrugged, "So I telephoned Dr. Kassell and asked him to contact the Shergold family."

I knew the British doctors had done everything they possibly could for Craig, but Mr. Kluge's intuition had led to Craig's life being saved, I was sure of that. "I believe in following my hunches too," I told him and I explained how chance had led me to find his letter. And how I had been so convinced Craig had to come to America, even after Dr. Hayward had offered to operate.

He listened nodding. "Always listen to your instincts, Marion. Sometimes it's God's way of telling you what to do."

As a thank-you present for Mr. Kluge, dear Arthur had made a metal plaque with a photograph of Craig in his Rocky pose mounted in the center. I thought this would be a good moment to present it, so I nudged Craig and he handed it to Mr. Kluge. Under the photo Arthur had engraved, *Thank you for helping me win the biggest fight of all, March 1st 1991.* When he read that, Mr. Kluge wiped away another tear, then he felt in his pocket and brought out a small silver coin. "Craig, this is for you," he said. "It's my lucky two-headed quarter. I've had it since I was a small boy about your age and it's always brought me luck. With one of these you can't ever lose."

While Craig held the coin up for the cameras Mr. Kluge leaned toward me and said quietly, "I'm very sorry I didn't see you before today, Marion. I wanted to meet you earlier. But if the outcome had been different I could never have faced you. I have been following Craig's progress though. Professor Kassell has kept me informed ever since his first examination back in November."

"So you really were watching over us like a guardian angel," I said. "It's how I'd always thought of you when I imagined you—a big kind guardian angel.'

"Thank you," Mr. Kluge smiled. "I'm so pleased it's turned out like this. You know when I spoke to Professor Kassell back in November after he'd first seen Craig, he told me he didn't want to operate. He said some things were beyond medical help."

"I told Ernie that's how he felt," I said. "I knew I was right."

"I begged him to think again. In the end he said it was something you said that changed his mind. He said you'd asked what he'd do if one of his daughters had a tumor like Craig's, and he decided he would give his own child a chance whatever the risks." He looked across at Craig, still posing and joking with the camera crew. "You know, Marion, you have a very special human being there. You think your son is famous now but believe me he is going on to much greater things."

Before I had time to respond the *Progress* reporter intervened. "What did you do when you heard the news about the operation, Mr. Kluge?"

"I got down on my knees and I thanked God," Mr. Kluge said.

I smiled. "That's what I did too." I felt so close to this wonderful man.

The reporter looked pleased. "That's great. I think we almost have enough material now. Just one more thing." He turned to Craig. "Do you have any special ambition, now that you can look forward to a normal life, Craig?"

Craig considered the question. "Yeh, I want to learn to play squash," he said suddenly. "Cos Dr. Kassell plays squash every day. And I want to come back and play Dr. Kassell, and beat him."

The reporter smiled. "And how long do you think that'll take you?"

"Oh, I reckon about ten years."

Mr. Kluge let out a roar of laughter. "I only hope I'm around to see it."

"You can be the umpire," I promised.

Chapter 18

—⁓—

IN THE whole two years he'd been ill I had never seen Craig cry. But at Heathrow Airport on Friday, April 19 his self-control broke down at last. As he flung his arms around Steven, his chin wobbled and tears of sheer happiness poured down his face.

"Hello, Ugly. I'm home," he said.

Poor Steven was too overcome to speak. Everyone was overcome. Granddad, Carol, Kylie, Kate and Sharon all jostled to kiss him, their faces wet with tears. They'd been waiting patiently for hours for us to come through the customs door. Little Kylie had spotted us before anyone else, "Uncle Craig, Uncle Craig," she'd screamed, and she'd squeezed through the barrier and run toward us with her little arms outstretched and wrapped herself around his legs. Craig had bent down and hugged her, grinning from ear to ear—he'd been so worried she wouldn't recognize him after nine weeks away.

As we pushed our luggage trolley up the walkway, flashbulbs started to pop and everyone began applauding. The whole world seemed to be waiting for us at the end of the barriers. Not just our family, but TV cameramen, reporters, even a party of Japanese tourists, were clapping and cheering as we walked toward them. Craig had been so determined to walk off the plane today and with a bit of help from Ernie, he made it. As he reached the end of the barrier at last and wobbled into Steve's arms there was a loud chorus of "For He's a Jolly Good Fellow!" Talk about a hero's welcome!

Our old friend Stuart Maister had organized a big limo to take us back to Carshalton and we arrived home to find the whole house covered with Union Jacks, Stars and Stripes, balloons and bunting. Over a hundred people were waiting in the street to welcome us and someone had set up speakers so that as the limo doors opened the first thing we heard was Stevie Wonder singing "I Just Called to Say I Love You" at the top of his voice. It was the crowning moment to a magic day.

Stuart Maister had come home with us in the limo and afterward, sitting in our front room, he interviewed Craig briefly. "What would you say to other people who've had the same illness that you've had, Craig?" he asked.

Craig didn't hesitate. "Never give up," he said. "Keep smiling and you'll beat it ..."

It's now more than two years since that wonderful day. And, please God, Craig has beaten it. His recovery has continued. The latest scan shows that the remains of the tumor have shrunk even further. It really does seem that God has answered our prayers and the prayers of millions of people around the world.

Craig's convalescence has been a long slow process. Some things have got better more quickly than others. His speech has improved dramatically. It's wonderful to hear him now. There's no slurring or hesitation and it's only very slightly slower than normal speech.

His physical recovery has taken longer. His left leg and the whole left side have taken a long time to get their strength back. For months he needed us to support his arms when he climbed stairs, and for months after that he was constantly tired and took long naps every day. Today he still has to use his wheelchair for traveling and shopping, and his walking still looks odd because his left knee won't obey him properly. So for now simple pleasures like playing football and riding a bike are beyond him. But slowly, with hard work, his control over his body is improving. There are still eight years to go until that squash match with Dr. Kassell, and I know he's going to make it.

We have had to accept that other things won't improve. Craig's appetite center has gone for good and he's having to learn to live with that. He put on a lot of weight in the first twelve months after the operation, though as he's got more active he has started to slim down again. His pituitary gland, too, has been permanently damaged which means he has to have regular injections of growth hormone to compensate. But to me those are minor problems. He may always be on the plump side, and he may never be as tall as Steven. But at least he has a future now. Beside that, nothing else matters.

In September 1992, three and a half years after he last sat in a classroom, Craig went back to school. Chartfield is a special state school for children who have missed lessons through illness or other problems. The classes are small so the pupils can get individual attention and be given special care and love. They follow the normal national curriculum and eventually take GCSE exams. Craig loves it and is doing well. His reading age is back to normal and the teachers are hopeful that in two or three months he will have caught up with the other children in most subjects. He loves English, music and maths but his favorite lesson is drama. He still wants to be an actor, and he had a part in his first school play last Christmas. He pronounced each word so distinctly that you could hear and understand him right at the back of the hall. No one listening would have guessed that only two years earlier he had hardly been able to make himself understood. How I wished Dr. Kassell and Mr. Kluge could have been there.

The Press turned out in force for Craig's first day back at school. I thought the media attention would die down but they are still as interested in him as ever. His story has been told in every magazine from *Reader's Digest* to *Hello!* and hardly a week goes by without him being invited to appear on television or radio. Craig regularly opens fêtes, tees off in charity golf matches, and attends film premieres, and he has been given the most wonderful trips—to Las Vegas to stay in the famous Mirage Hotel, to Finnish Lapland to see Santa Claus, to Germany for a special Christmas TV show, and to Italy to appear again on the *Nino de Marti Show* in front of a live audience in Rome.

That Italian evening was magical. Craig was treated like someone back from the dead. People in the audience were calling out *"Ciao!,"* "Bravo, Craig" and after the show it was just kisses, kisses, kisses. After half an hour Craig needed a flannel to get the lipstick off his face. But he has had to get used to that. Everywhere he goes, people want to kiss him, to touch him. It's as if they hope some of our blessings will rub off on them.

The avalanche of cards continues. We stopped counting cards individually in 1990 but the Post Office still keeps a tally of the number of sacks and by Charlie's estimate we have now received well over one hundred million cards. Even now, in early 1993, Craig is still receiving 15,000 a day, and the group of wonderful friends we call the card people are still meeting regularly to open them.

All Craig's fame hasn't brought us riches—we still live in our two-up, two-down house on the St. Helier housing estate in Carshalton. In December Ernie was made redundant from his job at the Electricity Board, so life isn't a bed of roses. Sometimes friends say, "Don't you wish you'd asked people to send Craig a pound coin instead of a get-well card?" But with my hand on my heart I can honestly say no. Love is worth more than money any time. If it wasn't for the get-well cards and the love they carried with them Craig wouldn't be here today. I'm certain of that. Ernie and I are the richest parents in the world, because we have our son. And every day we count our blessings.

Craig is a teenager now. He's no longer the little boy who was taken ill four years ago. He's grown up quickly since starting school. He's learning to let go of the apron strings which held us together for so long and he's starting to have a life of his own away from Ernie and me. I try not to fuss over him. I know I must begin to let him take chances and risks like any normal boy. All the same it's hard. I still worry every time he has a cold. And I'm sure it will be years before my heart stays calm when he says, "Mum, I've got a headache."

Only God knows what the future holds. And we're in His hands the same as we have been for the past four years. We continue to live one day at a time. But we're full of hope. God hasn't let us down so far. For me the most wonderful thing about what happened to Craig is that it shows how many good people there still are in the world. When the news is full of wars and people doing terrible things to each other, it's easy to lose your faith in human nature and to think there isn't any goodness or generosity left. Craig has proved differently.

Sometimes when I'm putting him to bed in the evening I say to him, "Can you imagine an island, Craig, with all the people who sent you a card and all the people who've been good to you living on it? What a wonderful place that would be." Craig always smiles. Thank you, world, for giving my son back to me . . .

Epilogue

In September 1991 we went back to the University of Virginia Medical Center so that Dr. Kassell and the staff there could assess Craig's progress since the operation.

While we were there Dr. Kassell told us something very strange had happened on the day of Craig's operation. Something no one could explain.

"In the ceiling of the operating room we have some very hi-tech cameras," he said. "We use them to film the operations so we can show them to medical students later. But when we ran the recording of Craig's operation we found we only had three minutes of film. Just as I was about to make the first incision everything went black. It's very disappointing. No one can understand what happened."

I stared at him. "I understand," I said.

He frowned. "You do?"

"God didn't want you to film a miracle," I said slowly. "That's what happened."

Dr. Kassell smiled. "Well, I haven't any better explanation, Marion," he said. "Who knows? Perhaps you're right."

UNIVERSITY OF VIRGINIA

HEALTH
SCIENCES
CENTER

DEPARTMENT OF
NEUROLOGICAL SURGERY

Craig Shergold first came to the University of Virginia in November 1990. We recognized immediately that Craig was a unique patient, but more importantly he proved to be a unique human being. Craig was fortunate in the sense that the University possessed cutting edge equipment like the Gamma Knife and highly-trained personnel, but without Craig's courage and determination the operation would have likely had a different outcome.

John Kluge and I have been friends for a number of years and he asked if I would take a look at Craig. The first time I saw the boy, he was essentially completely disabled, spent most of his day in bed, was unable to write, and could speak and be understood only with extreme difficulty.

Based on early discussions, we thought Craig was suffering from a malignant pineal region tumor and we were thinking in terms of treatment with the Gamma Knife to achieve a palliation of Craig's symptoms. However when the films arrived and we examined Craig, it was apparent that the tumor, about 5 cm in diameter or the size of a hen's egg, was too large for the Gamma Knife, which is really effective only for tumors up to about 3 cm in diameter—the size of a golf ball.

It appeared that our best option was to debulk the tumor, that is, to partially remove it in order to reduce its size so that it could be treated with the Gamma Knife. I was not very enthusiastic about the approach. My concern was that the procedure could only prolong Craig's life for a year or so and not improve his neurological condition.

We sat down with Craig's parents and presented this option to them. Mr. and Mrs. Shergold said that they wanted their son to make the decision himself. This Craig did by stating "no pain, no gain." Parenthetically, had it not been for Kluge's persistent urging to try and do something, I might not have offered this option to the Shergolds.

At the time of the surgery, we were very surprised to learn that the tumor appeared benign. It did not invade the brain as we expected from a malignant tumor and the lesion had a very good plane of separation from the normal brain structures.

We attempted to do a total removal of the tumor. The resection was difficult because of the proximity of vital blood vessels and brain structures. The operation was extremely complicated due to the scarring from the previous surgery and radiation. At several points during the surgery, my assistants urged me to stop, fearing that I was penetrating too deeply into the brain. However, I felt that as long as we had gone this far, we should go for a cure, working on the assumption that we were dealing with a benign tumor.

Using very high magnification in the operating microscope, we were able to resect at least 75% and perhaps 80% of the tumor, and maybe even more. The remaining portion was densely scarred to the brain from the previous surgery, and it appeared to be relatively inactive. Postoperatively, Craig's neurological condition improved immediately. However, during the night following surgery, his condition deteriorated and a brain scan showed that he had developed a very large blood clot in the space between the covering of the brain and his skull. This blood clot was actually distant from the surgery and resulted because when the large tumor was removed, the brain collapsed upon itself, leaving a dead space.

Later, the pathological examination of the tumor demonstrated that it was benign.

Over the past two years Craig has experienced a dramatic neurological improvement. The repeat scans performed this March, two years after the surgery, demonstrated that the residual tumor was, if anything, smaller. Craig has a very good chance of being cured of this tumor. In the unlikely event that the tumor starts to grow again, further surgery can be performed.

Again, Craig's courage and John Kluge's intuition and generosity were the overwhelming success factors in Craig's dramatic improvement. At this writing I am told Craig is playing soccer again for the first time, a dream that kept his spirits high during treatment. There can be no doubt that he has his tremendous character and strength of will to thank for miraculous recovery.

Dr. Neal F. Kassell, M.D.
Professor and Vice Chairman of the Department of
Neurological Surgery
University of Virginia School of Medicine